The Association Between Depression and Suicidal Behavior

Edited by

Francisco Manuel Morales-Rodríguez

Published in London, United Kingdom

The Association Between Depression and Suicidal Behavior
http://dx.doi.org/10.5772/intechopen.1004500
Edited by Francisco Manuel Morales-Rodríguez

Contributors
Arzu Gülbahçe, Blanca-Rosa García-Rivera, Chiaki Konishi, Chisom Precious Anodebe, Emmanuel Jonah Osiri, Esma Gökçe, Fatih Kara, Fredrick Sunday Isaac, Handan Zincir, Hao Huang, Ignacio-Alejandro Mendoza-Martínez, Julia Tesolin, Junting Chen, Maryamsadat Mirpour, Nuray Simsek, Soheil Behdarvandirad, Ukamaka Gloria Mgbeojedo

First published in London, United Kingdom, 2024 by IntechOpen
IntechOpen is the global imprint of INTECHOPEN LIMITED, registered in England and Wales, registration number: 11086078, 167-169 Great Portland Street, London, W1W 5PF, United Kingdom

British Library Cataloguing-in-Publication Data
A catalogue record for this book is available from the British Library

Additional hard and PDF copies can be obtained from orders@intechopen.com

The Association Between Depression and Suicidal Behavior
Edited by Francisco Manuel Morales-Rodríguez
p. cm.
Print ISBN 978-1-83769-853-0
Online ISBN 978-1-83769-852-3
eBook (PDF) ISBN 978-1-83769-854-7

Meet the editor

Francisco Manuel Morales-Rodríguez has a Ph.D. in Psychology and a degree in Labour Sciences. He is a full professor at the University of Granada, Spain. He is active in research and coordinates and participates in innovation projects in education, training, and employment. He has published several books and articles in academic journals and has worked as a referee for journals and congresses. He is currently investigating affective sexual and gender diversities and coordinating the advanced innovation project "Transversal Education for Affective-Sexual, Gender and Corporal Diversities." He was awarded one of nine research prizes from the General Foundation of the University of Málaga, Spain. Dr. Morales-Rodríguez is the recipient of the William James Award for Psychopedagogical Innovation from the International Scientific Association of Psychopedagogy.

Contents

Preface

This book explores the construct of depression and provides valuable insights for developing psychoeducational interventions in health care, as well as designing activities and programs to prevent suicidal behavior in diverse contexts. Through its eight chapters, the book presents recent knowledge and advances in both theoretical and practical aspects of depression and suicidal behavior.

The book is organized as follows:

Chapter 1: "Are Mexican University Students on the Brink? Unraveling the Impact of Psychosocial Factors on Suicidal Ideation Amidst COVID-19"

Chapter 2: "Depression and Burnout Syndrome in Healthcare Workers: Psychological Health and Reflections on Patient Safety"

Chapter 3: "Depression and Suicidal Ideations in Older Adults"

Chapter 4: "Fostering Healthy Growth of Sexual and Gender Diverse Young People: The Role of Parents/Caregivers and Social-Emotional Learning"

Chapter 5: "Loneliness, Depression, Suicide"

Chapter 6: "The Influence of Big Five Personality Traits on Depression and Suicidal Behavior"

Chapter 7: "The Relationship between Depression and Suicide"

Chapter 8: "The Role of Self-Rumination from Psychological, Neurological, and Linguistic Viewpoints"

Francisco Manuel Morales-Rodríguez
Department of Developmental and Educational Psychology,
University of Granada,
Grenada, Spain

Chapter 1

Are Mexican University Students on the Brink? Unraveling the Impact of Psychosocial Factors on Suicidal Ideation Amidst COVID-19

Blanca-Rosa García-Rivera
and Ignacio-Alejandro Mendoza-Martínez

Abstract

This research examines the psychosocial determinants of suicidal ideation among students in Mexican higher education during the COVID-19 pandemic. It explores factors such as Academic Pressure, Work Overload, Emotional Responses to COVID-19, Pandemic-Induced Uncertainty, Media Exposure, Resource Deprivation, Moral Distress, and Emotional Regulation. Using a methodologically robust approach, the study reveals the complex relationship between these factors and suicidal ideation, highlighting the challenges students face during the pandemic. Findings emphasize the need to address psychosocial factors in educational settings and call for targeted interventions and support mechanisms to reduce the risk of suicidal ideation. This research advances scientific understanding and underscores the urgency of evidence-based strategies to protect student well-being and foster resilience in times of crisis.

Keywords: academic pressure, moral distress, pandemic-induced uncertainty, emotional dysregulation, suicidal ideation

1. Introduction

In the wake of the COVID-19 pandemic, the mental health of university students has emerged as a pressing concern worldwide. Amidst the myriad challenges brought about by the pandemic, students enrolled in higher education institutions in Mexico face a unique set of circumstances that warrant careful examination. Of particular concern is the alarming rise in suicidal ideation among this demographic, signaling an urgent need for comprehensive understanding and targeted intervention strategies. The transition to remote learning during the quarantine, coupled with the uncertainties surrounding the pandemic, compounded existing stressors for students, exacerbating feelings of isolation, academic pressure, and financial strain. As the educational landscape continued to evolve in response to the pandemic, it became imperative to unravel the complex interplay of psychosocial factors that contributed to the emergence of suicidal ideation among Mexican university students to prevent future crisis-related emergencies.

Numerous scholarly inquiries have been directed toward discerning the ramifications of pandemics on suicidal ideation. A cursory exploration of academic literature yielded a substantial corpus, with Google Scholar returning 3,280,000 results within a mere 0.32 seconds. These findings underscore the heightened scholarly attention dedicated to unraveling the multifaceted interplay between pandemics and suicidal ideation. Within this expansive realm of inquiry, diverse methodological approaches have emerged, each endeavoring to elucidate the nuanced effects of psychosocial risks stemming from quarantine measures on the manifestation of suicidal ideation.

The scholarly landscape surrounding the impact of pandemics on suicidal ideation is vast and multifaceted, reflecting a convergence of interdisciplinary perspectives and methodological approaches. Early investigations by Hawton et al. [1] delved into the psychological ramifications of infectious disease outbreaks, shedding light on the complex interplay between societal stressors and mental health outcomes. Building upon this foundation, Holmes et al. [2] elucidated the psychosocial sequelae of quarantine measures, emphasizing the heightened risk of psychological distress and suicidal ideation among affected populations. Similarly, research by Gunnell and Appleby [3] underscored the need for proactive interventions to mitigate the adverse mental health effects of pandemics, particularly among vulnerable demographics. Within the realm of psychological inquiry, studies by Czeisler et al. [4] and Torales et al. [5] have elucidated the psychological toll of the COVID-19 pandemic, highlighting the intricate interplay of fear, uncertainty, and social isolation in precipitating suicidal ideation. Moreover, examinations by Ornell et al. [6] and Gunnell and Appleby [3] have underscored the disproportionate burden of mental health challenges borne by marginalized populations during periods of crisis, emphasizing the imperative for equitable access to mental health resources. Complementing these findings, investigations by Xiong et al. [7] and Mamun et al. [8] have delved into the mediating role of psychological resilience and coping mechanisms in buffering against the adverse mental health effects of pandemics, offering insights into potential avenues for intervention and support. Together, these seminal contributions illuminate the intricate psychosocial dynamics underpinning suicidal ideation during pandemics, providing a foundation for evidence-based interventions and policy responses aimed at safeguarding public mental health in times of crisis.

This study seeks to address this critical gap in the literature by meticulously examining the complex web of factors contributing to suicidal ideation among students enrolled in Mexican higher education institutions. Specifically, the research endeavors to explore the influence of academic pressure, work overload, emotional responses to COVID-19, pandemic-induced uncertainty, media exposure, resource deprivation, moral distress, emotional regulation, and emotional dysregulation on students' susceptibility to suicidal ideation. Through the application of a rigorous research methodology, underpinned by established theoretical frameworks from the realms of psychology and sociology, this study endeavors to illuminate the nuanced interplay between these psychosocial determinants and suicidal ideation. By elucidating these dynamics with precision and depth, the research aims to offer invaluable insights into the multifaceted challenges encountered by students as they navigate the unprecedented circumstances precipitated by the ongoing pandemic.

Through an examination of the nuanced relationship between psychosocial factors and suicidal ideation, this research endeavors to inform evidence-based intervention strategies aimed at safeguarding student well-being and fostering resilience in the face of adversity. By shedding light on the underlying determinants of suicidal ideation among Mexican university students, this study seeks to catalyze dialog and action toward creating a supportive and inclusive educational environment that prioritizes mental health and holistic well-being.

1.1 Objective

This study aims to ascertain the significant impact of various psychosocial determinants, including Academic Pressure, Work Overload, Emotional Responses to COVID-19, Pandemic-Induced Uncertainty, Media Exposure, Resource Deprivation, Moral Distress, Emotional Regulation, and Emotional Dysregulation, on suicidal ideation among students enrolled in Mexican higher education institutions during the COVID-19 pandemic.

1.2 Research question

To what extent do academic, professional, and socioemotional factors, namely Academic Pressure, Work Overload, Emotional Responses to COVID-19, Pandemic-Induced Uncertainty, Media Exposure, Resource Deprivation, Moral Distress, Emotional Regulation, and Emotional Dysregulation, exert significant influence on suicidal ideation among students enrolled in Mexican higher education institutions during the COVID-19 pandemic, as perceived by scientific inquiry and scholarly rigor?

1.3 Justification

This research holds significant practical implications for public health policy, clinical practice, and community intervention efforts amidst the ongoing COVID-19 pandemic. By elucidating the intricate interplay of psychosocial factors in precipitating suicidal ideation among students in Mexican higher education institutions, this study provides actionable insights for the development and implementation of targeted intervention strategies aimed at mitigating the adverse mental health effects of the pandemic. Understanding the specific stressors and vulnerabilities faced by this demographic is crucial for tailoring support services and resources to address their unique needs effectively.

Furthermore, this research contributes to the existing body of literature by shedding new light on the complex nexus between pandemics, psychosocial risks, and suicidal ideation. By employing a comprehensive framework that encompasses academic, professional, and socioemotional dimensions, this study advances our understanding of the underlying mechanisms driving suicidal ideation among university students during times of crisis. Such insights not only enrich theoretical models of suicide risk but also inform evidence-based practices and interventions across diverse settings and populations.

Beyond its academic contributions, this research carries significant social and economic benefits for Mexican society at large. By identifying and addressing the psychosocial determinants of suicidal ideation among university students, this study has the potential to reduce the prevalence of mental health disorders and associated socioeconomic burdens. By promoting student well-being and resilience, interventions informed by this research can enhance academic performance, workforce productivity, and overall societal flourishing. Moreover, by fostering a culture of mental health awareness and support within educational institutions, this research lays the groundwork for building a more resilient and compassionate society that prioritizes the holistic well-being of its citizens.

In sum, this research serves as a catalyst for positive change, offering practical solutions, advancing scholarly discourse, and promoting societal well-being in the face of unprecedented challenges posed by the COVID-19 pandemic. Through its interdisciplinary approach and real-world applicability, this study exemplifies the transformative potential of scientific inquiry in addressing pressing social issues and fostering a healthier, more resilient future for all.

Regarding the objective and research question, a Structural Equation Model with Latent Variables was developed using the Partial Least Squares method (SEM-PLS), which is presented in **Figure 1**.

In **Figure 1**, the anticipated effects of the exogenous variables on the endogenous variables are illustrated as suggested in the SEM model.

1.4 Initial structural equation model framework proposal

Figure 1 shows a direct and inverse influence of the exogenous variables on the endogenous variables, aligned with their expected theoretical relationships.

1.5 Specific hypotheses

The initial SEM-PLS model integrated the following specific hypotheses, presented in **Table 1**.

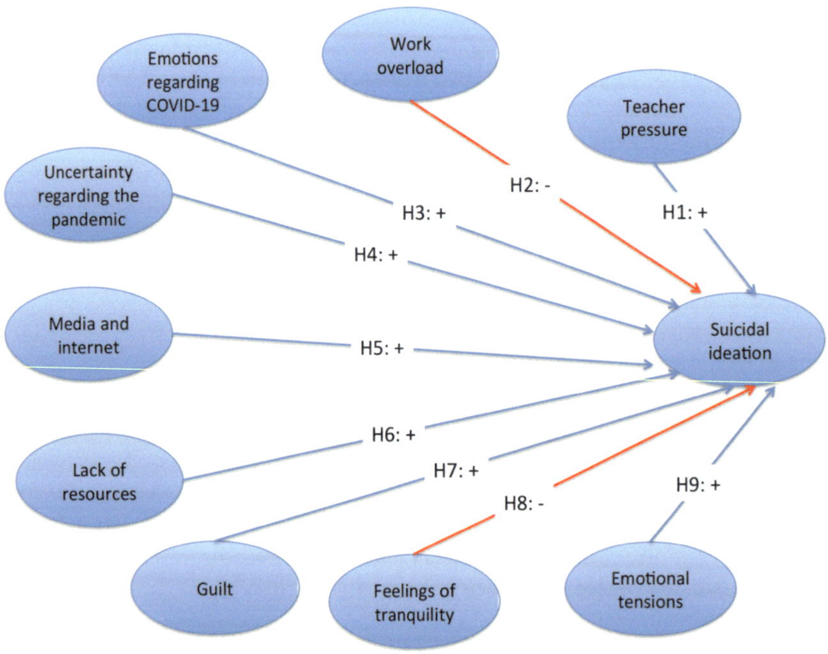

Figure 1.
Source: Self-research.

Hypotheses	Hypotheses statement
H1:	"Teacher pressure has a significant direct influence on suicidal ideation."
H2:	"Work overload has a significant inverse influence on suicidal ideation."
H3:	"Emotions regarding COVID-19 have a significant direct influence on suicidal ideation."
H4:	"Uncertainty regarding the pandemic has a significant direct influence on suicidal ideation."
H5:	"Media and internet have a significant direct influence on suicidal ideation."
H6:	"Lack of resources has a significant direct influence on suicidal ideation."
H7:	"Feelings of guilt have a significant direct influence on suicidal ideation."
H8:	"Feelings of tranquility have a significant inverse influence on suicidal ideation."
H9:	"Emotional tensions have a significant direct influence on suicidal ideation."
Source: Self-research.	

Table 1.
Specific hypotheses.

The specific hypotheses are expressed in **Table 2**, considering their statistical expression.

1.6 Suicidal ideation

The COVID-19 pandemic has significantly impacted mental health worldwide, and higher education students in Mexico have been no exception. The increase in suicidal ideation among this group can be attributed to several interconnected factors, including Academic pressure and overload, uncertainty and anxiety, emotions regarding COVID-19, media and internet, lack of resources, feelings of guilt, and other psychological risks that youngsters experienced during the Pandemic. Martinez-Libano and Yeomans [9] made a systematic review of suicidal ideation in University Students during the pandemic finding that almost 18% of

Hypothesis	Exogenous or independent variables.	Expected influence	Endogenous or dependent Variable
H1:	Teacher pressure	+	Suicidal Intent
H2:	Work overload	–	
H3:	Emotions regarding COVID-19	+	
H4:	Uncertainty regarding the pandemic	+	
H5:	Media and internet	+	
H6:	Lack of resources	+	
H7:	Guilt	+	
H8:	Feelings of tranquility	–	
H9:	Emotional tensions	+	
Source: Self-research.			

Table 2.
Statistical expression of hypotheses.

the University Students population had suicidal ideation thoughts regarding psychological, contextual, and health factors. Despite extensive research on suicidal ideation, there is a notable lack of studies in Mexico. Therefore, investigating suicidal ideation among students by analyzing variables such as gender, sociodemographic characteristics, and mediating factors is essential. Recent studies have shown increased levels of suicidal ideation among students during the COVID-19 pandemic [9–12].

1.7 Hypotheses theoretical support

"H1 and H2: Teacher pressure and Work overload versus Suicidal Ideation."

Addressing suicidal behavior among university students presents an important challenge in the realm of public health, often hindered by societal stigma and a reluctance to engage with this critical issue [13]. The World Health Organization (WHO) reports that approximately 700,000 individuals deliberately end their own lives each year, rendering suicide the second leading cause of mortality among individuals aged 15 to 24 [14, 15]. Moreover, the WHO extends this age bracket to encompass individuals aged 10 to 24 in numerous countries, underscoring the alarming prevalence of suicide within this demographic (WHO). Beyond these alarming statistics, it is crucial to acknowledge the spectrum of suicidal behavior, which encompasses varying degrees of severity. This spectrum spans from fleeting thoughts of not wanting to live to concrete contemplation of suicide, progressing to suicide threats and attempts, and ultimately culminating in death by suicide, representing the most severe manifestation [16, 17]. Notably, death by suicide comprises only a fraction of all suicide attempts, constituting approximately 10% annually [18]. Despite the fact that many suicide attempts do not result in death, they carry significant risks, including severe injury, physical pain, and an increased vulnerability to future suicide attempts [19, 20]. Moreover, suicidal behaviors can exacerbate broader mental health struggles among university students, leading to considerable suffering and impairments across various aspects of their lives.

Being a university student is renowned for its demanding nature, characterized by a plethora of stressors such as heavy workloads, challenging interactions with professors, administrative demands, and societal expectations [21, 22]. The convergence of these stressors can exact a profound toll on students' mental health and well-being, potentially precipitating adverse outcomes [23]. Likewise, suicidal ideation, defined as the contemplation of self-harm or ending one's life, presents a significant concern for mental health [24]. This phenomenon can stem from a multitude of factors, including psychological distress, interpersonal conflicts, and a perceived lack of social support [25, 26]. The intersection of these stressors with the unique challenges faced by university students underscores the imperative of comprehensively understanding the relationship between stress and suicidal ideation within the educational context.

A burgeoning body of literature has illuminated the intricate interplay between stressors inherent in university life and the manifestation of suicidal ideation among students [27, 28]. Research studies, as detailed in **Table 3**, underscore the profound impact of stress on students' mental health and the prevalence of suicidal ideation within this population. By acknowledging and addressing the complex interplay between stress and suicidal ideation among university students, stakeholders can implement targeted interventions and support mechanisms to safeguard the psychological well-being of students and mitigate the risk of adverse outcomes. Following

Model	Author	Theory explained:
Job Demands-Control-Support Model (JDCS)	Karasek and Theorell [23]	This model suggests that job demands (e.g., workload) and control (e.g., autonomy) influence employees' stress levels. High job demands coupled with low control are associated with increased stress, which may contribute to the development of suicidal ideation among individuals experiencing a sense of helplessness or lack of agency in their work environment.
Effort-Reward Imbalance Model (ERI)	Siegrist [29]	The ERI model posits that when individuals perceive an imbalance between the efforts they exert at work and the rewards they receive (e.g., salary, recognition), they experience stress. This chronic stress may lead to feelings of frustration and hopelessness, which are risk factors for suicidal ideation.
Transactional Model of Stress and Coping	Lazarus and Folkman [30]	This model proposes that stress arises from the interaction between individuals and their environment. Coping strategies, such as problem-solving or seeking social support, mediate the relationship between stressors and psychological outcomes. Maladaptive coping responses to work-related stressors may exacerbate feelings of despair and hopelessness, contributing to suicidal ideation.
Demand-Control Model (DCM)	Johnson and Hall [22]	The DCS model extends the JDC model by incorporating social support as a buffering factor against job strain. Perceived support from colleagues and supervisors may mitigate the impact of high job demands and low control on stress levels, reducing the likelihood of suicidal ideation among employees.
Conservation of Resources (COR) Theory	Hobfoll [31]	COR theory suggests that individuals strive to acquire, retain, and protect valuable resources such as job security, social support, and self-esteem. Loss of these resources or failure to gain them may lead to stress and emotional distress, increasing vulnerability to suicidal ideation.
Occupational Stress Theory	Cooper and Marshall [32]	Occupational stress theory focuses on the relationship between work-related stressors and adverse health outcomes. Persistent exposure to job stressors, such as role ambiguity or interpersonal conflict, may erode individuals' resilience and coping resources, increasing susceptibility to suicidal ideation as a maladaptive response to overwhelming stress.
Cognitive Activation Theory of Stress (CATS)	Ursin and Eriksen [33]	CATS suggests that stress results from the activation of cognitive processes aimed at maintaining psychological equilibrium in response to environmental demands. Maladaptive cognitive activation patterns, such as rumination or catastrophizing, may amplify stress responses and contribute to the emergence of suicidal ideation.
Biopsychosocial Model	Engel [34]	This holistic model considers the interplay of biological, psychological, and social factors in shaping individuals' health outcomes. Biopsychosocial stressors, such as chronic illness, interpersonal conflicts, or socioeconomic disadvantage, may interact to increase vulnerability to suicidal ideation through their cumulative impact on individuals' mental and emotional well-being.
Dual Process Model (DPM)	Lazarus and Folkman [30]	The DPM proposes that stress-related psychopathology results from the interplay between cognitive appraisal processes and emotion regulation strategies. Dysfunctional cognitive appraisals of stressors, such as perceived threat or loss, coupled with ineffective emotion regulation, may contribute to the development of suicidal ideation.
Person-Environment Fit (P-E Fit) Model	Caplan [21]	This model emphasizes the importance of congruence between individuals and their work environment in determining well-being. A mismatch between an individual's abilities, needs, and values, and the demands and rewards of their job, may lead to stress and psychological distress, increasing susceptibility to suicidal ideation.

Source: Self-research.

Table 3.
Classic models supporting Stress and Suicidal Ideation.

this, **Table 3** provides a succinct comparison of models and authors pertinent to this relationship.

As seen in **Table 3**, several theoretical models have been proposed to understand the relationship between teacher stress and suicidal ideation. These models offer insights into the complex interplay of individual and environmental factors that contribute to teachers' mental health outcomes. By examining these models and their respective authors, researchers can gain a deeper understanding of the mechanisms underlying teacher stress and its implications for suicidal ideation. Overall, these theoretical models provide valuable information into the multifaceted nature of work-related stress and its implications for mental health, including suicidal ideation. By understanding the underlying mechanisms, researchers and practitioners can develop targeted interventions to prevent and address suicidal ideation in educational institutions. Identifying the predictors of suicidal behavior assumes paramount importance in crafting efficacious prevention strategies and interventions tailored to university students amidst the backdrop of the COVID-19 pandemic. A comprehensive understanding of these predictors not only enriches the design of preventative measures but also informs the development of interventions aimed at bolstering the therapeutic alliance and curtailing dropout rates among students currently undergoing treatment.

Drawing from this understanding, two hypotheses can be proposed:

H1: "Teacher pressure has a significant direct influence on suicidal ideation."

H2: "Work overload has a significant inverse influence on suicidal ideation."

These hypotheses are grounded in the literature linking Teacher pressure, work overload, and suicidal ideation, and they highlight the unique challenges faced by university students during the pandemic. By empirically testing these hypotheses, researchers can gain insights into the specific mechanisms underlying the relationship between teacher pressure, work overload, and suicide intent among university students, informing targeted interventions and support strategies to mitigate suicide risk during times of crisis [35].

"H3 and H4 Negative Emotions and Uncertainty regarding Covid-19 versus Suicide Intent."

Investigating the relationship between negative emotions and uncertainty regarding COVID-19 and suicide intent among university students requires a nuanced understanding of various psychological and situational factors. Negative emotions, such as depression, anxiety, and hopelessness, have long been recognized as significant contributors to suicidal ideation and behavior [36, 37]. These emotions often arise from stressors, such as academic pressure, financial strain, social isolation, and personal challenges, all of which are prevalent among university students, particularly during the COVID-19 pandemic [38, 39]. Furthermore, the uncertainty surrounding the COVID-19 pandemic introduces an additional layer of stress and anxiety, as individuals grapple with fears about their health, the health of their loved ones, economic instability, and disruptions to daily life [40, 41]. Uncertainty about the future and the unpredictability of the pandemic's trajectory can exacerbate feelings of powerlessness and distress, further amplifying negative emotions and increasing susceptibility to suicidal thoughts and behaviors [8, 42].

In the context of university students, who are already navigating the challenges of academic demands, social pressures, and developmental transitions, the confluence of negative emotions and uncertainty regarding COVID-19 may heighten vulnerability to suicide intent. Students may experience a sense of overwhelm and hopelessness, feeling trapped in a situation where they perceive few options for relief or improvement [43, 44]. This heightened distress may manifest as increased thoughts of suicide as a means of escape or relief from psychological pain [45, 46]. Drawing from this understanding, two hypotheses can be proposed:

H3: "Emotions regarding COVID-19 have a significant direct influence on suicidal ideation."

H4: "Uncertainty regarding the pandemic has a significant direct influence on suicidal ideation."

These hypotheses are grounded in the literature linking negative emotions, uncertainty, and suicidal ideation, and they highlight the unique challenges faced by university students during the pandemic. By empirically testing these hypotheses, researchers can gain insights into the specific mechanisms underlying the relationship between negative emotions, uncertainty, and suicide intent among university students, informing targeted interventions and support strategies to mitigate suicide risk during times of crisis.

H5: "Media and internet have a significant direct influence on suicidal ideation."

While the COVID-19 pandemic has not impacted as many individuals as some other historical crises, nor is it the most lethal, its repercussions have been profound due to the interconnectedness of today's globalized world. Initially, many societies adopted a passive stance, believing that modern advancements and infrastructures provided adequate control. This misconception, amplified by the constant influx of information and misinformation through media and the internet, significantly hampered timely and effective responses. The rapid spread of COVID-19 dismantled the perceived sense of security, demonstrating how quickly a virus could exploit the vulnerabilities of a globalized society. The unique characteristics of this pandemic, coupled with the overwhelming flow of information on digital platforms, created confusion and anxiety, further straining individuals' resources. This scenario highlighted the critical need for better media literacy, responsible reporting, and more robust international health strategies to address future global health threats effectively [47, 48].

H6: "Lack of resources has a significant direct influence on suicidal ideation."

Hopelessness is identified as a significant individual risk factor in various models [49], leading people to perceive their current problems as insurmountable. Additionally, adverse living conditions, combined with certain personal characteristics such as low educational levels, inadequate problem-solving strategies, impulsivity, and lack of self-control, can create high-risk environments for families facing psychosocial challenges. These factors particularly impact the well-being and biopsychosocial development, as they contribute to a chaotic environment with dysfunctional communication. Studies indicate that diminished displays of affection and poorly defined family rules correlate with increased psychological stress and reduced problem-solving abilities. During the COVID-19 pandemic, many professors faced significant challenges due to a lack of resources, exacerbating feelings of hopelessness. The sudden shift to online teaching, often without adequate technological support or training, left many educators struggling to cope. This lack of resources, combined with the overwhelming stress of adapting to new teaching methods and maintaining student engagement, contributed to a sense of helplessness. In some cases, this profound despair and inability to see a resolution led to tragic outcomes, including suicidal ideation. The pandemic highlighted the urgent need for better support systems and resources for educators to ensure their mental health and well-being during crises [50].

H7: "Feelings of guilt have a significant direct influence on suicidal ideation."

Research has demonstrated that the emotion of shame induces toxic experiences of worthlessness, inferiority, and incompetence, leading to a desire to escape and socially withdraw. Recurring experiences of shame can exacerbate a global negative self-attribution, often associated with adverse effects on mental well-being, including poor psychological adjustment, interpersonal difficulties, and overall poor life functioning. The psychopathological symptoms elicited by shameful experiences can vary from eating disorders and depression to anxiety disorders. The highly distressing and cumulative nature of COVID-19-related stressors can often provoke a shame response, potentially leading to traumatic consequences based on perceptions of having no value to others or, worse, of being dangerous to them. The fear of possible shameful experiences and of being rejected by others can prevent individuals from disclosing relevant facts about their clinical situation and their actual risk of contagion. Such attitudes may be observed in traumatized patients treated for COVID-19 or those exhibiting symptoms of the disease, potentially contributing to the further spread of the virus in other social contexts. Personal experiences of COVID-19 may elicit shame related to thoughts of inferiority and weakness. After becoming infected, individuals may perceive themselves as defective and powerless, triggering self-criticism and negative self-assessment. Furthermore, COVID-19 patients or individuals who have recovered from the disease may experience shameful feelings induced by social rejection from family members or friends. Given that shame can make individuals want to withdraw from social interactions for extended periods, living with COVID-19 may become a far more negative experience than necessary [51].

H8: "Feelings of tranquility have a significant inverse influence on suicidal ideation."

Feelings of tranquility play a critical role in mitigating suicidal ideation, serving as a significant protective factor against the emergence of self-destructive thoughts. Tranquility, characterized by a state of calmness, peace, and emotional stability, can counterbalance the overwhelming stress and negative affective states that often precipitate suicidal ideation. Research indicates that individuals experiencing higher levels of tranquility are better equipped to cope with life's adversities, demonstrating enhanced resilience and a greater capacity for positive problem-solving. This emotional state reduces the psychological impact of adverse experiences, thereby diminishing the intensity and frequency of suicidal thoughts. Moreover, tranquility fosters a sense of hope and well-being, which are essential for maintaining mental health and preventing the descent into severe depressive states. By promoting emotional equilibrium and reducing internal turmoil, feelings of tranquility significantly decrease the likelihood of suicidal ideation, underscoring their vital role in mental health interventions and suicide prevention strategies [52].

H9: "Emotional tensions have a significant direct influence on suicidal ideation."

Emotional tensions significantly contribute to the onset and intensification of suicidal ideation, acting as a direct influence on individuals' mental states. Emotional tensions, often arising from prolonged stress, interpersonal conflicts, and unresolved psychological issues, can lead to overwhelming feelings of distress and hopelessness. These tensions exacerbate negative thought patterns, creating a fertile ground for suicidal ideation as individuals struggle to find relief from their emotional pain. Research consistently shows that high levels of emotional turmoil are closely associated with an increased risk of suicide, as they impair cognitive functioning and limit the ability to engage in effective problem-solving and coping strategies. This emotional strain can lead to feelings of entrapment and a perceived lack of alternatives, driving individuals toward considering suicide as a means of escape. Additionally, emotional tensions can amplify underlying mental health conditions such as depression and anxiety, further heightening the risk of suicidal thoughts and behaviors. Therefore, addressing and mitigating emotional tensions is crucial in reducing suicidal ideation and enhancing overall mental well-being [53].

2. Methods

2.1 Type of study

This is ex-post-facto, observational, cross-sectional study that is somewhat explanatory due to the use of Structural Equation Models.

2.2 Unit of analysis

The study focused on a sample of 17,046 Mexican university students. The sociodemographic composition of the sample was as follows: 63.9% were females (n = 10,255), and 36.1% were males (n = 6791). Regarding marital status, 91.3% of the participants were single (n = 15,575), 3.8% were in a civil union (n = 646), 3.8% were married (n = 655), and 1% fell into other categories (n = 170). In terms of educational attainment, 90.3% were pursuing a Bachelor's degree (n = 15,396), 6.4% were enrolled in specialization programs (n = 1088), 2.3% were pursuing a Master's degree (n = 392), and 1% were categorized as "other" (n = 170). The age distribution was as follows: 73.2% were between 17 and 22 years old (n = 12,488), 19.4% were between 23 and 27 years old (n = 3314), and 7.3% were aged 28 years or older (n = 1244). All participants received detailed information about the study's objectives and provided informed consent online. No financial compensation was provided to participants.

2.3 Data collection

Data collection was conducted electronically between early April 2020 and late May 2020. The survey was distributed to the entire population of students and professors at Northern Mexican universities, resulting in a final sample of 17,057 students. Professors were excluded from this analysis. Responses were compiled into a database, which was subsequently edited and analyzed using IBM SPSS Statistics version 23 for Windows and Smart PLS version 3.

2.4 Instruments

The data collection instrument consisted of several sections, including questions about the students' sociodemographic characteristics such as gender, marital status, age, and academic information like program enrollment and scholarship status. The instrument also included a section on uncertainty related to the COVID-19 pandemic, which was developed specifically for this study. This section comprised five Likert-scale questions measuring uncertainty as a unidimensional variable, with sample items such as: "I was afraid when facing the pandemic," "I felt that life is very fragile," "I feared being infected," and "I was terrified to imagine someone dear was going to die." Although this instrument had not been previously validated in Mexico, its internal consistency was tested using Cronbach's alpha, along with assessments of content validity, construct validity, and concurrent validity, all of which yielded reliable results. The reliability of the constructs was confirmed, with Cronbach's alpha and Rho coefficients exceeding 0.70. For validity, the Average Variance Extracted (AVE) scores for all subscales met or exceeded 0.50, and discriminant validity coefficients were above 0.70, consistent with the Fornell-Larcker criterion.

The study also employed a modified version of the Scale for Suicide Ideation (SSI-W) to evaluate suicidal thoughts among students during the pandemic. This adaptation comprised six questions, each rated on a binary scale, based on the original SSI-W developed by Beck et al. [54]. Initially created and validated for use with psychiatric patients in the United States, the SSI-W has been extensively utilized in both clinical and outpatient environments.

The questionnaire administered to students included inquiries about their sociodemographic characteristics, such as gender, marital status, age, educational background, academic program, and scholarship status. These variables were categorized to facilitate demographic analysis.

The SBI (Gil-Monte) burnout questionnaire was also utilized, focusing specifically on the Guilt Dimension, which includes items 4, 9, 13, 16, and 20. This scale has been tested and validated in Latin America and Mexico with satisfactory outcomes [55]. The reliability and validity of the constructs measured by this instrument were confirmed through similar methods, with all subscales demonstrating reliability coefficients above 0.70, AVE scores of 0.50 or greater, and discriminant validity coefficients above 0.70.

The adaptation of the SSI-W focused on assessing suicidal ideation among students during the pandemic. While the SSI-W has been widely applied in the United States since its standardization for psychiatric patients [54], its use among university students in Mexico has been limited. Although few studies have applied the scale in the Mexican context, those that did reported positive results. As with the other instruments, the reliability of the SSI-W adaptation was confirmed, with all subscales exhibiting alpha and Rho coefficients above 0.70. The validity was supported by AVE scores meeting or exceeding 0.50, and discriminant validity coefficients consistent with the Fornell-Larcker criterion.

2.5 Psychometric properties of the scales

2.5.1 Reliability

The Cronbach's Alpha exceeded the level of $\alpha = 0.70$ for all subscales. The hierarchy from the highest to lowest is as follows:

1. Emotions regarding COVID-19 ($\alpha = 0.92$)
2. Guilt ($\alpha = 0.91$)
3. Work overload ($\alpha = 0.89$)
4. Suicidal ideation ($\alpha = 0.87$)
5. Uncertainty regarding the pandemic ($\alpha = 0.87$)
6. Pressure from faculty ($\alpha = 0.81$)
7. Media and internet ($\alpha = 0.79$)
8. Lack of resources ($\alpha = 0.79$)
9. Emotions of calm ($\alpha = 0.79$)
10. Emotional tensions ($\alpha = 0.74$)

The reliability analysis was completed with the calculation of the composite reliability coefficient (Rho), showing the following results:

1. Emotions regarding COVID-19 (Rho = 0.93)

2. Guilt (Rho = 0.93)

3. Work overload (Rho = 0.91)

4. Suicidal ideation (Rho = 0.90)

5. Uncertainty regarding the pandemic

6. Lack of resources (Rho = 0.88)

7. Media and internet (Rho = 0.88)

8. Emotions of calm (Rho = 0.88)

9. Pressure from faculty (Rho = 0.87)

10. Emotional tensions (Rho = 0.85)

These results confirm that the instrument used in this study strongly meets the criteria for reliability and internal consistency in measuring the constructs.

2.5.2 Validity

Regarding convergent validity, the Average Variance Extracted (AVE) exceeded the score of 0.50 for all subscales. The hierarchy from the highest to lowest is as follows:

1. Guilt (AVE = 0.74)

2. Media and internet (AVE = 0.70)

3. Lack of resources (AVE = 0.70)

4. Emotions of calm (AVE = 0.70)

5. Emotions regarding COVID-19 (AVE = 0.67)

6. Emotional tensions (AVE = 0.65)

7. Suicidal ideation (AVE = 0.65)

8. Uncertainty regarding the pandemic (AVE = 0.65)

9. Pressure from faculty (AVE = 0.63)

10. Work overload (AVE = 0.63)

The validity was further confirmed with the calculation of the discriminant validity coefficient (Square Root of AVE), exceeding 0.70 for all subscales:

1. Guilt (0.86)
2. Lack of resources (0.84)
3. Media and internet (0.84)
4. Emotions of calm (0.84)
5. Emotions regarding COVID-19
6. Uncertainty regarding the pandemic
7. Emotional tensions (0.81)
8. Suicidal ideation (0.81)
9. Work overload (0.79)
10. Pressure from faculty (0.79)

Considering the above data, it can be affirmed that the instrument demonstrated adequate levels of validity, encompassing both convergent and discriminant validities.

2.5.3 Correlations

The Pearson Product–Moment correlations corroborated the expected theoretical assumptions regarding inverse correlations between subscales. The correlations between Emotions of calm and the other subscales at the 0.95% level are as follows:

- Pressure from faculty (r = −0.24)
- Work overload (r = −0.37)
- Emotions regarding COVID-19 (r = −0.57)
- Uncertainty regarding the pandemic (r = −0.41)
- Media and internet (r = −0.33)
- Lack of resources (r = −0.26)
- Guilt (r = −0.12)
- Emotional tensions (r = −0.55)
- Suicidal ideation (r = −0.25)

3. Results

The generation of structural equation models using partial least squares (SEM-PLS) was developed using the R Studio PLSPM software.

3.1 SEM results

The results of structural modeling are seen in **Figure 2** and **Tables 4** and 5.

In **Figure 2**, the observed effects of the exogenous variables on the endogenous variable are shown in the SEM model.

Figure 2 shows a direct influence f Emotions regarding COVID-19 AND Guilt and inverse influence of Work overload on Suicidal Ideation, accordingly to the expected theoretical relationships. Moreover, on **Table 4**, we can observe the results from the SEM in detail.

As noticed in **Table 4** in the SEM results, we observed six hypotheses that were not accepted. Moreover, in **Table 5**, we present results from the SEM.

3.2 Statistical analysis and hypothesis testing

3.2.1 Results of hypothesis testing

The results of the hypothesis testing are presented in **Figure 2** below. As observed, hypotheses H2, H3, and H7 were accepted.

3.2.2 Rejected hypotheses

Of the nine hypotheses derived from the SEM, six were rejected for not being statistically significant, as shown in **Table 6**.

3.2.3 Accepted hypotheses

The specific hypotheses derived from the SEM that were accepted were 3, and the statistical results are presented in **Table 7**.

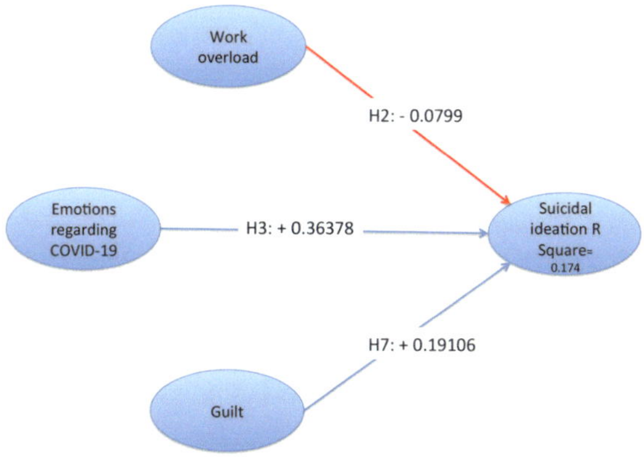

Figure 2.
Source: Self-research.

	Subscales	Items	Alpha de Cronbach	Composite reliability	AVE	E1	E2	E3	E4	E5	E6	E7	E8	E9	E10
E1	Pressure from Faculty	4	0.81	0.87	0.63	**0.79**									
E2	Work Overload	6	0.89	0.91	0.63	0.43	**0.79**								
E3	Emotions regarding COVID-19	7	0.92	0.93	0.67	0.38	0.54	**0.82**							
E4	Uncertainty about the Pandemic	5	0.87	0.90	0.65	0.28	0.40	0.69	**0.81**						
E5	Media and internet	3	0.79	0.88	0.70	0.25	0.33	0.55	0.66	**0.84**					
E6	Lack of Resources	3	0.79	0.88	0.70	0.27	0.41	0.37	0.27	0.29	**0.84**				
E7	Guilt	5	0.91	0.93	0.74	0.18	0.11	0.24	0.21	0.23	0.20	**0.86**			
E8	Feelings of Calm	3	0.79	0.88	0.70	−0.24	−0.37	−0.57	−0.41	−0.33	−0.26	−0.12	**0.84**		
E9	Emotional Tensions	3	0.74	0.85	0.65	0.29	0.44	0.63	0.53	0.43	0.32	0.19	−0.55	**0.81**	
E10	Suicidal Ideation	5	0.87	0.90	0.65	0.19	0.14	0.37	0.32	0.28	0.18	0.27	−0.25	0.28	**0.81**

Source: Self-research.
As shown in this table, the bolded high-value loadings suggest that these items are strong indicators of their respective underlying constructs. This bold formatting highlights the items that contribute significantly to the measurement of each sub-scale, reinforcing the validity and reliability of the constructs assessed.

Table 4.
Results from the SEM.

Subscales	Original	Mean. Boot	Std. Error	perc.025	perc.975
Workoverload - > SuicidalIdeation	−0.08	−0.08	0.01	−0.09	−0.07
EmoCovid - > SuicidalIdeation	0.36	0.36	0.01	0.35	0.38
Guilt - > SuicidalIdeation	0.19	0.19	0.01	0.18	0.21

Source: Self-research.

Table 5.
Results from the SEM.

H:	Hypotheses statement:
H1:	"Teacher pressure has a significant direct influence on suicidal ideation."
H4:	"Uncertainty regarding the pandemic has a significant direct influence on suicidal ideation."
H5:	"Media and the Internet have a significant direct influence on suicidal ideation."
H6:	"Lack of resources has a significant direct influence on suicidal ideation."
H8:	"Emotions of tranquility have a significant inverse influence on suicidal ideation."
H9:	"Emotional tensions have a significant direct influence on suicidal ideation."

Source: Self-research.

Table 6.
Rejected hypotheses.

H:	Exogenous variable	Expected influence	Endogenous variable	R Square	Decision
H2:	Work overload	−0.08	Suicidal ideation	0.174	Accept
H3:	Emotions in the face of COVID-19	0.36			Accept
H7:	Guilt	0.19			Accept

Source: Self-research.

Table 7.
Accepted hypotheses.

With the above-accepted Hypotheses, the following can be affirmed:

H2: "Work overload has a significant inverse influence (−0.08) based on its standardized regression coefficient on suicidal ideation." Although its influence is very small, it was shown to be significant, and if it increases, it could be thought to influence more in reducing suicidal ideation, as students would be engaged in their work as students.

H3: "Emotions regarding COVID-19 have a significant direct influence (0.36) based on their standardized regression coefficient on suicidal ideation." The influence of emotions regarding COVID-19 was relevant, as no previous pandemic had been experienced with the impacts that COVID-19 had.

H7: "Guilt has a significant direct influence (0.19) based on its standardized regression coefficient on suicidal ideation." Guilt had a relevant influence in increasing suicidal ideation; it is important to consider this variable in future studies, as we could observe which emotional variables are related to guilt and could trigger greater suicidal thoughts.

These psychosocial subscales were able to explain approximately 17% of suicidal ideation based on their R-squared value; 17% is a yellow indicator on a "psychosocial traffic light" or a warning indicator for all faculty and educational administration, giving feedback to Educational authorities to direct strategies to address this issue so that it does not progress to actual suicides among students.

3.2.4 Significant differences by gender

To complement the study, it was necessary to run the final SEM PLS to assess possible significant differences by the gender of the students. A bootstrapping test was conducted, yielding the following results shown in **Table 8**.

Table 8 shows results from the group comparison analyzed in PSL-PM for the path coefficients.

As observed, **Table 8** confirms only one significant difference in the influence of Guilt on Suicidal Ideation, based on its p-value, which was less than 0.05. Therefore, it was necessary to run the SEM separately for the group of women and the group of men.

Also, below in **Figure 3**, the results of the observed effects of the exogenous variables on the endogenous variables are illustrated as suggested in the SEM model.

Figure 3 represents the Final SEM of the Students, observing the following results in **Table 9**.

Table 9 shows the exogenous variables expected influence on the endogenous variable.

Scale of Data:	**TRUE**					
Weighting Scheme:	centroid					
Selected method:	permutation					
Number of replicates:	100					
$test						
Subscales	**global group**	**group. Female**	**group. Male**	**diff. Abs**	**p. value**	**sig.05**
workoverload->suicidalideation	−0.08	−0.0813	−0.0801	0.0012	0.9505	no
emocovid->suicidalideation	0.3638	0.3807	0.3513	0.0294	0.1089	no
guilt->suicidalideation	0.1911	0.1459	0.2313	0.0855	0.0099	yes
Inner models in the	following objects:					
$global						
$group1						
$group2						

Source: Self-research.

Table 8.
The analysis employed a permutation method with 100 replicates and a centroid weighting scheme, with the data scaled to ensure comparability. The results indicate that there is no statistically significant difference between males and females for the paths from work overload ("workoverload -> suicidalideation," p = 0.9505) and the emotional impact of COVID-19 ("emocovid -> suicidalideation," p = 0.1089) to suicidal ideation. However, a significant difference is observed in the path from guilt to suicidal ideation ("guilt -> suicidalideation"), with males showing a stronger association (p = 0.0099). This finding suggests that guilt is a more potent predictor of suicidal ideation in males compared to females, indicating a potential area for targeted intervention.

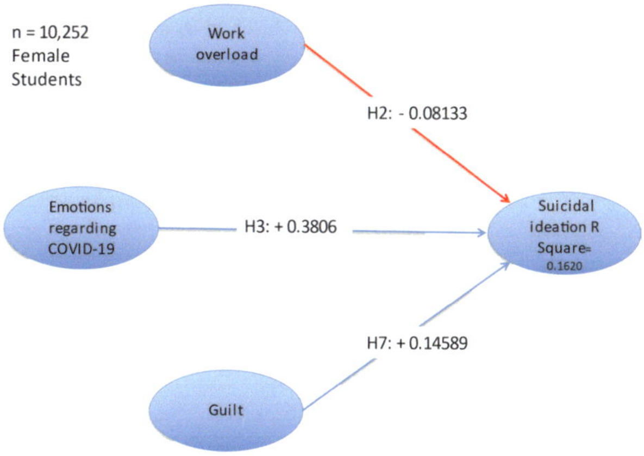

Figure 3.
SEM final female students. Source: Self-research.

H:	Exogenous variable	Expected influence	Endogenous variable	R Square	Decision
H2:	Work overload	−0.08	Suicidal ideation	0.162	Accept
H3:	Emotions in the face of COVID-19	0.38			Accept
H7:	Guilt	0.15			Accept

Source: Self-research.
This table displays the results of hypothesis testing for the relationships between exogenous and endogenous variables. It includes the expected influence, R-squared values, and decisions for each hypothesis. The exogenous variables considered are "Work overload," "Emotions in the face of COVID-19," and "Guilt," with the endogenous variable being "Suicidal ideation." The R-squared values indicate the proportion of variance explained by the exogenous variables, and the decision column reflects whether each hypothesis is supported by the data.

Table 9.
Results of hypothesis testing in structural equation modeling.

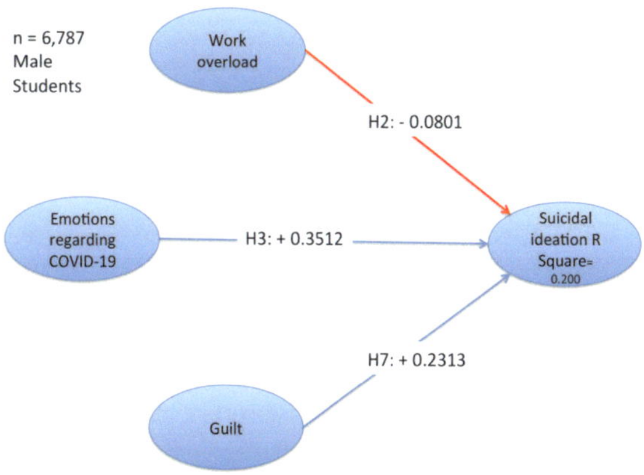

Figure 4.
SEM final male students. Source: Self-research.

H:	Exogenous or independent variable	Expected influence	Endogenous or dependent variable	R Square	Decision
H2:	Work overload	−0.08	Suicidal ideation	0.20	Accept
H3:	Emotions in the face of COVID-19	0.35			Accept
H7:	Guilt	0.23			Accept

Source: Self-research.

Table 10.
Final SEM for Male Students' results.

As observed in **Table 9**, all three Hypotheses were accepted, showing an inverse effect of Work overload on Suicidal Ideation and a direct influence of Emotions in the Face of COVID-19 and Guilt on Suicidal Ideation. Following, in **Figure 4**, we can observe the male students' final SEM.

Figure 4 represents the Final SEM for male Students, observing the results presented in **Table 10**.

As observed in **Table 10**, male students' results present a similar behavior; however, lower Emotions in the face of COVID and a higher Guilt in Males toward Suicidal Ideation are observed.

Scale of Data:	TRUE					
Weighting Scheme:	centroid					
Selected method:	permutation					
Number of replicates:	100					
$test						
Subscales	**global group**	**group. Do not work**	**group. If they work**	**diff. Abs**	**p. value**	**sig.05**
WORKOVERLOAD- > SUICIDALIDEATION	−0.08	−0.081	−0.0842	0.0033	0.8218	no
EMOCOVID- > SUICIDALIDEATION	0.3638	0.3749	0.3555	0.0194	0.2277	no
GUILT- > SUICIDALIDEATION	0.1911	0.169	0.2172	0.0482	0.0198	yes
Inner models in the following objects:						
$global						
$group1						
$group2						

Source: Self-research.

Table 11.
The differential impact of work overload, emotional effects related to COVID-19, and feelings of guilt on suicidal ideation across groups with different work statuses. The results indicate no statistically significant difference between groups ("Do Not Work" and "If They Work") for the paths from work overload (p = 0.8218) and emotional effects of COVID-19 (p = 0.2277) to suicidal ideation. However, a significant difference was found for the path from guilt to suicidal ideation (p = 0.0198), suggesting that guilt may differently influence suicidal ideation depending on whether individuals are working or not.

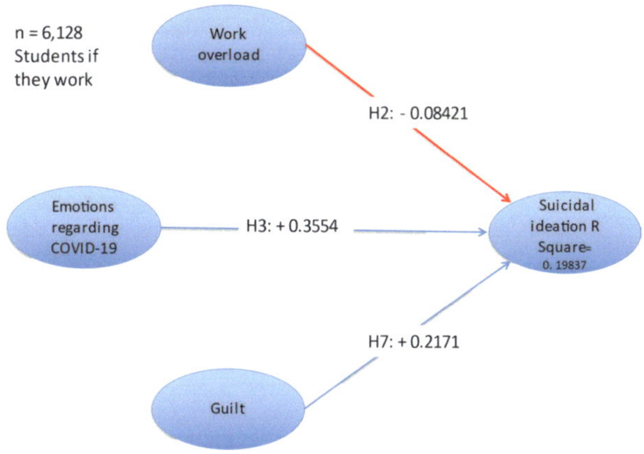

Figure 5.
Final SEM for students if they work. Source: Self-research.

Hypotheses	Exogenous or independent variable	Expected influence	Endogenous or dependent variable	R Square	Decision
H2:	Work overload	−0.0842	Suicidal ideation	0.19837	Accept
H3:	Emotions in the face of COVID-19	0.3555			Accept
H7:	Guilt	0.2172			Accept

Source: Self-research.

Table 12.
Decision to accept or reject Hypotheses According to their expected influence.

3.2.5 Significant differences by the work overload variable

To complement the study, it was necessary to run the final SEM PLS to assess possible significant differences by the work variable of the students. Therefore, a

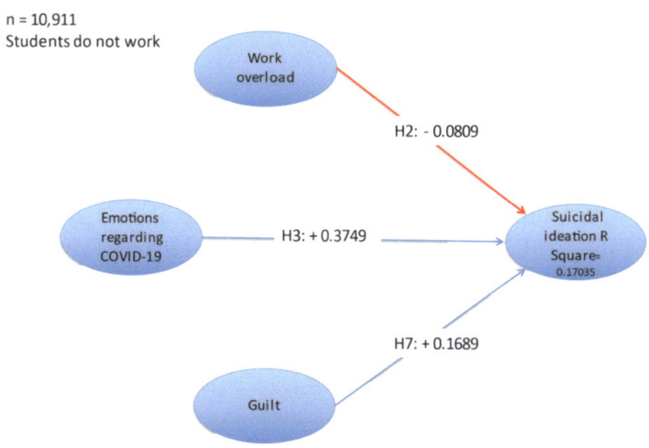

Figure 6.
Final SEM for students who do not work. Source: Self-research.

H:	Exogenous	Expected influence	Endogenous	R Square	Decisión
H2:	Work Overload	−0.081	Suicidal ideation	0.17035	Accept
H3:	Emotions in the face of COVID-19	0.3749			Accept
H7:	Guilt	0.169			Accept

Source: Self-research.

Table 13.
SEM results of students who do not work.

bootstrapping test was conducted, yielding the following results as shown in **Table 11**.

Table 11 shows the path coefficients for the different groups, showing the results if they work and if they do not work.

Table 11 confirms only one significant difference in the influence of Guilt on Suicidal Ideation, based on its p-value, w was less than 0.05. Therefore, it was necessary to run the SEM separately for the group of students who work and the group of students who do not work.

Figure 5 represents the Final SEM of the students who work showing the results observed in **Table 12**.

As noticed in **Table 12**, there was a higher influence of Emotions in the Face of COVID-19 for Students who work; however, they seem to experience the same influence of Guilt as the other group that does not work.

Finally, in **Figure 6**, we can find the SEM for the Students who do not work, observing even a higher influence of Emotions in the Face of COVID-19 vs. the ones who work, showing, however, a lower influence of Guilt and a lower inverse influence of Work overload.

Figure 6 represents the Final SEM of the Students who do not work, observing the results as shown in **Table 13**.

Table 13 shows the results of the students who do not work and their expected influence on the endogenous variable.

Table 13 shows a higher direct influence of Emotions in the face of COVID-19, a lower direct influence of Guilt, and a lower inverse influence of Work Overload.

4. Discussion

Our review explored the prevalence of suicidal ideation among university students amidst the COVID-19 pandemic, focusing on several critical psychological variables. The findings highlight a profound impact on students' mental health, emphasizing guilt, work overload, and emotional responses to COVID-19 as significant factors. Work overload among university students has intensified during the pandemic, exacerbating stress levels and contributing to mental health challenges [56]. The abrupt shift to online learning, combined with academic demands and uncertainties about the future, has placed unprecedented pressure on students, increasing their vulnerability to suicidal ideation [57].

Guilt has emerged as another potent psychological factor affecting students during the pandemic. Feelings of guilt may stem from perceived failures in academic performance, inability to meet personal or familial expectations, or even survivor guilt related to the health and economic impacts of COVID-19. These feelings amplify stress and contribute to a sense of hopelessness, further exacerbating suicidal ideation among vulnerable students. Media exposure to pandemic-related news and social media discussions has played a dual role in shaping students' emotional responses. While information dissemination is crucial, excessive exposure to negative news and misinformation can heighten anxiety and distress among students. Social media platforms, though intended for connectivity, have also become conduits for stress and exacerbate feelings of isolation and uncertainty.

In discussing these findings, our review aligns with similar studies emphasizing the significant impact of emotional responses and suicidal ideation among university students during the COVID-19 pandemic [58]. Consistent with prior research, our findings emphasize that while suicidal ideation is prevalent, actual suicidal behaviors may not always manifest [59]. Moreover, several studies have documented an increase in the intensity of self-harm behaviors, underscoring the need for targeted interventions aimed at mitigating these concerning trends [60].

These observations are consistent with the recommendations of other researchers who advocate for preventive actions focusing on enhancing life-protective factors amidst the challenges posed by the pandemic [61]. By highlighting these converging findings, our study underscores the urgent need for comprehensive mental health strategies tailored to support young individuals in navigating the emotional turmoil exacerbated by global health crises like COVID-19. Further research is warranted to elucidate the underlying mechanisms driving these trends and to evaluate the effectiveness of intervention programs aimed at reducing emotional distress and self-harm behaviors in this vulnerable population.

Addressing suicidal ideation among university students necessitates a multifaceted approach. Interventions should prioritize promoting effective emotional regulation strategies, such as mindfulness and cognitive-behavioral techniques, to help students manage stress and negative emotions effectively [62, 63]. Providing accessible mental health resources and fostering supportive environments within university settings are critical steps in mitigating the adverse psychological impacts of the pandemic.

4.1 Opportunities of future research

Future research should continue to explore these interconnected factors to develop targeted interventions tailored to the evolving needs of university populations in the post-pandemic era. Longitudinal studies are needed to assess the long-term effects of pandemic-induced stressors on students' mental health and to evaluate the effectiveness of interventions aimed at reducing suicidal ideation and improving overall well-being.

4.2 Limitations

Limitations of our study should be considered when interpreting the findings. First, the variability in methodologies across studies examining emotional responses and suicidal ideation during the COVID-19 pandemic may affect the comparability and generalizability of results. Differences in study designs, assessment tools, and sampling techniques could introduce biases and limit the ability to draw definitive conclusions.

Second, the reliance on self-report measures in many studies may introduce response biases, particularly regarding sensitive topics such as suicidal ideation and self-harm behaviors. The subjective nature of self-reported data could lead to underreporting or overreporting of symptoms, affecting the accuracy of prevalence estimates.

Third, the cross-sectional nature of most studies included in our review limits causal inferences. Longitudinal studies are needed to elucidate the temporal relationships between emotional responses, suicidal ideation, and other variables such as media exposure, emotional regulation, and stressors related to the pandemic.

Fourth, the majority of studies focused on specific demographic groups or geographical regions, potentially limiting the generalizability of findings to broader populations. Variations in cultural contexts and healthcare systems could influence the prevalence and manifestation of emotional distress and suicidal ideation across different populations.

Fifth, the rapid evolution of the COVID-19 pandemic and public health responses may have influenced the mental health outcomes studied. Changes in public policies, vaccination campaigns, and social restrictions could have impacted individuals' emotional responses and mental health status during different phases of the pandemic.

Finally, the dynamic nature of emotional responses and suicidal ideation suggests that our findings represent a snapshot in time. Ongoing research is needed to capture the evolving impact of the pandemic on mental health outcomes and to evaluate the long-term effects of preventive measures and interventions.

Despite these limitations, our study contributes valuable insights into the complex interplay of emotional responses and suicidal ideation during the COVID-19 pandemic. Future research should address these limitations to provide a more comprehensive understanding of the psychological consequences of global health crises and inform effective strategies for mental health support and intervention.

In conclusion, while the COVID-19 pandemic has profoundly affected university students' mental health, proactive measures can mitigate these impacts. By addressing guilt, work overload, and emotional responses to COVID-19 through evidence-based interventions and supportive environments, universities can play a crucial role in safeguarding the mental well-being of their students during and after global health crises.

In discussing the implications of our findings, it becomes evident that while our study provides valuable insights into the immediate impact of the COVID-19 pandemic on emotional responses and suicidal ideation among various populations, there are significant implications for long-term public health strategies. The pandemic has underscored the importance of proactive mental health preventive measures. Policymakers and public health officials must prioritize the development and implementation of safety nets and mechanisms for mental health support in preparation for future health crises. This includes integrating mental health services into primary care settings, enhancing community-based support networks, and promoting resilience-building strategies at both individual and societal levels.

Moreover, investments in mental health infrastructure, including workforce training and resource allocation, are crucial to ensure timely and effective responses to emerging mental health challenges during future pandemics or other global crises. By adopting a proactive approach, policymakers can mitigate the impact of future health emergencies on mental health outcomes and promote overall resilience within communities.

Conflict of interest

The authors declare no conflict of interest.

Institutional review board statement

The study was conducted according to the guidelines of the Declaration of Helsinki. The final questionnaire was presented to the Ethics and Bioethics Commission of the Universidad Autonoma de Baja California for its evaluation and authorization, according to NOM-0035.

Author details

Blanca-Rosa García-Rivera[1]* and Ignacio-Alejandro Mendoza-Martínez[2]

1 Facultad de Ciencias Administrativas y Sociales, Universidad Autónoma de Baja California, Ensenada, Baja California, México

2 Departamento de Posgrado e Investigación, Universidad Anáhuac México Norte, Cd. de México, México

*Address all correspondence to: blanca_garcia@uabc.edu.mx

References

[1] Hawton K, Rodham K, Evans E, Harriss L. Adolescents who self harm: A comparison of those who go to hospital and those who do not. Child and Adolescent Mental Health. 2009;**14**(1):24-30. DOI: 10.1111/j.1475-3588.2008.00485.x

[2] Holmes E, O'Connor R, Perry V, Tracey I, Wessely S, Arseneault L, et al. Multidisciplinary research priorities for the COVID-19 pandemic: a call for action for mental health science. The Lancet Psychiatry. 2020;7(6):547-560. ISSN 2215-0366. DOI: 10.1016/S2215-0366(20)30168-1

[3] Gunnell D, Appleby L. Suicide risk and prevention during the COVID-19 pandemic. The Lancet Psychiatry. 2020;7(6):468-471. DOI: 10.1016/S2215-0366(20)30171-1

[4] Czeisler MÉ, Lane RI, Petrosky E, Wiley JF, Christensen A, Njai R, et al. Mental health, substance use, and suicidal ideation during the COVID-19 pandemic - United States, June 24-30, 2020. MMWR: Morbidity and Mortality Weekly Report. 2020;**69**(32):1049-1057. DOI: 10.15585/mmwr.mm6932a1

[5] Torales J, O'Higgins M, Castaldelli-Maia JM, Ventriglio A. The outbreak of COVID-19 coronavirus and its impact on global mental health. International Journal of Social Psychiatry. 2020;**66**(4):317-320. DOI: 10.1177/0020764020915212

[6] Ornell F, Schuch JB, Sordi AO, Kessler FHP. "Pandemic fear" and COVID-19: mental health burden and strategies. Brazilian Journal of Psychiatry. 2020;**42**(3):232-235. DOI: 10.1590/1516-4446-2020-0008. Epub 2020 Apr 3. Erratum in: Braz J Psychiatry. 2020;42(3):333, 10.1590/1516-4446-2020-0011

[7] Xiong J, Lipsitz O, Nasri F, Lui LMW, Gill H, Phan L, et al. Impact of COVID-19 pandemic on mental health in the general population: A systematic review. Journal of Affective Disorders. 2020;**1**(277):55-64. DOI: 10.1016/j.jad.2020.08.001

[8] Mamun MA, Griffiths MD. First COVID-19 suicide case in Bangladesh due to fear of COVID-19 and xenophobia: Possible suicide prevention strategies. Asian Journal of Psychiatry. 2020;**51**:102073. DOI: 10.1016/j.ajp.2020.102073

[9] Martínez-Líbano J, Yeomans Cabrera MM. Suicidal ideation and suicidal thoughts in university students during the COVID-19 pandemic: A systematic review. Revista Argentina de Clínica Psicológica. 2021;**XXX**(2):390-405. DOI: 10.24205/03276716.2020.4038

[10] Wang X, Hegde S, Son C, Keller B, Smith A, Sasangohar F. Investigating mental health of US College students during the COVID-19 pandemic: Cross-sectional survey study. Journal of Medical Internet Research. 2020;**22**(9):e22817. DOI: 10.2196/22817

[11] Wathelet M, Duhem S, Vaiva G, Baubet T, Habran E, Veerapa E, et al. Factors associated with mental health disorders among university students in France confined during the COVID-19 pandemic. JAMA Network Open. 2020;**3**(10):1-13. DOI: 10.1001/jamanetworkopen.2020.25591

[12] Žilinskas E, Žulpaitė G, Puteikis K, Viliūnienė R. Mental health among

higher education students during the COVID-19 pandemic: A cross-sectional survey from Lithuania. International Journal of Environmental Research and Public Health. 2021;**18**(23):12737. DOI: 10.3390/ijerph182312737

[13] Al-Halabí S, Fonseca-Pedrero E. Suicidal behavior prevention: The time to act is now. Clinic Health. 2021;**32**:89-92. DOI: 10.5093/clysa2021a17

[14] Fonseca-Pedrero E, Pérez de Albéniz A, Fonseca-Pedrero E, Pérez de Albéniz A. Evaluación de La Conducta Suicida En Adolescentes: A Propósito de La Escala Paykel de Suicidio. Papeles Psicólogo. 2020;**41**:106-115. Available online: https://scielo.isciii.es/scielo.php?pid=S0214-78232020000200106&script=sci_abstract [Accessed: June 6, 2024]

[15] WHO Suicide. Available from: https://www.who.int/news-room/fact-sheets/detail/suicide [Accessed: November 20, 2023]

[16] American Psychiatry Association Diagnostic and Statistical Manual of Mental Disorders (DSM-5-TR). Available online: https://www.psychiatry.org:443/psychiatrists/practice/dsm [Accessed: December 13, 2023]

[17] Pedreira JL. Conductas suicidas en la adolescencia: Una guía práctica para la intervención y la prevención. Revista de psicopatología y psicología clínica. 2019;**24**:217-237. Available online: https://pdfs.semanticscholar.org/24c7/21a841d4b1746227fa6095dfff63438c0945.pdf [Accessed: June 21, 2024]

[18] Vázquez P, Armero P, Martínez L, Garcia J, Bonet LC, Notario HF, et al. Autolesiones y conducta suicida en niños y adolescentes. Lo que la pandemia nos ha desvelado. Anales de Pediatría. 2023;**98**:204-212. DOI: 10.1016/j.anpedi.2022.11.006

[19] Espandian A, González M, Reijas T, Florez G, Ferrer E, Saiz PA, et al. Factores predictores de riesgo de repetición de intento de suicidio en una muestra de pacientes ambulatorios. Revista de Psiquiatria y Salud Mental. 2020;**13**:11-21. DOI: 10.1016/j.rpsm.2019.03.003

[20] Sarti P, Colliva C, Varrasi S, Guerrera CS, Platania GA, Boccaccio FM, et al. A network study to differentiate suicide attempt risk profiles in male and female patients with major depressive disorder. Clinical Psychology & Psychotherapy. 2023;**31**(1):1-14. DOI: 10.1002/cpp.2924

[21] Caplan R. Person-environment fit theory and organizations: Commensurate dimensions, time perspectives, and mechanisms. Journal of Vocational Behavior. 1987;**31**(3):1-9 ISSN 0001-8791. DOI: 10.1016/0001-8791(87)90042-X

[22] Johnson JV, Hall EM. Job strain, work place social support, and cardiovascular disease: A cross-sectional study of a random sample of the Swedish working population. American Journal of Public Health. 1988;**78**(10):1336-1342. DOI: 10.2105/ajph.78.10.1336

[23] Karasek R. Healthy Work-Stress. Productivity and the Reconstruction of Working Life. 1990. Available from: https://cir.nii.ac.jp/crid/1570572700117643520 [Accessed: June 26, 2024]

[24] Joiner TE, Hom MA, Hagan CR, Silva C. Suicide as a derangement of the self-sacrificial aspect of eusociality. Psychological Review. 2016;**123**(3):235-254. DOI: 10.1037/rev0000020

[25] Klonsky ED, May AM, Saffer BY. Suicide, suicide attempts, and suicidal ideation. Annual Review of Clinical

Psychology. 2016;**12**:307-330. DOI: 10.1146/annurev-clinpsy-021815-093204

[26] Bryan CJ, Cukrowicz KC, West CL, Morrow CE. Combat experience and the acquired capability for suicide. Journal of Clinical Psychology. 2010;**66**(10):1044-1056. DOI: 10.1002/jclp.20703

[27] McIntyre RS, Lee Y. Projected increases in suicide in Canada as a consequence of COVID-19. Psychiatry Research. 2020;**290**:113104. DOI: 10.1016/j.psychres.2020.113104

[28] Smith AP, Smith HN. An international survey of the wellbeing of employees in the business process outsourcing industry. Psychology. 2017;**8**:160-167. DOI: 10.4236/psych.2017.81010

[29] Siegrist J. Adverse health effects of high-effort/low-reward conditions. Journal of Occupational Health Psychology. 1996;**1**(1):27-41. DOI: 10.1037/1076-8998.1.1.27

[30] Lazarus R, Folkman S. Stress, Appraisal, and Coping. New York: Springer. Available from: https://www.scirp.org/reference/ReferencesPapers?ReferenceID=1927117&btwaf=84565988; 1984 [Accessed: June 26, 2024]

[31] Hobfoll SE. Conservation of resources: A new attempt at conceptualizing stress. American Psychologist. 1989;**44**(3):513-524. DOI: 10.1037/0003-066X.44.3.513

[32] Cooper CL, Marshall J. Occupational sources of stress: A review of the literature relating to coronary heart disease and mental ill health. Journal of Occupational Psychology. 1976;**49**(1):11-28. DOI: 10.1111/j.2044-8325.1976.tb00325.x

[33] Ursin H, Eriksen HR. The cognitive activation theory of stress. Psychoneuroendocrinology. 2004;**29**(5):567-592. DOI: 10.1016/S0306-4530(03)00091-X

[34] Engel GL. The need for a new medical model: A challenge for biomedicine. Science. 1977;**196**(4286):129-136. DOI: 10.1126/science.847460

[35] Mendoza-Martínez I, García-Rivera B, García Alcaraz J. Exploring the Dynamics of Suicidal Ideation, Negative Emotional States, Uncertainty, Work Overload, Illusion for Study, and Persistence among University Students during COVID-19: A Comprehensive Study. London, UK: IntechOpen; 2023. DOI: 10.5772/intechopen.1003219

[36] Liu Y, Cao L, Li J. The relationship between suicidal ideation and social support in college students: The mediating role of negative emotions. Frontiers in Psychology. 2017;**8**:2150. DOI: 10.1080/13811118.2013.826155

[37] Smith PN, Cukrowicz KC, Poindexter EK, Hobson V, Cohen LM, Eddington AR. The acquired capability for suicide: A comparison of suicidal ideation and attempts. Archives of Suicide Research. 2020;**24**(1):27-42. DOI: 10.1002/da.20701

[38] Cao W, Fang Z, Hou G, Han M, Xu X, Dong J, et al. The psychological impact of the COVID-19 epidemic on college students in China. Psychiatry Research. 2020;**287**:112934. DOI: 10.1016/j.psychres.2020.112934

[39] Son C, Hegde S, Smith A, Wang X, Sasangohar F. Effects of COVID-19 on college students' mental health in the United States: Interview survey study. Journal of Medical Internet Research. 2021;**23**(9):e21279. DOI: 10.2196/21279

[40] Polsek D, Huremović D, editor. Psychiatry of Pandemics: A Mental

Health Response to Infection Outbreak. Croatia: Springer Nature, Springer International Publishing; 2019. p. 185; ISBN978-3-030-15346-5 (e-book), ISBN978-3-030-15345-8 (softcover). Croatian Medical Journal. 2020 Jun;61(3):306. DOI: 10.3325/cmj.2020.61.306

[41] Tull MT, Edmonds KA, Scamaldo KM, Richmond JR, Rose JP, Gratz KL. Psychological outcomes associated with stay-at-home orders and the perceived impact of COVID-19 on daily life. Psychiatry Research. 2020;**289**:113098. DOI: 10.1016/j.psychres.2020.113098

[42] Moutier C. Suicide prevention in the COVID-19 era: Transforming threat into opportunity. JAMA Psychiatry. 2020;**77**(11):1093-1094. DOI: 10.1001/jamapsychiatry.2020.3746

[43] Beasley C, Thompson T, Davidson J. Resilience in response to life stress: The effects of coping style and cognitive hardiness. Personality and Individual Differences. 2015;**86**:343-348. Available online: https://nursingacademy.com/wp-content/uploads/2020/01/resiliencecoping.pdf [Accessed: December 13, 2023]

[44] Wilcox HC, Arria AM, Caldeira KM, Vincent KB, Pinchevsky GM, O'Grady KE. Prevalence and predictors of persistent suicide ideation, plans, and attempts during college. Journal of Affective Disorders. 2010;**127**(1-3):287-294. DOI: 10.1016/j.jad.2010.04.017

[45] Kleiman EM, Riskind JH, Schaefer KE, Weingarden H. Cognitive factors as moderators of the relationship between stress and suicide risk. Crisis. 2018;**39**(4):259-269. DOI: 10.1027/0227-5910/a000159

[46] Smith AR, Velkoff M, Ribeiro J, Franklin J. Are eating disorders and related symptoms risk factors for suicidal thoughts and Behaviors? A meta-analysis. Current Opinion in Psychology. 2019;**30**:6-10. DOI: 10.1111/sltb.12427

[47] Culebras JM, San Mauro Martin I, Vicente-Vacas L. COVID-19 y otras pandemias. JONNPR. 2020;**5**(6):644-664. DOI: 10.19230/jonnpr.3750

[48] Mukhtar F, Candilis P. Pandemics and suicide risk: Lessons from COVID and its predecessors. The Journal of Nervous and Mental Disease. 2022;**210**(10):799-807. DOI: 10.1097/NMD.0000000000001536

[49] Wenzel A, Beck A. A cognitive model of suicidal behavior: Theory and treatment. Applied and Preventive Psychology. 2008;**12**(4):189-201, ISSN 0962-1849. DOI: 10.1016/j.appsy.2008.05.001

[50] Amer S, AAM, Fouad AM, El-Samahy M, Anan M, Saati AA, Sarhan AA, et al. Cognitive function and work resilience of healthcare professionals: A comparative cross-sectional study. Journal of Family and Community Medicine. 2024:**31**(2):153-159. DOI: 10.4103/jfcm.jfcm_304_23

[51] Brooks SK, Webster RK, Smith LE, Woodland L, Wessely S, Greenberg N, et al. The psychological impact of quarantine and how to reduce it: Rapid review of the evidence. Lancet. 2020;**395**(10227):912-920. DOI: 10.1016/S0140-6736(20)30460-8

[52] Mann JJ, Michel CA, Auerbach RP. Improving suicide prevention through evidence-based strategies: A systematic review. The American Journal of Psychiatry. 2021;**178**(7):611-624. DOI: 10.1176/appi.ajp.2020.20060864

[53] Zhong W, Liang Q, Yang A, Yan R. Why emotional neglect brings suicidal

ideation? The mediating effect of meaning in life and the moderating effect of post-stress growth. Child Abuse & Neglect. 2024;**149**:106700, ISSN 0145-2134. DOI: 10.1016/j.chiabu.2024.106700

[54] Beck AT, Brown GK, Steer RA. Psychometric characteristics of the scale for suicide ideation with psychiatric outpatients. Behaviour Research and Therapy. 1997;**35**(11):1039-1046. DOI: 10.1016/s0005-7967(97)00073-9

[55] Gil-Monte P, Zúñiga-Caballero L. Validez factorial del Cuestionario para la Evaluación del Síndrome de Quemarse por el Trabajo (CESQT) en una muestra de médicos mexicanos. Universitas Psychologica. Revista Salud Mental. Colombia: Pontificia Universidad Javeriana Bogotá. 2010;**9**(1):169-178. de 2023. Available from: https://www.redalyc.org/pdf/647/64712156014.pdf [Accessed: June 24 2024]

[56] Palladini M, Mazza MG, Scalabrini A, Rovere Querini P, Poletti S, Benedetti F. The burden of survivorship: Survivor guilt and its association with psychiatric sequelae in COVID-19 patients. Journal of Clinical Medicine. 2023;**12**:3117. DOI: 10.3390/jcm12093117

[57] Chi X, Becker B, Yu Q, Willeit P, Jiao C, Huang L, et al. Prevalence and psychosocial correlates of mental health outcomes among chinese college students during the coronavirus disease (COVID-19) pandemic. Frontiers in Psychiatry. 2020;**11**:803. DOI: 10.3389/fpsyt.2020.00803

[58] Grzejszczak J, Strzelecki D, Gabryelska A, Kotlicka-Antczak M. Evaluation of COVID-19 effect on mental health, self-harm, and suicidal Behaviors in children and adolescents population. Journal of Clinical Medicine. 2024;**13**(3):744. DOI: 10.3390/jcm13030744

[59] Hawes MT, Szenczy AK, Klein DN, Hajcak G, Nelson BD. Increases in depression and anxiety symptoms in adolescents and young adults during the COVID-19 pandemic. Psychological Medicine. 2022;**52**(14):3222-3230. DOI: 10.1017/S0033291720005358

[60] Elharake JA, Akbar F, Malik AA, et al. Mental health impact of COVID-19 among children and college students: A systematic review. Child Psychiatry and Human Development. 2023;**54**:913-925. DOI: 10.1007/s10578-021-01297-1

[61] Chang J, Yuan Y, Wang D. Mental health status and its infuencing factors among college students during the epidemic of COVID-19. Nan Fang Yi Ke Da Xue Xue Bao. 2020;**40**(2):171-176. DOI: 10.12122/j.issn.1673-4254.2020.02.06

[62] Giurgiu LR, Damian C, Sabău AM, Caciora T, Călin FM. Depression related to COVID-19, coping, and hopelessness in sports students. Brain Sciences. 2024;**14**:563. DOI: 10.3390/brainsci14060563

[63] McKay S, Veresova M, Bailey E, Lamblin M, Robinson J. Suicide prevention for international students: A scoping review. International Journal of Environmental Research and Public Health. 2023;**20**(2):1500. DOI: 10.3390/ijerph20021500

Chapter 2

Depression and Burnout Syndrome in Healthcare Workers: Psychological Health and Reflections on Patient Safety

Esma Gökçe

Abstract

Depression and burnout syndrome among healthcare workers can have detrimental effects on psychological well-being and patient safety. The prevalence of such psychological difficulties is increasing among healthcare workers, often caused by various factors such as high workload, stress, and occupational trauma. When the effects of conditions such as burnout and depression on patient safety are examined, it is revealed that they contribute to an increased propensity of healthcare workers to make mistakes and to a decrease in the quality of patient care. On the other hand, depression and burnout among healthcare workers also affect their own health, leading to a high rate of attrition from the profession and even suicide. All of this causes serious harm to health workers, patients, and institutions. Therefore, intervention strategies to improve the psychological well-being of healthcare workers and enhance patient safety are of great importance. These strategies focus on various areas such as organizational culture, flexible working hours, support groups, counseling services, and professional development opportunities. The objective of this chapter is to examine the effects of depression and, especially burnout syndrome on both employee health and patient safety, as well as to evaluate prevention strategies.

Keywords: burnout syndrome, depression, healthcare workers, patient safety, psychology

1. Introduction

The Diagnostic and Statistical Manual of Mental Disorders-5 (DSM-5) defines depression as a mental disorder characterized by the presence of at least five of the following symptoms over a period of at least 2 weeks: Depressed mood, decreased interest in activities or anhedonia, lack of energy, decreased or increased appetite, decreased or increased sleep, psychomotor agitation or retardation, feelings of worthlessness or guilt, decreased concentration or indecisiveness, recurrent thoughts of self-harm or suicide attempts, and a decrease in previous levels of functioning [1].

Burnout is more prevalent in professions that necessitate direct interaction with individuals [2]. The concept of "burnout syndrome" was first presented by Freudenberger in 1974 to describe the fatigue, frustration, and turnover observed among volunteer healthcare workers. Freudenberger defined this emerging phenomenon as "failure, weariness, and exhaustion by creating excessive demands on energy, strength, or resources" [3]. Following Freudenberger, Christina Maslach is credited with the most widely accepted definition of burnout, largely due to her extensive research in this field and the development of a comprehensive burnout assessment tool. Maslach defines burnout as a syndrome that occurs in individuals who are exposed to intense emotional demands due to their profession and who are required to work with proximity to others on a regular basis. The syndrome is characterized by exhaustion, prolonged physical fatigue, feelings of helplessness and hopelessness, and negative reactions to the work, the outside world and other people [4].

Depression and burnout are two common symptoms of stress that can impair psychosocial functioning and cognition [5]. Although burnout and depression are moderately related and sometimes share similar characteristics, they have been reported to be distinct mental health conditions that require special attention and approach [5, 6]. Burnout is characterized as a state of emotional exhaustion, particularly in response to the cumulative effects of workplace stress [7]. Depression is characterized by core symptoms such as sadness and anhedonia but also includes additional emotional, somatic, and cognitive symptoms that are heterogeneous across individuals [1]. However, although both burnout and depression are associated with chronic stress, it has been theorized that burnout is dependent on the context of occupational stress, whereas depression is more independent of this context [7]. It has been reported that the presence of depression and burnout among healthcare workers can have significant effects on patients [8]. Several studies have indicated that physicians who screen positive for depression or burnout are more likely to make errors [2, 5, 8, 9]. Results from studies in nursing have shown that higher levels of burnout and depressive symptoms are associated with lower perceptions of patient safety and higher rates of objectively measured errors [6, 7, 10].

2. Depression

Depression is a significant public health concern due to its high prevalence and impaired functioning. It is the second leading cause of years of disability worldwide. When deaths due to suicide and other diseases are taken into consideration, depression is the third disease with the highest burden of disease in the world and is predicted to rise to first place in 2030 [11]. Biological, genetic, and environmental factors contribute to the etiology of depression, with these factors interacting with each other in complex ways. Some structural and functional changes observed in depression are thought to result from these factors [12]. Psychosocial stressors, psychodynamic processes, early attachment problems, interpersonal factors, or individual behaviors and cognitions are also suggested to play a role in the development of depression [1, 2].

One of the most significant consequences of depression is suicide. It has been estimated that between 50 and 70% of suicides are attributable to depression. In 2015, 788,000 individuals lost their lives due to suicide, representing one of the top 20 causes of death with a prevalence of 1.5% [13]. On the other hand, international evidence suggests that health professionals have an increased risk of developing common mental illnesses, including anxiety and depression, compared to the general population [14]. It has been postulated that healthcare workers may be at increased risk of suicide compared to other individuals due to high job demands, avoidance of mental health services due to fear of stigma, and greater access to medication-assisted suicide [15, 16].

Nurses are a group with a high prevalence of mental health issues, including depression. This may have a significant impact on nurses' perceptions of patient safety [15, 16]. Johnson et al. provide further evidence for a correlation between depressive symptoms and patient perceptions of safety in nurses [10]. Conversely, although nursing is the largest healthcare profession, there is a paucity of knowledge regarding suicide among nurses. Recent studies have reported a higher incidence of suicide among nurses than the general population [15–17]. It has been documented that over 70% of individuals who die by suicide have not received the necessary mental health services in the 2 months prior to their demise, and only a small percentage of affected nurses have received these services [17].

Previous research has demonstrated that the prevalence of depression among physicians ranges from 7–65%, which is considerably higher than the 4–5% found in the general population [18, 19]. A study of depressive symptoms in doctors found that doctors who reported work-related illnesses had double the odds of depressive symptoms [5]. It is well established that depression has a detrimental impact on neurocognitive functions, particularly attention, processing speed, and elements of executive function [1, 2]. It has been proposed that depressed physician assistants may exhibit a reduced capacity to self-correct or halt the progression of errors before they cause harm [18]. In a study conducted by Brunsberg et al., it was found that 2% of physician assistants expressed suicidal ideation. The study found that physicians who screened positive for depression demonstrated a threefold increased likelihood of committing errors that resulted in patient harm [8].

These findings collectively indicate that the mental health of nurses and physicians is not only crucial for their own general well-being but also be a significant determinant of patient safety.

3. Depression and burnout syndrome

The common aspects of burnout and depression include their potential to impact work performance in various ways and their tendency to become chronic if left untreated. This poses a threat to both job performance and individual well-being, leading to persistent symptoms of burnout and depression [5–9, 20]. Additionally, akin to burnout, depressive symptoms among healthcare workers can result in consequences for patient care such as cognitive failures and increased likelihood of medical errors [18–20]. On the other hand, the different aspects of burnout and depression, while interventions for depressive symptoms may focus on individual-level approaches (e.g., awareness), interventions for burnout encompass a broader spectrum including restructuring work processes and organizational-level changes [10]. Therefore, understanding and identifying the relationships between burnout, depressive symptoms, and patient safety is crucial.

Some studies in the literature have examined both burnout and depressive symptoms and reported that depressive symptoms increase the risk of burnout. Thus, it has been concluded that burnout due to depression is a more consistent indicator of reported errors and that errors by healthcare workers are related to work-related stressors, fatigue, and burnout [9, 18–21]. On the contrary, some studies have reported that burnout in healthcare workers may lead to depressive symptoms and other mental disorders. Specifically, burnout has been reported to lead to depression, post-traumatic stress disorder, substance abuse disorders, and suicidal tendencies, in addition to affecting the ability to enjoy work [22–25]. In summary, when examining the answer to the question of whether burnout causes depression or depression causes burnout, the literature provides a positive answer to both.

One study found an inverse causal relationship between burnout and job satisfaction, and depressive symptoms were reported to be a consequence of burnout [26]. In addition, psychological distress, such as depression and suicidal ideation, was strongly associated with burnout in healthcare workers [27, 28]. Another study reported that burnout symptoms affect patient safety more than depression symptoms. Based on this finding, it has been suggested that staff-level interventions for depressive symptoms, such as mindfulness, may have benefits in terms of patient safety, while interventions for burnout may be more effective in improving patient safety [10].

As a result of these studies, it is hypothesized that burnout mediates the relationship between depressive symptoms and perceptions of patient safety. This hypothesis suggests that interventions that focus on burnout symptoms may be more effective in ensuring both healthcare worker well-being and patient safety. For these reasons, the remainder of this chapter focuses on the causes, consequences, and prevention strategies of burnout.

4. Burnout syndrome

Burnout has become a syndrome consisting of constant malaise, cynicism, that is, the loss of a critical/interested view of the profession, and a decrease in professional effectiveness or personal accomplishment. These symptoms can manifest as a feeling of having nothing left to give, emotional exhaustion, depersonalization, seeing patients as objects, and feeling ineffective [29]. Burnout is recognized because of chronic work stress that is not successfully managed [30]. As of January 1, 2012, burnout has been recognized as a medical diagnosis in the International Classification of Diseases, 11th Revision (ICD-11) [31]. It is listed as an occupational disease by nine European countries (Denmark, Estonia, France, Hungary, Latvia, the Netherlands, Portugal, Slovakia, and Sweden) [32]. Denmark, France, Latvia, Portugal, and Sweden have set a precedent for the recognition of burnout through the payment of compensation for burnout [33].

Burnout, a psychological syndrome, is considered in three dimensions. It is a combination of emotional exhaustion, depersonalization, and low personal functioning [34]. Burning, also, is an extended and sustained response to sustained emotional and interpersonal job stress and stressful events that may affect both personal and organizational issues [35]. Emotional exhaustion caused by the experience of stress is associated with the depletion of emotional and physical resources. The individual who begins to experience emotional exhaustion does not want to go to work. Therefore, they begin to come to work late with various excuses, leave work early, or even do not go to work at all. Depersonalization refers to people who become callous and unresponsive to the people who perform their duties and responsibilities in the institutions where they work. Individuals may have negative attitudes toward people they encounter because of their work or pretend they do not exist. Individuals with this structure are usually distant from their jobs. They may have lost the first day's excitement and sense of responsibility in their work. Personal failure refers to the development of a sense of low professional productivity and lack of work efficiency. Feelings of failure, unloved, and guilt can even lead to depression because they lower self-esteem. Another factor that causes these feelings of guilt is the individual's belief that they are not progressing or even regressing in their work [34].

In general, healthcare workers have been reported to have higher rates of burnout and exhaustion due to work stress than other occupational groups [36, 37]. In addition, physicians and nurses have been reported to have the highest prevalence of burnout [5, 38]. Unfortunately, burnout among healthcare workers is a serious problem worldwide. Healthcare workers have reached a breaking point, and the threat of burnout to public health is growing to significant levels. Staff shortages are among the top concerns of hospital administrators, and the threat of physician/nurse walkouts is increasing [39]. In one urban, academic, level 1 trauma center, the prevalence of burnout among hospital staff was as high as 60% [36]. Magnet hospitals are officially recognized as good places to work. However, a study by Aiken et al. shows that even in these hospitals, work-related problems exist among physicians and nurses. According to the study results, only 10% of clinicians enjoy their hospital practice. In addition, one-third of physicians and nearly half of nurses experience high levels of burnout. These findings are important for understanding the challenges facing health professionals [39]. A randomized controlled trial conducted at two large academic medical centers found that burnout rates among critical care clinicians (physicians, nurses, pharmacists, therapists) exceeded 50% [25].

Stress and burnout are becoming increasingly important occupational issues for healthcare workers, particularly as they have been associated with poor care outcomes [21–26, 32–36]. Healthcare workers may be particularly vulnerable as they may experience emotional exhaustion when caring for patients and their families [37]. However, the psychological and physical effects on healthcare providers are clear, and the impact on the healthcare workforce is of concern. In the United States, it is estimated to cost approximately $5 billion per year and is associated with decreased clinical productivity and increased physician walkouts [40]. Research has shown that physicians are often unable to recognize symptoms of burnout or depression and are even less likely to seek help [41]. A burned-out physician is reported to be "angry, irritable, impatient, have increased absenteeism, decreased productivity, and decreased quality of care" [29]. Of 15,000 US physicians who responded to an online survey in 2018, 42% showed evidence of burnout. The highest incidence of burnout (50%) was found among physicians aged 45–54, the age group in which work productivity should peak [42]. The findings repeated in 2019 were similar, with an overall rate of 44% reporting feelings of burnout and an alarming 14% reporting suicidal ideation. Only one-third of those with suicidal ideation reported seeking treatment [43]. Compared with professionals in other fields, physicians work longer hours, are less satisfied with their work-life balance, and experience significantly higher rates of burnout symptoms [41, 44]. A recent multispecialty systematic review of surgeons found that 31% of participating surgeons and 42% of residents experienced high levels of emotional exhaustion, and high levels of depersonalization were reported by 26% of participating surgeons and 53% of residents [45].

International research indicates that nurses frequently encounter significant levels of burnout [35, 46–48]. Research conducted in the United States has specifically explored burnout among nurse practitioners, nurse managers, and emergency department nurses, revealing varying degrees of burnout among these professionals [47]. A study by Aiken et al. extended this inquiry to nine countries, including the USA, China, South Korea, Thailand, Japan, New Zealand, the UK, Germany, and Canada, revealing that approximately 30–60% of nurses in eight of these nations experience elevated levels of burnout [48]. Given the increasingly demanding nature of the healthcare system and the resultant nursing shortages, the prevalence of burnout among nurses is unsurprising and constitutes a significant global challenge [35].

5. Causes of burnout syndrome

Many factors that contribute to the realization of burnout can be listed and these factors are generally explained as individual factors and environmental factors. Individual factors that influence burnout are age, gender, marital status, educational status, personality structure, empathy, emotional control, individual needs, and expectation levels [49, 50]. Environmental factors are organizational factors such as the nature of the job, patient intensity, working hours, workload, job security, communication in the work environment, relationships with coworkers and supervisors, institutional plans and policies, equity, inadequate pay, lack of advancement opportunities, increased electronic documentation, lack of rewards, physical conditions of the workplace [49–51].

5.1 Workload and work control

Physicians and nurses frequently experience elevated levels of burnout, job dissatisfaction, and a desire to leave their current positions within hospitals characterized by challenging work environments, excessive workloads that exceed clinicians' control, and shortages in staffing [48–51]. Low job control refers to the extent to which an employee has control over his or her work and has been found to be associated with burnout [32, 50]. For physicians, lack of control over workload, lack of quality of work environment, and insufficient number of nurses have been shown to be of great importance in terms of burnout levels [39]. Multiple studies have identified a correlation between workload and emotional exhaustion, depersonalization [52–54]. Furthermore, staffing levels [53] and time constraints [54] have been linked to all aspects of burnout. Research indicates that reducing the number of patients assigned to nurses corresponds with lower overall burnout scores [55, 56].

5.2 Rewards, values, fairness and community

Fairness refers to the fair and equal application of workplace decisions and practices and has been found to be associated with burnout [57]. Value congruence refers to the extent to which an individual's personal values are compatible with workplace values, and value conflict has been found to be associated with burnout [55–58]. The research findings indicate that nurses who exhibit high-value congruence report lower levels of emotional exhaustion, whereas those with low-value congruence tend to experience higher levels of depersonalization [58]. Compensation, referred to as reward, plays a significant role in employee satisfaction, and studies have shown that an imbalance between effort and reward is linked to burnout [59]. Social capital, defined as the benefits derived from social relationships within a community, has been identified as a predictor of emotional exhaustion among hospital staff, particularly in settings with low social capital [60].

5.3 Working patterns

Overtime has been found to be associated with burnout, and shorter shifts have been found to be protective against burnout [49–51, 55–61]. Working night shifts were found to be associated with burnout, but this association was not always significant [62]. In contrast to rotating shift patterns, working on permanent shift patterns did not affect burnout, but working irregular shifts were found to affect burnout [63]. Recent studies indicate that nurses working longer hours are more likely to experience higher levels of burnout compared to those working shifts of less than 8 hours [64]. Time spent on non-clinical tasks has also been found to increase burnout, as physicians' primary role and natural tendency is to care for patients [39–41].

5.4 Psychological demands and job complexity

Conditions such as work overload and psychological demands [62, 63], and role conflict [65] are often associated with emotional exhaustion, meaning that the difficulty and stress of the job can drain individuals' energy and lead them to feel exhausted. In addition, patient complexity is also associated with burnout, because as patients' conditions become more complex, healthcare workers' stress may increase, leading to burnout [51]. However, factors such as task variety, autonomy, and decision-making freedom [66] can reduce feelings of burnout. Rouxel et al. found that increased job demands were positively correlated with higher levels of emotional exhaustion and personal failure among healthcare workers [67]. Also, healthcare workers decisions to care for patients with multiple needs, to care for a dying patient, and to withhold life-sustaining treatment were found to increase the likelihood of burnout [68].

5.5 Work environment and leadership

Negative work environment, institutional disorganization, environmental uncertainty, mistrust of the institution (especially in organizational support and structural empowerment), and underinvestment in quality of care have been found to be associated with all dimensions of burnout [56, 69]. According to a report [39], almost half of doctors and nurses lacked confidence in management's commitment to addressing issues identified in patient care. Additionally, nearly one-third of these healthcare providers felt their values did not align well with those of management. Research indicates that inadequate workplace conditions for nursing practice contribute to burnout and compromise patient safety [46].

5.6 Information technology

The healthcare environment exhibits a dynamic and diverse organizational culture. Electronic medical record (EMR) systems have been identified as sources of stress and increased burnout among healthcare professionals [70–72]. The additional burdens imposed on physicians by EMRs can be categorized into technical factors, software design flaws, and socio-technical factors related to workflow incompatibilities [71]. These issues can heighten frustration and demand greater documentation efforts to meet organizational and regulatory requirements, consequently reducing time spent on direct patient care. This situation exacerbates burnout symptoms such as fatigue, depersonalization, and reduced sense of accomplishment [29]. A survey of community oncologists revealed that 67% experienced moderate to severe stress from EMR responsibilities, with 79% performing these tasks outside regular clinic hours [72]. Similarly, a Canadian study indicated that 74.5% of physicians displaying burnout symptoms attributed EMR use as a contributing factor [71]. The likelihood of burnout was reported to be 2.8 times higher among physicians who reported insufficient documentation time and frustration with the EMR [70]. Both nurses and physicians reported spending too much time on EMR and feeling frustrated with the task [39].

6. Consequences of burnout syndrome

Factors contributing to burnout affect healthcare workers and institutions, imposing significant financial burdens. Research highlighting the detrimental effects of burnout underscores its potential to jeopardize patients and colleagues through increased absenteeism, presenteeism, turnover, and medical errors [10, 49, 50]. In essence, individuals experiencing burnout in their careers may not only endanger themselves but also those in their vicinity.

6.1 Consequences for healthcare workers

The consequences of burnout have three distinct effects on health workers: Physical, psychological, and behavioral. Physical symptoms of burnout generally include fatigue and exhaustion, headaches, gastrointestinal disorders, high blood pressure, and sleep disturbances. Psychological and behavioral symptoms include family problems, disrupted sleep patterns, anxiety, depression, and even death [73].

Physicians experiencing burnout show markers of abnormal glucose metabolism [74]. A study of 2000 nurses revealed prevalent physical and psychological symptoms such as tension, irritability, sadness, feelings of inferiority, and sleep disturbances [75]. Burnout is moderately linked to sickness absence, impaired work performance, and overall health issues [30, 41, 46, 50]. In a survey across 10 European countries, nurses' intentions to leave the profession varied from 5–17% [76].

The presence of burnout in an organization increases the likelihood of individuals developing a diagnosable medical condition by 50%, surpassing the health impact of exposure to secondhand smoke [77]. Workplace stress is estimated to contribute to over 120,000 deaths annually, with health problems stemming from burnout costing between $125 billion and $190 billion annually [32, 77].

Nursing and physician turnover, a consequence of burnout, imposes significant costs on the healthcare community. According to the most recent national nursing sample survey (Health Resources & Services Administration-HRSA 2020), 40% of nurses who left their jobs attributed burnout as the primary reason [78]. While nurse turnover due to burnout is inevitable, it also leads to other detrimental outcomes such as decreased unit morale, staffing shortages, and disruptions in teamwork [79]. Physician turnover, including reduced clinic hours, is estimated to exceed $4 billion annually, with nurse turnover costs projected to be even higher [40]. The NSI National Health Care Retention & RN Staffing Report 2020 indicates that the cost associated with each departing nurse ranges from $37,700 to $58,400, translating to potential losses of $5 million to $8 million per hospital annually, based on a current hospital nurse turnover rate of 17.6% [80].

6.2 Consequences for patient safety

Burnout remains a persistent challenge for healthcare organizations worldwide, impacting the health and safety of healthcare workers, staff turnover, job satisfaction, and job performance, while posing a potential risk to patient safety [8, 32, 35, 39, 41]. These adverse effects associated with burnout diminish the quality of patient care and contribute to preventable errors, which annually result in harm or fatalities for thousands of individuals [44, 46, 48, 50, 51].

Numerous studies have demonstrated that all facets of burnout correlate negatively with the patient safety climate [10, 26, 63, 72]. According to a systematic review conducted by Dall'Ora et al. findings from 17 studies underscored burnout's detrimental impact on various aspects of care quality, including patient safety, adverse events, error reporting, medication errors, infections, patient falls, patient dissatisfaction, and family complaints [51]. Both colleagues and patients contribute to assessing the quality of patient care, with collective evaluations of nursing units revealing that all three subdimensions of burnout exert a negative influence on care quality [59].

Studies of nurses have reported that emotional exhaustion has a negative impact on the reporting of patient safety events [53, 56, 59, 81, 82]. A similar study reported that when nurses experienced high levels of emotional exhaustion, they were less likely to report near misses and adverse events [81]. Burnout has been found to have negative consequences, including negative effects on team communication and effectiveness, increased infection rates, and decreased infection control compliance [56, 59]. Specifically, high levels of emotional exhaustion and depersonalization have been reported to be associated with infections, particularly catheter-associated urinary tract infections, surgical site infections, and nosocomial infections [59, 82]. In addition, depersonalization and low personal accomplishment were found to be important predictors of patient falls, and all dimensions of burnout were found to be associated with medication errors [82]. Kalemam et al. reported that high levels of burnout were associated with increased medication errors, patient falls and infections, as well as patient and family complaints and family verbal abuse [35].

Looking at other reviews of physician burnout and patient outcomes, two recent systematic reviews found moderate evidence of an inverse association between physician burnout and patient safety [8, 50]. Burnout has been found to increase medical errors among physicians [18, 21]. Several studies have reported that an increase in the number of errors and poor quality of patient care among physicians is associated with high levels of burnout [18, 35]. A recent meta-analysis of 47 studies involving more than 42,000 physicians found that physician burnout doubled the risk of adverse patient safety events and led to lower overall quality of care and patient satisfaction [83]. Physicians who reported symptoms of burnout were found to have lower job performance and higher turnover rates than those who were not affected [21]. Burnout among primary care physicians also increases turnover and thus costs [84]. Physician burnout and the resulting decline in productivity could exacerbate the projected shortage of 45,000–90,000 physicians in the United States by 2025 [41]. Another study reported that surgeon burnout was associated with poor physician empathy and professionalism, leading to a higher risk of being involved in medical errors [44].

7. Strategies to prevent burnout syndrome

There is concern in the medical community that complacency in addressing burnout in the healthcare sector will jeopardize the global delivery of quality healthcare in the future, with "profound consequences for billions of people worldwide" [27]. Effective interventions are needed to ameliorate the problems and consequences of burnout and increased psychosocial distress in healthcare workers [85]. It is imperative that national and international action be taken to address this issue. At the International Council of Nurses (ICN) International Labour Forum, nurse leaders called on governments to take action to ensure safe staffing levels and decent working conditions for patients and nurses [86]. The National Academy of Medicine published a report entitled "Taking Action Against Clinician Burnout: A Systems Approach to Professional Well-Being" [87]. These are all efforts to develop solutions through systemic changes at the health care, organizational, and governmental levels.

7.1 Organizational support

The most prominent strategy for preventing burnout among healthcare workers is organizational support and the creation of a healthy organizational culture [37, 44]. Organizational support and structural empowerment provided to healthcare workers increase trust in hospital management and organization and reduce burnout [56, 69]. In addition, the fact that healthcare workers could participate in the policy decisions of organizations will be effective in all dimensions of burnout [51]. Healthcare workers are particularly negatively affected by job insecurity, and to prevent this, providing opportunities for career advancement and satisfactory wages will be effective on emotional exhaustion and depersonalization [65]. Hospitals' investment in quality of care will have a positive effect on both health professionals and patients [51]. Higher schedule flexibility and the ability to plan days off were found to protect against burnout. Having more than 8 days off per month was found to be associated with less burnout [58]. Healthcare workers' top priorities include an improved work environment, including better nurse/physician staffing, uninterrupted scheduled breaks, no unscheduled work, more control over scheduling, and additional resources for new work [39]. Organizational policies that support flexible work arrangements and schedules can provide employees with adequate rest, reduce symptoms of fatigue, and improve patient safety [37]. Solutions to electronic document processes that increase burnout among healthcare workers will contribute to quality of care and patient safety [70].

7.2 Social support and coping skills training

Efforts to mitigate burnout often emphasize enhancing social support, coping skills, and fostering interprofessional collaboration [25, 46]. Research indicates that nearly 90% of physicians and nurses acknowledge the positive impact of social support on professional relationships and team effectiveness [39]. Nurses frequently rely on peer support mechanisms to manage stress, and interventions promoting teamwork can potentially enhance collective resilience among nursing teams [21]. For instance, a cross-sectional study involving 127 emergency department nurses in China, conducted by Lu and colleagues, highlighted that nursing leadership's attention to coping strategies significantly enhanced the quality of care delivered [88].

Furthermore, external support systems, such as family or friend support and emotional and informational support, have been shown to reduce work-life conflict and alleviate burnout among employees [37].

7.3 Wellness programs

Efforts to combat burnout have led to the development of wellness programs aimed at achieving systemic and sustainable change. These programs incorporate both individual-focused approaches, such as mindfulness practices, and structural and organizational strategies, including reduced duty hours and revised inpatient rotations, to achieve significant reductions in burnout [89]. Approximately 80% of interventions targeted at healthcare workers have successfully lowered burnout rates, with comprehensive approaches that combine individual interventions like cognitive behavioral training and organizational strategies like communication workshops and management skills training showing enduring effects [90]. Furthermore, recommendations from studies advocate for the appointment of a wellness officer at the administrative level to prioritize clinician well-being, establish policies, and offer self-care and mental health resources to support healthcare professionals in need [91].

7.4 Employee assistance programs

Disruptive behaviors among healthcare workers contribute to prolonged burnout. Identifying the root causes of these behaviors and implementing effective interventions are crucial to promoting the well-being of both patients and staff, as well as reducing turnover and organizational costs [29]. Consequently, numerous organizations are prioritizing the implementation of employee assistance programs (EAPs). EAPs serve as a resource utilized by many large healthcare organizations to offer assessments, personalized plans, counseling, and referrals. These programs assist employees in addressing personal issues proactively, thereby mitigating disruptive behaviors that may otherwise impact their work performance [92].

7.5 Death cafés

Death cafés are virtual spaces for informal conversations about death, dying, loss, and illness to alleviate distress [25]. Death cafés for healthcare professionals have been described as similar in structure and function to community initiatives, with the goal of fostering a sense of community and collaboration among staff while encouraging reflection on distressing patient events. Studies of the impact of death cafés, particularly the effectiveness of virtual debriefing sessions in preventing burnout in the intensive care unit setting, are ongoing [25, 89].

7.6 Art therapy

Art therapy is a psychological therapy that uses art making and creative expression through visual arts media as a core element of treatment. Art therapy-based interventions have been found to be widely accepted by a variety of health professionals in international contexts [27, 93]. It is strongly suggested that art therapy-based methods should be strongly considered as an acceptable and effective treatment for symptoms of burnout and psychosocial distress in health care workers [27].

7.7 Conservation of resources

This theory, developed by Hobfoll, defines stress as an individual's response to environmental demands and his or her perception of meeting those demands [94]. Stress arises when there is a perceived threat of resource loss, actual loss of resources, or when individuals lack the means to replenish resources through personal investment. These resources encompass various aspects such as tangible objects, personal attributes, circumstances, and energies. When essential resources are consistently jeopardized, it can contribute to burnout, impacting work performance and potentially compromising patient safety. Tangible resources include physical items like shelter and clothing, often linked to socioeconomic status. Situational resources encompass constructs such as social relationships, job status, and health, influencing decisions regarding job retention. Personal characteristic resources involve individual traits and coping abilities, while social support, from family or colleagues, can bolster or diminish one's sense of self. Energy resources represent valuable skills and capabilities that can be leveraged for acquiring other resources such as time, money, and knowledge. As a result of this theory, the conservation of resources can help prevent or reduce burnout in healthcare workers [46, 94]. Prapanjaroensin et al. conceptualize burnout in a new way using resource conservation theory, which helps to prevent burnout [46].

8. Conclusion

Burnout and depression symptoms occur in healthcare workers, particularly due to stress and deteriorating well-being. Even in institutions that are known to be good places to work, serious stress can be experienced. Although burnout and depression are different diagnoses, they have an important relationship and can trigger each other. In any case, both conditions cause serious material and moral damage to health workers themselves, patients, institutions, and countries. In other words, the continuity and vitality of the hospital workforce and patient safety are threatened. The findings that burnout is a more serious threat to patient safety than depression and that interventions to reduce burnout are also effective for depression, are drawing more attention to this issue. To overcome burnout, clinicians want to solve problems in patient care, create a supportive work environment, create a work culture that promotes patient safety, and create an environment of trust, especially in management. In addition, organizations that meet these demands of the healthcare team and improve their dynamics will be able to ensure both patient safety and the continued retention of healthcare professionals.

Author details

Esma Gökçe
Toros University, Mersin, Türkiye

*Address all correspondence to: esmagokce0@gmail.com

References

[1] American Psychiatric Association. Diagnostic and Statistical Manual of Mental Disorders. 21st ed. Washington, DC: American Psychiatric Association; 2013

[2] Ertek IE, Özkan S, Candansayar S, İlhan MN. Stress, burn-out and depression in medical students. Gazi Journal of Health Sciences. 2020;**5**(1):10-20

[3] Freudenberger HJ. The staff burnout syndrome in alternative institutions. Psychology and Psychotherapy: Theory, Research and Practice. 1975;**12**(1):73-82. DOI: 10.1037/h0086411

[4] Maslach C, Jackson SE. The measurement of experienced burnout. Journal of Occupational Behaviour. 1981;**2**:99-113. DOI: 10.1002/job.4030020205

[5] Villarreal-Zegarra D, Lázaro-Illatopa WI, Castillo-Blanco R, Cabieses B, Blukacz A, Bellido-Boza L, et al. Relationship between job satisfaction, burnout syndrome and depressive symptoms in physicians: A cross-sectional study based on the employment demand-control model using structural equation modelling. BMJ Open. 2022;**12**(10):e057888. DOI: 10.1136/bmjopen-2021-057888

[6] Koutsimani P, Montgomery A, Georganta K. The relationship between burnout, depression, and anxiety: A systematic review and meta-analysis. Frontiers in Psychology. 2019;**10**:284. DOI: 10.3389/fpsyg.2019.00284

[7] Potter G, Hatch D, Hagy H, Radüntz T, Gajewski P, Falkenstein M, et al. Slower information processing speed is associated with persistent burnout symptoms but not depression symptoms in nursing workers. Journal of Clinical and Experimental Neuropsychology. 2021;**43**(1):33-45. DOI: 10.1080/13803395.2020.1863340

[8] Brunsberg KA, Landrigan CP, Garcia BM, Petty CR, Sectish TC, Simpkin AL, et al. Association of pediatric resident physician depression and burnout with harmful medical errors on inpatient services. Academic Medicine. 2019;**94**(8):1150-1156. DOI: 10.1097/ACM.0000000000002778

[9] de Oliveira GS, Chang R, Fitzgerald PC, Almeida MD, Castro-Alves LS, Ahmad S, et al. The prevalence of burnout and depression and their association with adherence to safety and practice standards: A survey of United States anesthesiology trainees. Anesthesia and Analgesia. 2013;**117**(1):182-193. DOI: 10.1213/ANE.0b013e3182917e85

[10] Johnson J, Louch G, Dunning A, Johnson O, Grange A, Reynolds C, et al. Burnout mediates the association between depression and patient safety perceptions: A cross-sectional study in hospital nurses. Journal of Advanced Nursing. 2017;**73**(7):1667-1680. DOI: 10.1111/jan.13251

[11] Whiteford HA, Degenhardt L, Rehm J, Baxter AJ, Ferrari AJ, Erskine HE, et al. Global burden of disease attributable to mental and substance use disorders: Findings from the global burden of disease study 2010. Lancet. 2013;**382**(9904):1575-1586. DOI: 10.1016/S0140-6736(13)61611-6

[12] Camkurt MA. MicroRNAs as a new hope for depression. Journal of Mood Disorder. 2015;**5**(1):23-30. DOI: 10.5455/jmood.20141013124845

[13] World Health Organization. Depression and Other Common Mental Disorders: Global Health Estimates. Geneva: World Health Organization; 2017

[14] Brand SL, Thompson Coon J, Fleming LE, et al. Whole-system approaches to improving the health and wellbeing of healthcare workers: A systematic review. PLoS One. 2017;**12**:e0188418. DOI: 10.1371/journal.pone.0188418

[15] Davidson J, Mendis J, Stuck AR, DeMichele G, Zisook S. Nurse Suicide: Breaking the Silence. [Internet]. National Academy of Medicine Perspectives; 8 January 2018:1-18. Available from: https://nam.edu/nurse-suicide-breaking-the-silence/ [Accessed: March 19, 2024]

[16] Davis MA, Cher BAY, Friese CR, Bynum JPW. Association of US nurse and physician occupation with risk of suicide. JAMA Psychiatry. 2021;**78**(6):651-658. DOI: 10.1001/jamapsychiatry.2021.0154

[17] Melnyk BM, Davidson JE, Mayfield C, Zisook S, Tucker S, Hsieh AP, et al. A study protocol for the modified interactive screening program plus MINDBODYSTRONG© RCT: A mental health resiliency intervention for nurses. PLoS One. 2024;**19**(6):e0303425. DOI: 10.1371/journal.pone.0303425

[18] Fahrenkopf AM, Sectish TC, Barger LK, et al. Rates of medication errors among depressed and burnt out residents: Prospective cohort study. BMJ. 2008;**336**(7642):488-491. DOI: 10.1136/bmj.39469.763218.BE

[19] Sen S, Kranzler HR, Krystal JH, Speller H, Chan G, Gelernter J, et al. A prospective cohort study investigating factors associated with depression during medical internship. Archives of General Psychiatry. 2010;**67**(6):557-565. DOI: 10.1001/archgenpsychiatry.2010.41

[20] Hatch DJ, Freude G, Martus P, Rose U, Muller G, Potter GG. Age, burnout and physical and psychological work ability among nurses. Occupational Medicine. 2018;**68**(4):246-254. DOI: 10.1093/occmed/kqy033

[21] Shanafelt TD, Hasan O, Dyrbye LN, Sinsky C, Satele D, Sloan J, et al. Changes in burnout and satisfaction with work-life balance in physicians and the general US working population between 2011 and 2014. Mayo Clinic Proceedings. 2015;**90**(12):1600-1613. DOI: 10.1016/j.mayocp.2015.08.023

[22] Naveen R. Mental health in the workplace: World mental health day 2017. Indian Journal of Occupational and Environmental Medicine. 2017;**21**:99-100. DOI: 10.4103/ijoem.IJOEM_148_17

[23] Vigo D, Thornicroft G, Atun R. Estimating the true global burden of mental illness. Lancet Psychiatry. 2016;**3**:171-178. DOI: 10.1016/S2215-0366(15)00505-2

[24] Moss M, Good VS, Gozal D, Kleinpell R, Sessler CN. An official critical care societies collaborative statement - burnout syndrome in critical care health-care professionals: A call for action. Chest. 2016;**150**:17-26. DOI: 10.1016/j.chest.2016.02.649

[25] Bateman ME, Hammer R, Byrne A, Ravindran N, Chiurco J, Lasky S, et al. Death Cafés for prevention of burnout in intensive care unit employees: Study protocol for a randomized controlled trial (STOPTHEBURN). Trials. 2020;**21**(1):1019. DOI: 10.1186/s13063-020-04929-4

[26] Lopes MCC, Oliva CCC, Bezerra NMS, Silva MT, Galvão TF.

Relationship between depressive symptoms, burnout, job satisfaction and patient safety culture among workers at a university hospital in the Brazilian Amazon region: Cross-sectional study with structural equation modeling. São Paulo Medical Journal. 2022;**140**(3):412-421. DOI: 10.1590/1516-3180.2021.0614.15092021

[27] Tjasink M, Keiller E, Stephens M, Carr CE, Priebe S. Art therapy-based interventions to address burnout and psychosocial distress in healthcare workers - a systematic review. BMC Health Services Research. 2023;**23**(1):1059. DOI: 10.1186/s12913-023-09958-8

[28] Chen C, Meier ST. Corrigendum to "burnout and depression in nurses - a systematic review and meta-analysis". International Journal of Nursing Studies. 2022;**127**:104180, International Journal of Nursing Studies, Volume 124 (2021) 104099. DOI: 10.1016/j.ijnurstu.2022.104180

[29] Gerlach KE, Phalak KA, Parikh JR. The disruptive radiologist. Clinical Imaging. 2022;**87**:5-10. DOI: 10.1016/j.clinimag.2022.04.002

[30] Chen YC, Guo YL, Chin WS, Cheng NY, Ho JJ, Shiao JS. Patient-nurse ratio is related to nurses' intention to leave their job through mediating factors of burnout and job dissatisfaction. International Journal of Environmental Research and Public Health. 2019;**16**(23):4801. DOI: 10.3390/ijerph16234801

[31] World Health Organization. ICD-11 for Mortality and Morbidity Statistics. [Internet]. 2024. Available from: https://icd.who.int/browse11/l-m/en#/http://id.who.int/icd/entity/129180281 [Accessed: April 12, 2024]

[32] Jun J, Ojemeni MM, Kalamani R, Tong J, Crecelius ML. Relationship between nurse burnout, patient and organizational outcomes: Systematic review. International Journal of Nursing Studies. 2021;**119**:103933. DOI: 10.1016/j.ijnurstu.2021.103933

[33] Lastovkova A, Carder M, Rasmussen HM, Sjoberg L, Groene GJ, Sauni R, et al. Burnout syndrome as an occupational disease in the European Union: An exploratory study. Industrial Health. 2018;**56**(2):160-165. DOI: 10.2486/indhealth.2017-0132

[34] Maslach C, Schaufeli WB, Leiter MP. Job burnout. Annual Review of Psychology. 2001;**52**(1):397-422. DOI: 10.1146/annurev.psych.52.1.397

[35] Kakemam E, Chegini Z, Rouhi A, Ahmadi F, Majidi S. Burnout and its relationship to self-reported quality of patient care and adverse events during COVID-19: A cross-sectional online survey among nurses. Journal of Nursing Management. 2021;**29**(7):1974-1982. DOI: 10.1111/jonm.13359

[36] Hammer R, Ravindran N, Nielsen N. Can death Cafés resuscitate morale in hospitals? Medical Humanities. 2021;**47**(1):2-3. DOI: 10.1136/medhum-2018-011607

[37] Wolff MB, O'Connor PJ, Wilson MG, Gay JL. Differences in work and non-work support associations with job stress, burnout, and well-being between types of healthcare workers. Journal of Occupational and Environmental Medicine. 2021;**63**(3):e145-e152. DOI: 10.1097/JOM.0000000000002134

[38] Maticorena-Quevedo J, Beas R, Anduaga-Beramendi A, et al. Prevalence of burnout syndrome in Peruvian physicians and nurses, ENSUSALUD 2014. Revista Peruana de Medicina

Experimental y Salud Pública. 2016;**33**:241-247. DOI: 10.17843/rpmesp.2016.332.2170

[39] Aiken LH, Lasater KB, Sloane DM, Pogue CA, Fitzpatrick Rosenbaum KE, Muir KJ, et al. US clinician wellbeing study consortium. Physician and nurse well-being and preferred interventions to address burnout in hospital practice: Factors associated with turnover, outcomes, and patient safety. JAMA Health Forum. 2023;**4**(7):e231809. DOI: 10.1001/jamahealthforum.2023.1809

[40] Han S, Shanafelt TD, Sinsky CA, Awad KM, Dyrbye LN, Fiscus LC, et al. Estimating the attributable cost of physician burnout in the United States. Annals of Internal Medicine. 2019;**170**(11):784-790. DOI: 10.7326/M18-1422

[41] Yates SW. Physician stress and burnout. The American Journal of Medicine. 2020;**133**(2):160-164. DOI: 10.1016/j.amjmed.2019.08.034

[42] Nicholls M. Cardiologists and the burnout scenario. European Heart Journal. 2019;**40**(1):5-6. DOI: 10.1093/eurheartj/ehy788

[43] Medscape. Medscape National Physician Burnout, Depression & Suicide Report. [Internet]. 2019. Available from: https://www.medscape.com/2019-lifestyle-burnout [Accessed: April 13, 2024]

[44] Tmam A, Al-Ghunaim A, Johnson J, Biyani CS, Alshahrani KM, Dunning AD, et al. Surgeon burnout, impact on patient safety and professionalism: A systematic review and meta-analysis. American Journal of Surgery. 2022;**224**(1 Pt A):228-238. DOI: 10.1016/j.amjsurg.2021.12.027

[45] Pulcrano M, Evans SR, Sosin M. Quality of life and burnout rates across surgical specialties: A systematic review. JAMA Surgery. 2016;**151**(10):970-978. DOI: 10.1001/jamasurg.2016.1647

[46] Prapanjaroensin A, Patrician PA, Vance DE. Conservation of resources theory in nurse burnout and patient safety. Journal of Advanced Nursing. 2017;**73**(11):2558-2565. DOI: 10.1111/jan.13348

[47] Browning L, Ryan CS, Thomas S, Greenberg M, Rolniak S. Nursing specialty and burnout. Psychology, Health & Medicine. 2007;**12**(2):248-254. DOI: 10.1080/13548500600568290

[48] Aiken LH, Sloane DM, Clarke S, Poghosyan L, Cho E, You L, et al. Importance of work environments on hospital outcomes in nine countries. International Journal for Quality in Health Care. 2011;**23**(4):357-364. DOI: 10.1093/intqhc/mzr022

[49] Kieft RA, de Brouwer BB, Francke AL, Delnoij DM. How nurses and their work environment affect patient experiences of the quality of care: A qualitative study. BMC Health Services Research. 2014;**14**:249. DOI: 10.1186/1472-6963-14-249

[50] Garcia CDL, Abreu LCD, Ramos JLS, Castro CFDD, Smiderle FRN, Santos JAD, et al. Influence of burnout on patient safety: Systematic review and meta-analysis. Medicina (Kaunas, Lithuania). 2019;**55**(9):553. DOI: 10.3390/medicina55090553

[51] Dall'Ora C, Ball J, Reinius M, Griffiths P. Burnout in nursing: A theoretical review. Human Resources for Health. 2020;**18**(1):41. DOI: 10.1186/s12960-020-00469-9

[52] Andela M, Truchot D, Van der Doef M. Job stressors and burnout in hospitals: The mediating role of

emotional dissonance. International Journal of Stress Management. 2016;**23**(3):298-317. DOI: 10.1037/str0000013

[53] Liu X, Zheng J, Liu K, Baggs JG, Liu J, Wu Y, et al. Hospital nursing organizational factors, nursing care left undone, and nurse burnout as predictors of patient safety: A structural equation modeling analysis. International Journal of Nursing Studies. 2018;**86**:82-89. DOI: 10.1016/j.ijnurstu.2018.05.005

[54] Cao X, Naruse T. Effect of time pressure on the burnout of home-visiting nurses: The moderating role of relational coordination with nursing managers. Japan Journal of Nursing Science. 2019;**16**(2):221-231. DOI: 10.1111/jjns.12233

[55] Akman O, Ozturk C, Bektas M, Ayar D, Armstrong MA. Job satisfaction and burnout among paediatric nurses. Journal of Nursing Management. 2016;**24**(7):923-933. DOI: 10.1111/jonm.12399

[56] Galletta M, Portoghese I, Ciuffi M, Sancassiani F, Aloja E, Campagna M. Working and environmental factors on job burnout: A cross-sectional study among nurses. Clinical Practice and Epidemiology in Mental Health. 2016;**12**:132-141. DOI: 10.2174/1745017901612010132

[57] Leiter MP, Maslach C. Nurse turnover: The mediating role of burnout. Journal of Nursing Management. 2009;**17**(3):331-339. DOI: 10.1111/j.1365-2834.2009.01004.x

[58] Shao J, Tang L, Wang X, Qiu R, Zhang Y, Jia Y, et al. Nursing work environment, value congruence and their relationships with nurses' work outcomes. Journal of Nursing Management. 2018;**26**(8):1091-1099. DOI: 10.1111/jonm.12641

[59] Colindres CV, Bryce E, Coral-Rosero P, Ramos-Soto RM, Bonilla F, Yassi A. Effect of effort-reward imbalance and burnout on infection control among Ecuadorian nurses. International Nursing Review. 2018;**65**(2):190-199. DOI: 10.1111/inr.12409

[60] Van Bogaert P, Kowalski C, Weeks SM, Van Heusden D, Clarke SP. The relationship between nurse practice environment, nurse work characteristics, burnout and job outcome and quality of nursing care: A cross-sectional survey. International Journal of Nursing Studies. 2013;**50**(12):1667-1677. DOI: 10.1016/j.ijnurstu.2013.05.010

[61] Khamisa N, Peltzer K, Ilic D, Oldenburg B. Work related stress, burnout, job satisfaction and general health of nurses: A follow-up study. International Journal of Nursing Practice. 2016;**22**(6):538-545. DOI: 10.1111/ijn.12455

[62] Vidotti V, Ribeiro RP, Galdino MJQ, Martins JT. Burnout syndrome and shift work among the nursing staff. Revista Latino-Americana de Enfermagem. 2018;**26**:e3022. DOI: 10.1590/1518-8345.2550.3022

[63] Bagheri Hosseinabadi M, Ebrahimi MH, Khanjani N, Biganeh J, Mohammadi S, Abdolahfard M. The effects of amplitude and stability of circadian rhythm and occupational stress on burnout syndrome and job dissatisfaction among irregular shift working nurses. Journal of Clinical Nursing. 2019;**28**(9-10):1868-1878. DOI: 10.1111/jocn.14778

[64] Stimpfel AW, Sloane DM, Aiken LH. The longer the shifts for hospital nurses, the higher the levels of burnout and patient dissatisfaction. Health Affairs (Millwood). 2012;**31**(11):2501-2509. DOI: 10.1377/hlthaff.2011.1377

[65] Konstantinou AK, Bonotis K, Sokratous M, Siokas V, Dardiotis E. Burnout evaluation and potential predictors in a Greek cohort of mental health nurses. Archives of Psychiatric Nursing. 2018;**32**(3):449-456. DOI: 10.1016/j.apnu.2018.01.002

[66] Madathil R, Heck NC, Schuldberg D. Burnout in psychiatric nursing: Examining the interplay of autonomy, leadership style, and depressive symptoms. Archives of Psychiatric Nursing. 2014;**28**(3):160-166. DOI: 10.1016/j.apnu.2014.01.002

[67] Rouxel G, Michinov E, Dodeler V. The influence of work characteristics, emotional display rules and affectivity on burnout and job satisfaction: A survey among geriatric care workers. International Journal of Nursing Studies. 2016;**62**:81-89. DOI: 10.1016/j.ijnurstu.2016.07.010

[68] Laeeque SH, Bilal A, Babar S, Khan Z, Rahman SU. How patient-perpetrated workplace violence leads to turnover intention among nurses: The mediating mechanism of occupational stress and burnout. Journal of Aggression, Maltreatment & Trauma. 2018;**27**(1):96-118. DOI: 10.1080/10926771.2017.1410751

[69] Moloney W, Boxall P, Parsons M, Cheung G. Factors predicting registered nurses' intentions to leave their organization and profession: A job demands-resources framework. Journal of Advanced Nursing. 2018;**74**(4):864-875. DOI: 10.1111/jan.13497

[70] Gardner RL, Cooper E, Haskell J, Harris DA, Poplau S, Kroth PJ, et al. Physician stress and burnout: The impact of health information technology. Journal of the American Medical Informatics Association. 2019;**26**(2):106-114. DOI: 10.1093/jamia/ocy145

[71] Tajirian T, Stergiopoulos V, Strudwick G, Sequeira L, Sanches M, Kemp J, et al. The influence of electronic health record use on physician burnout: Cross-sectional survey. Journal of Medical Internet Research. 2020;**22**(7):e19274. DOI: 10.2196/19274

[72] Gajra A, Bapat B, Jeune-Smith Y, Nabhan C, Klink AJ, Liassou D, et al. Frequency and causes of burnout in US community oncologists in the era of electronic health records. JCO Oncology Practice. 2020;**16**(4):e357-e365. DOI: 10.1200/JOP.19.00542

[73] Salvagioni DAJ, Melanda FN, Mesas AE, Gonzalez AD, Gabani FL, Andrade SM. Physical, psychological and occupational consequences of job burnout: A systematic review of prospective studies. PLoS One. 2017;**12**(10):e0185781. DOI: 10.1371/journal.pone.0185781

[74] Deneva T, Ianakiev Y, Keskinova D. Burnout syndrome in physicians-psychological assessment and biomarker research. Medicina (Kaunas, Lithuania). 2019;**55**(5):209. DOI: 10.3390/medicina55050209

[75] Lee HF, Yen M, Fetzer S, Chien TW. Predictors of burnout among nurses in Taiwan. Community Mental Health Journal. 2015;**51**(6):733-737. DOI: 10.1007/s10597-014-9818-4

[76] Heinen MM, van Achterberg T, Schwendimann R, Zander B, Matthews A, Kózka M, et al. Nurses' intention to leave their profession: A cross sectional observational study in 10 European countries. International Journal of Nursing Studies. 2013;**50**(2):174-184. DOI: 10.1016/j.ijnurstu.2012.09.019

[77] Goh J, Pfeffer J, Zenios SA. The relationship between workplace stressors

and mortality and health costs in the United States. Management Science. 2016;**62**(2):608-628. DOI: 10.1287/mnsc.2014.2115

[78] Health Resources & Services Administration. Nursing Workforce Survey. [Internet]. Available from: https://data.hrsa.gov/topics/health-workforce/nursing-workforce-survey-data [Accessed: April 18, 2024]

[79] Dewanto A, Wardhani V. Nurse turnover and perceived causes and consequences: A preliminary study at private hospitals in Indonesia. BMC Nursing. 2018;**17**(Suppl. 2):52. DOI: 10.1186/s12912-018-0317-8

[80] Nursing Solutions, Inc. 2020 NSI National Healthcare Retention & RN Staffing Report. [Internet]. 2020. Available from: https://www.nsinursingsolutions.com/Documents/Library/NSI_National_Health_Care_Retention_Report.pdf [Accessed: March 8, 2024]

[81] Halbesleben JR, Wakefield BJ, Wakefield DS, Cooper LB. Nurse burnout and patient safety outcomes: Nurse safety perception versus reporting behavior. Western Journal of Nursing Research. 2008;**30**(5):560-577. DOI: 10.1177/0193945907311322

[82] Nantsupawat A, Nantsupawat R, Kunaviktikul W, Turale S, Poghosyan L. Nurse burnout, nurse-reported quality of care, and patient outcomes in Thai hospitals. Journal of Nursing Scholarship. 2016;**48**(1):83-90. DOI: 10.1111/jnu.12187

[83] Panagioti M, Geraghty K, Johnson J, Zhou A, Panagopoulou E, Chew-Graham C, et al. Association between physician burnout and patient safety, professionalism, and patient satisfaction: A systematic review and meta-analysis. JAMA Internal Medicine. 2018;**178**(10):1317-1331. DOI: 10.1001/jamainternmed.2019.0155

[84] Willard-Grace R, Knox M, Huang B, Hammer H, Kivlahan C, Grumbach K. Burnout and health care workforce turnover. Annals of Family Medicine. 2019;**17**(1):36-41. DOI: 10.1370/afm.2338

[85] Dijxhoorn A-FQ, Brom L, van der Linden YM, Leget C, Raijmakers NJH. Prevalence of burnout in healthcare professionals providing palliative care and the effect of interventions to reduce symptoms: A systematic literature review. Palliative Medicine. 2021;**35**(1):6-26. DOI: 10.1177/0269216320956825

[86] International Council of Nurses. ICN International Workforce Forum Calls for Urgent Action from Governments to Address Global Nursing Shortage. [Internet]. Available from: https://www.icn.ch/news/icn-international-workforce-forum-calls-urgent-action-governments-address-global-nursing. [Accessed: May 11, 2024]

[87] Lancet T. Physician burnout: The need to rehumanise health systems. Lancet. 2019;**394**(10209):1591. DOI: 10.1016/S0140-6736(19)32669-8

[88] Lu DM, Sun N, Hong S, Fan YY, Kong FY, Li QJ. Occupational stress and coping strategies among emergency department nurses of China. Archives of Psychiatric Nursing. 2015;**29**(4):208-212. DOI: 10.1016/j.apnu.2014.11.006

[89] West CP, Dyrbye LN, Erwin PJ, Shanafelt TD. Interventions to prevent and reduce physician burnout: A systematic review and meta-analysis. Lancet. 2016;**388**(10057):2272-2281. DOI: 10.1016/S0140-6736(16)31279-X

[90] Jarden RJ, Sandham M, Siegert RJ, Koziol-McLain J. Strengthening

workplace well-being: Perceptions of intensive care nurses. Nursing in Critical Care. 2019;**24**(1):15-23. DOI: 10.1111/nicc.12386

[91] Kishore S, Ripp J, Shanafelt T, Melnyk B, Rogers D, Spisso J. Making the Case for the Chief Wellness Officer in America's Health Systems: A Call to Action. Health Affairs Forefront. [Internet]. 26 October 2024. Available from: https://www.healthaffairs.org/do/10.1377/hblog20181025.308059/full [Accessed: May 12, 2024]

[92] Fallon LF Jr, Fleming L, McConnell CR. Human Resource Management in Health Care. Section IV Discipline, Chapter 14 Managers and Employee Problems, Employee Assistance Programs. The United States of America: Jones & Bartlett Publishers; 2013. p. 288

[93] Depret OR, Maia EBS, de Borba RIH, Ribeiro CA. Health and well-being: Art therapy for health professionals working in outpatient care settings. Escola Anna Nery - Revista de Enfermagem. 2020;**24**(1):e20190177. DOI: 10.1590/2177-9465-EAN-2019-0177

[94] Hobfoll SE. Conservation of resources: A new attempt at conceptualizing stress. The American Psychologist. 1989;**44**(3):513-524. DOI: 10.1037//0003-066x.44.3.513

Chapter 3

Depression and Suicidal Ideations in Older Adults

Ukamaka Gloria Mgbeojedo, Emmanuel Jonah Osiri, Fredrick Sunday Isaac and Chisom Precious Anodebe

Abstract

With advancing age, older adults are usually faced with psychological challenges as a result of intense feelings of loneliness, anxiety, and loss, leading to depression and, consequently, suicidal ideations. Depression is a mood disorder that causes a persistent feeling of sadness and loss of interest, which erodes quality of life, negatively affecting the health and well-being of older adults. Suicidal thoughts and ideas occur to depressed people in an attempt to find a long-term solution to their problems. The older adult population has a notably high prevalence of depression and suicidal ideations. However, adequate social support, relationships, and networks, early medical interventions, etc., have been found to be important factors influencing depression and suicidal thoughts. This chapter examines depression and suicidal ideations among older adults in relation to prevalence, causes, and the role of social support and physical activity as possible management strategies. Studies have reported and recommended early major depression diagnosis and treatment as a means of lowering the risk of suicide.

Keywords: depression, suicidal ideations, older adults, prevalence, social support

1. Introduction

Aging is linked to certain challenges such as changes in one's level of independence, financial situation, interpersonal connections, and physical and mental capacities [1]. Furthermore, the loss of social support networks as one ages is frequently brought on by retirement, relocation, or bereavement. The growing number of older adults demands more attention be paid to mental and late-life healthcare [2]. If they live long enough, older adults may start losing loved ones to illness and old age. They might struggle with their own mortality and worry about death and dying. For most people, this "age of loss" is overwhelming and can exacerbate feelings of loneliness, hopelessness, helplessness, and depression.

Depression in older individuals is a major and expanding public health issue worldwide [3]. It is also one of the main factors reducing disability-adjusted life years [4]. It is a mood disorder that causes a persistent feeling of sadness and loss of interest [5, 6]. It has a detrimental impact on senior citizens' health and well-being [7]. Although depression is common among older adults, it is not a typical aspect of aging. Compared to most medical conditions, it is linked to a higher medical burden, higher use of health services, longer hospital stays, disability, and greater functional impairment. According to Zivin et al. [7], depression is also linked to poor socioeconomic position, bereavement, death, and suicide in later life. There are a number of risk factors for depression in older adults, including being female, single, divorced, or widowed, not having a supporting social network, experiencing stressful life events, having a poor socioeconomic position, having a chronic physical ailment, and having a family history [6].

Additional risk factors include a lack of social support or interaction, death and suicide in later life [7], and loss and sadness [8]. Depression is further increased by physical illnesses like dementia, cancer, diabetes mellitus, hypertension, and stroke. Depressive disorders are dangerous chronic illnesses that worsen morbidity and mortality [9], which lowers quality of life [10]. Depression in older persons is sometimes misdiagnosed as a side effect of many conditions and medications. Late-life depression symptoms are sometimes mistaken for signs of aging, bereavement, physical sickness, or dementia. As a result, many older persons battle with depression needlessly because healthcare professionals, family, and patients overlook the indicators of sadness and, more significantly, opportunities to begin therapy [11]. Suicidal thoughts and ideations are typically the result of depression in people who are trying to find a long-term solution to their problems [12].

Suicidal ideation is the deliberate attempt to end one's own life [13]. It can take many different forms, from passive thoughts to complex plans and objectives to actually executing suicide [14]. Suicidal ideation, non-fatal suicide attempts, and even successful suicides are all considered suicidal outcomes [15]. There is a strong correlation between suicidal ideation and suicide deaths as well as suicide attempts [15, 16]. The world community recognizes older adults' suicidal ideation as a serious public health issue [14, 17]. Compared to other age groups, older adults have greater suicide rates; and men are more likely to commit suicide than women [18, 19]. Mental health conditions like depression, physical health conditions like chronic illnesses and impairments, and social health conditions like social isolation and bereavement are risk factors linked to suicide behavior in older adults [18, 20]. Retirement, low socioeconomic status, social isolation, loss of a spouse, and living alone are among the specific experiences of aging that are linked to suicidal ideation [2, 18, 21–22]. Since targeted suicide prevention and treatment strategies focus on the population with suicide risks, suicide risk assessments often begin after finding evidence of suicidal ideation [23]. We therefore hypothesize that a deeper comprehension of suicidal ideation may enable health professionals to recognize older adults who are at risk earlier and offer them the assistance they require. This chapter thus focuses on the prevalence, causes, and possible management strategies of depression and suicidal ideations in older adults.

2. Prevalence of depression and suicidal ideations among older adults

The World Population Prospect [24] projects that the number of people over 80 will triple to 426 million between 2020 and 2050, contributing to the world's aging population, which is now increasing at an accelerated rate. As people age, they become more vulnerable to certain illnesses. Many people are vulnerable to mental health conditions like depression and anxiety. A mental disorder affects 14% of people 60 years of age and older [25]. 10.6% of the total impairment in older persons (measured in disability-adjusted life years) is attributed to these illnesses. There have been conflicting results from the numerous researches on the prevalence of depression. While a study reported the global point prevalence of serious depressive illness among individuals over 55 to be 4.7% [26], a recent meta-analysis and systematic review revealed that older individuals had a global prevalence of depression of 28.4% overall [27]. Diversity in study territories, attitudes toward mental health problems and stigma, accessibility to basic public health services, and screening tools [26, 28, 29] have all been linked to the wide variations in the prevalence of depression among older adults, which has been reported to range from 8.2 to 63.0% [30, 31].

According to some prior research, 10 to 20% of older adults worldwide suffer from depression [32–34], while 40% of those with mental illnesses were found to have a depressive condition [35]. Older adults often accept depressive symptoms such as exhaustion, anorexia, and insomnia as normal aging processes or appropriate reactions to life's challenges [36, 37]. Screening for mental health disorders such as depression is essential for older persons since it reduces the chance of suicide and other issues [28, 38–40]. Because of its links to risk factors for suicide, increased healthcare expenses, emotional discomfort, and death from other causes, depression in older adults is seen as a severe public health concern [41–43].

Global estimates of the lifetime prevalence of suicide ideation and attempts are 3 and 9%, respectively, for all age groups [44]. According to estimates, 3 to 25% of people worldwide experience suicidal thoughts in their later years [45–48]. Researchers have discovered that older individuals who are single, widowed, bereaved, live alone and/or are socially isolated, and have underlying medical and/or mental health difficulties are more likely to suffer a high incidence of suicidal ideation [49]. Compared to younger age groups, older adults are more likely to experience suicidal ideation and act on it even though they are less likely to kill themselves right away [50–52].

Research on psychological autopsies conducted in China and the West has shown that older adults with medical conditions have a higher risk of suicide [53, 54]. Older adults account for about 22% of suicides, even though they make up only 16.8% of the population [55, 56]. Individuals 65 years of age or older were responsible for 10,433 of the almost 49,449 suicides that occurred in the US in 2022 [55]. Thus, the first and most crucial step in effectively avoiding late-life suicide is screening for suicidal ideation.

3. Causes and risk factors of depression and suicidal ideations in older adults

Depression is one of the major contributing aspects to the reasons older adults have suicidal ideations [57]. Depression is the strongest direct correlate of suicide ideation and behavior in older adults, independent of other variables [58, 59]. A multitude of factors, including biological, psychological, social, economic, and demographic ones, have complex effects on depression in older adults. Health professionals do not view geriatric depression as a normal aspect of aging, despite the fact that it is the most prevalent mental health disorder among persons 65 years of age and older [60]. Nonetheless, there are a few factors that can make older adults more vulnerable to mental illnesses including depression and suicidal ideations. Studies have indicated that while these characteristics may increase an individual's risk of depression, they do not always result in depression or thoughts of suicide in the older adults population. Long-term health issues, inherited depression, stress, sleep issues, social isolation, loneliness, and functional restrictions are a few of them. Mental health issues are worldwide problems imposing huge burdens on individuals and health care systems. Among the population of older adults, depression, and suicidal ideations can be directly linked to the following factors:

3.1 Gender

Almost everywhere in the globe, women experience depression two to three times more frequently than men [61], making the gender gap in depression a global problem. This unequal burden also applies to other mental health issues. According to Vafaei et al. [62], women are more likely than men to experience depression, anxiety, or suicidal thoughts. They are also more likely to participate in risky behaviors that could negatively impact their health, like substance abuse, violent or antisocial behavior, or suicide. Women are more likely than men to encounter stressful situations and depression risk factors during the course of their life [63]. Women may also react differently to these factors, which contribute to the explanation of why depression rates are higher in women. Studies reveal that men's mood control systems tend to be more problem-solving oriented, while women's mechanisms tend to be more emotion-focused [64]. These gender differences in the ways that people express and cope with mental distress have been linked to the social roles that society values for men and women [62]. The acceptance of feminine roles by women may make depression worse.

3.2 Health conditions

Numerous studies have demonstrated a strong correlation between the chance of engaging in suicide behavior and higher levels of disability [65–68]. More specifically, multimorbidity in older adults [69] and poor health conditions [67, 70] have been associated with an increased risk of suicide behavior. According to McIntyre et al. [67], co-occurring anxiety and depression may point to a range of clinical severity, which can lead to a decline in self-reported health status, an increase in the number of medical illnesses, a reduction in mental functioning, and a rise in the demand for emergency services. Nonetheless, a surge in suicidal thoughts has been connected to chronic pain [71]. Furthermore, in older adults who had suffered severe poststroke depression, a postmortem analysis by Nishida et al. [72] showed a clear association between the severity of a stroke and the completion of suicide.

4. Relationship between depression and suicidal ideation

Depression and suicidal ideations in older adults are linked [59]. Depression is the strongest direct correlate of suicidal ideation and behavior in older adults, irrespective of other characteristics [57, 59]. According to Jang and Kim [73], stress affects older adults' depression, and depression is a major factor that encourages suicidal ideation. Depression had a greater effect on older adults in terms of suicidal thoughts and attempts [74]. Depression raises the risk of suicide among older adults more than it does for suicide in any other age group [75]. Depression directly affects suicide, while factors related to family and community integration, health, and economic status have an indirect effect. Higher levels of suicidal thoughts are more common among older adults with severe depression, according to a significant correlation between suicidal ideation and depression [59, 76, 77]. In a study among stroke survivors, depression was significantly associated with suicidal ideations [13].

5. Depression and suicidal ideation: the role of social support

It is well recognized that depression and suicidal ideations play a significant role in the worldwide disease burden. While depression is deleterious for people of all ages in terms of both their physical and mental health, it is particularly worse for older adults. In addition to being biologically more susceptible to depression [78], older adults also experience social deprivation; when their social networks deteriorate with age, they are more prone to feel alone, which has a detrimental impact on mental health [79].

Social support describes resource exchange between a minimum of two people in which one of them believes the other is trying to improve their own well-being [80]. It refers to positive interactions with a network that supports people, particularly older adults, in maintaining their health or overcoming adversity [81]. Social support has been defined in terms of both actualized and perceived social support. Perceived social support is the belief that one can get social assistance, whereas received social support is the reported exchange or use of social support resources by an individual [82].

Research has shown that older adults who have a spouse or partner have fewer depressive symptoms [83–85]. Additionally, it was found that living circumstances among older adults were significantly associated with symptoms of depression [86–88]. Moreover, studies have demonstrated a significant relationship between the extent of one's social support system and the lack of depressive symptoms [89–91].

The characteristics of a social network have also been connected to depression among older adults. In reference to the source of social support in relation to depression, contradictory findings exist. Research has indicated that older adults who receive support from friends report having fewer depressive symptoms [88]. A recent study reported that the friend domain of social support was not a significant predictor of depression [89]. Conversely, a small number of studies have reported a direct correlation between lower depressive symptoms and social support from family [92–94].

Adequate social support might be necessary to foster the resilience needed for a successful transition to the difficulties that come with aging [89]. This suggests that social support is essential for older adults' mental health. According to Tengku et al. [80], social support can be classified as structural versus functional and perceived versus received. A person's organizational ties to others are indicated by structural social support, which may be quantified in a variety of ways, including the size of their social network, the makeup of their network, how often they interact with one another, and the variety of their relationships with network members. Conversely, functional social support is the sharing of knowledge, appraisal, instrumental or practical support, and emotional support. The satisfaction that comes from having confidence and not being socially isolated is one facet of social support. Perceived and actualized social support are other ways to characterize social support. While received social support is the acknowledged exchange or use of social support resources by an individual, perceived social support is the idea that one can obtain social assistance. Therefore, social support is a complex idea that generally refers to the emotional, instrumental, or informational assistance that one receives from others (e.g., encouraging someone, helping with housework, or notifying them about a job opportunity) [95].

Older adults who are depressed frequently exhibit characteristics of inactivity, lethargic behavior, and listlessness because they feel helpless or incapable of changing their situation [96]. Reduced engagement in social and recreational activities is one potentially detrimental effect of depression, and it has been amply demonstrated that depression is a major predisposing factor for suicidal ideation and suicide completion in older persons [97]. A form of healthy aging known as active social engagement has also been studied; its many benefits and striking distinctions from lonely older adults have been noted [98]. According to Park et al. [99], participating in a variety of activities gives older adults the ability to connect emotionally and receive support from people who are more readily in line with their ideas and struggles in life. As a result, feelings of isolation, depression, and suicidal ideations decrease. Informal socializing, such as hanging out with friends, family, or neighbors, has been found to have the biggest positive impact on well-being in later life and can help ward off depression and suicidal ideations [100]. Supportive family members can help older adults with depressive symptoms in their late-life years develop good coping mechanisms by encouraging regular exercise and other healthy behaviors [101]. Thoughts like going to the movies, hanging out with friends, or other leisure activities away from home are not likely to be on the list of things that cross their minds; instead, they are provided by the people who are caring for them. Thoits [102] surmised that supportive significant others serve as good role models in addition to helping older adults with poor mental health cope. Strong supportive relationships can help older adults have access to more social resources, like community services that their pro-social family members attend. Family members that are supportive may also encourage changes in health-related activities, such as going outside and exercising, that either directly or indirectly lessen depressive symptomology [103]. The quantity and frequency of social connections have a significant role in assisting with depression. It has also been noted that having a neighborhood support system can assist in preventing depression and suicidal ideations [104]. It has also long been believed that older adults' surroundings affect their health. Formal friendships with neighbors have been suggested to have mitigating effects on depression [105].

6. Depression and suicidal ideation: the role of physical activity

According to Krämer et al. [106], depression affects older adults by reducing their motivation and volitional capacity, which includes their ability to translate intentions into actions. This intensifies feelings of loneliness, which heightens depressing ideas and thoughts of suicide. Their inability to perform their activities of daily living (ADL) is another factor contributing to depression [107]. When older adults are unable to perform simple tasks like eating, dressing, washing, and using the restroom, it can make them feel helpless and reliant, which can make them unhappy and pessimistic. This corresponds to research that reported a correlation between depression and functional disability in older adults [5]. In a similar vein, Takahashi et al. [108] discovered that older adults with depression exhibited balance and mobility issues in addition to a shorter lateral functional reach, which is positively connected with ADL. According to Gureje et al. [109], major depressive disorder is more common in older adults who struggle to complete their ADLs.

Given its role, physical activity—which has been linked to a decrease in depression symptoms—plays a significant role in the management of this disorder [110]. Endogenous opiates, brain neurotransmitters, anti-inflammatory cytokines, cerebral blood flow, and the function of the hypothalamic-pituitary-adrenal axis are some of the physiological or biochemical explanations for how physical activity affects depression and suicidal ideations [111, 112]. In addition, exercise controls depression and suicidal ideations via psychological processes. Distraction and improved self-efficacy, self-esteem, behavioral activation, sense of accomplishment/mastery, and self-determination are some ways in which this might occur [113, 114].

Creating intervention programs is crucial to shielding older adults from the crippling repercussions of not doing ADLs. Proactive measures to reduce depression include carefully working with older adults in community settings and using screening to assess a patient's depression risk, which can be done by medical experts like doctors, nurses, and social workers. Additionally, social workers who work with the families of older individuals are able to spot changes in the family's dynamics on an emotional or relational level. In these circumstances, they might play a critical role in assisting the family in making that evaluation and in screening their aging relative for depression. In addition, it is imperative that the government work in concert with mental health and suicide prevention service centers to develop required medical examination programs that incorporate depression testing.

7. Conclusion

Depression and suicidal ideations in older adults are common and serious public health concerns. Their debilitating effects are quite fatal. However, they are not part of the normal aging process.

Early diagnosis and management are key to salvaging the negative consequences. Adequate social support and networks, along with routine screening of these psychological variables, are recommended in order to enhance/improve their quality of life and general well-being.

Competing interest

The authors declare that they have no competing interest.

Author details

Ukamaka Gloria Mgbeojedo*, Emmanuel Jonah Osiri, Fredrick Sunday Isaac and Chisom Precious Anodebe
Department of Medical Rehabilitation, University of Nigeria, Enugu Campus, Enugu, Nigeria

*Address all correspondence to: amakamgbeojedo@yahoo.com

References

[1] Haigh EAP, Bogucki OE, Sigmon ST, Blazer DG. Depression among older adults: A 20-year update on five common myths and misconceptions (article in press). American Journal Geriatric Psychiatry. 2017;**1**(26):1-16

[2] Purcell B, Heisel MJ, Speice J, Franus N, Conwell Y, Duberstein PR. Family connectedness moderates the association between living alone and suicide ideation in a clinical sample of adults 50 years and older. American Journal Geriatric Psychiatry. 2012;**8**:717-723. DOI: 10.1097/JGP.0b013e31822ccd79

[3] Ustun TB, Ayuso-Mateos JL, Chatterji S, Mathers C, Murray CJL. Global burden of depressive disorders in the year 2000. British Journal of Psychiatry. 2004;**184**:386-392

[4] Murray CJ, Lopez AD. Measuring the global burden of disease. New England Journal of Medicine. 2013;**369**(5):448-457

[5] Akosile CO, Mgbeojedo UG, Maruf FA, Okoye EC, Umeonwuka IC, Ogunniyi A. Depression, functional disability and quality of life among Nigerian older adults: Prevalences and relationships. Archives of Gerontology and Geriatrics. 2017;**74**:39-43. DOI: 10.1016/j.archger.2017.08.011

[6] Park M, Reynolds CF. Depression among older adults with diabetes mellitus. Clinics in Geriatric Medicine. 2015;**31**(1):117-137. DOI: 10.1016/j.cger.2014.08.022

[7] Zivin K, Llewellyn DJ, Lang LA, Vijan S, Kabeto MU, Miller EM, et al. Depression among older adults in the United States and England. The American Journal of Geriatric Psychiatry. 2010;**18**(11):1036-1044. DOI: 10.1097/JGP.0b013e3181dba6d2

[8] Stroebe M, Schut H, Stroebe W. Health outcomes of bereavement. The Lancet. 2007;**370**(9603):1960-1973

[9] Park M, Katon WJ, Wolf FM. Depression and risk of mortality in individuals with diabetes: A meta-analysis and systematic review. General Hospital Psychiatry. 2013;**35**(3):217-225

[10] Cuijpers P, Beekman AT, Reynolds CF 3rd. Preventing depression: A global priority. JAMA: The Journal of the American Medical Association. 2012;**307**(10):1033-1034

[11] Forsström E, Hakko H, Nordström T, Räsänen P, Mainio A. Suicide in patients with stroke: A population-based study of suicide victims during the years 1988-2007 in northern Finland. Journal of Neuropsychiatry and Clinical Neurosciences. 2010;**22**:182-187

[12] Turecki G, Brent DA, Gunnell D, O'Connor RC, Oquendo MA, Pirkis J, et al. Suicide and suicide risk. Nature Reviews Disease Primers. 2019;**5**(1):74. DOI: 10.1038/s41572-019-0121-0

[13] Mgbeojedo UG, Osiri EJ, Akosile CO, Okoye EC, John JN, Akobundu UN, et al. Post-stroke depression and suicidal ideations: Relationship with gender and marital status: A cross sectional study. Journal of Primary Care & Community Health. 2024;**15**:1-7. DOI: 10.1177/21501319241233172

[14] Chang Q, Chan CH, Yip PSF. A meta-analytic review on social relationships and suicidal ideation among older adults. Social Science & Medicine. 2017;**191**:65-76. DOI: 10.1016/j.socscimed.2017.09.003

[15] Borges G, Angst J, Nock MK, Ruscio AM, Walters EE, Kessler RC. A risk index for 12-month suicide attempts in the National Comorbidity Survey Replication (NCS-R). Psychological Medicine. 2006;**36**(12):1747-1757. DOI: 10.1017/S0033291706008786

[16] Posner K, Brown GK, Stanley B, Brent DA, Yershova KV, Oquendo MA, et al. The Columbia-suicide severity rating scale: Initial validity and internal consistency findings from three multisite studies with adolescents and adults. The American Journal of Geriatric Psychiatry. 2011;**168**(12):1266-1277. DOI: 10.1176/appi.ajp.2011.10111704

[17] Okolie C, Dennis M, Thomas ES, John A. A systematic review of interventions to prevent suicidal behaviors and reduce suicidal ideation in older people. International Psychogeriatrics. 2017;**29**(11):1-24. DOI: 10.1017/S1041610217001430

[18] Conwell Y, Duberstein PR, Caine ED. Risk factors for suicide in later life. Biological Psychiatry. 2002;**52**(3):193-204. DOI: 10.1016/s0006-3223(02)01347-1

[19] O'Connell H, Chin A-V, Cunningham C, Lawlor BA. Recent developments: Suicide in older people. The British Medical Journal. 2004;**329**(7471):895-899. DOI: 10.1136/bmj.329.7471.895

[20] Dong X, Chang ES, Zeng P, Simon MA. Suicide in the global Chinese aging population: A review of risk and protective factors, consequences, and interventions. Aging and Disease. 2015;**6**:121-130. DOI: 10.14336/AD.2014.0223

[21] Lee H-Y, Hahm M-I, Park E-C. Differential association of socio-economic status with gender-and age-defined suicidal ideation among adult and elderly individuals in South Korea. Psychiatry Research. 2013;**210**(1):323-328

[22] Ju YJ, Park E-C, Han K-T, Choi JW, Kim JL, Cho KH, et al. Low socioeconomic status and suicidal ideation among elderly individuals. International Psychogeriatrics. 2016;**28**(12):2055-2066. DOI: 10.1017/S1041610216001149

[23] Han B, Crosby AE, Ortega LAG, Parks SE, Compton WM, Gfroerer J. Suicidal ideation, suicide attempt, and occupations among employed adults aged 18-64years in the United States. Comprehensive Psychiatry. 2016;**66**:176-186. DOI: 10.1016/j.comppsych.2016.02.001

[24] United Nations. World Population Prospect 2022: Release Note about Major Differences in Total Population Estimates for Mid2021 between 2019 and 2022 Revisions. New York: United Nations Department of Economic and Social Affairs, Population Division; 2022. Available from: http://population.un.org/wpp/Publications/Files/WPP2022_Release-Note-rev1.pdf [Accessed: September 12, 2023]

[25] Institute of Health Metrics and Evaluation. Global Health Data Exchange (GHDx). 2023. Available from: http://vizhub.healthdata.org/gbd-results/

[26] Ferrari AJ, Charlson FJ, Norman RE, Patten SB, Freedman G, Murray CJ, et al. Burden of depressive disorders by country, sex, age, and year: Findings from the global burden of disease study 2010. PLoS Medicine. 2013;**10**(11):e1001547. DOI: 10.1371/journal.pmed.1001547

[27] Hu S, Zhang X, Stamatiou M, Hambly C, Huang Y, Ma J, et al.

Higher than predicted resting energy expenditure and lower physical activity in healthy underweight Chinese adults. Cell Metabolism. 2022;**34**(10):1413-1415. DOI: 10.1016/j.cmet.2022.05.012

[28] Krishnamoorthy Y, Nagarajan R, Saya GK, Menon V. Prevalence of psychological morbidities among general population, healthcare workers and COVID-19 patients amidst the COVID-19 pandemic: A systematic review and meta-analysis. Psychiatry Research. 2020;**293**:113382. DOI: 10.1016/j.psychres.2020.113382

[29] Moreno-Agostino D, Wu YT, Daskalopoulou C, Hasan MT, Huisman M, Prina M. Global trends in the prevalence and incidence of depression: A systematic review and meta-analysis. Journal of Affective Disorders. 2021;**281**:235-243. DOI: 10.1016/j.jad.2020.12.035

[30] Manandhar K, Risal A, Shrestha O, Manandhar N, Kunwar D, Koju R, et al. Prevalence of geriatric depression in the Kavre district, Nepal: Findings from a cross sectional community survey. BMC Psychiatry. 2019;**19**:271. DOI: 10.1186/s12888-019-2258-5

[31] Pirkis J, Pfaff J, Williamson M, Tyson O, Stocks N, Goldney R, et al. The community prevalence of depression in older Australians. Journal of Affective Disorders. 2009;**115**:54-61. DOI: 10.1016/j.jad.2008.08.014

[32] Zenebe Y, Akele B, W/Selassie M, Necho M. Prevalence and determinants of depression among old age: A systematic review and meta-analysis. Annals of General Psychiatry. 2021;**20**(1):55. DOI: 10.1186/s12991-021-00375-x

[33] Eustache E, Gerbasi ME, Smith Fawzi MC, Fils-Aimé JR, Severe J, Raviola GJ, et al. High burden of mental illness and low utilization of care among school-going youth in Central Haiti: A window into the youth mental health treatment gap in a low-income country. The International Journal of Social Psychiatry. 2017;**63**(3):261-274. DOI: 10.1177/0020764017700174

[34] Mitchell AJ, Subramaniam H. Prognosis of depression in old age compared to middle age: A systematic review of comparative studies. The American Journal of Psychiatry. 2005;**162**(9):1588-1601

[35] Patel V, Saxena S. Transforming lives, enhancing communities–Innovations in global mental health. The New England Journal of Medicine. 2014;**370**(6):498-501. DOI: 10.1056/NEJMp1315214

[36] Sadavoy J. An integrated model for defining the scope of psychogeriatrics: The five Cs. International Psychogeriatrics. 2009;**21**(5):805-812. DOI: 10.1017/S104161020999010X

[37] Duo-Yu W, Guo M, Gao Y-S, Kang Y-H, Guo J-C, Jiang X-L, et al. Clinical effects of comprehensive therapy of early psychological intervention and rehabilitation training on neurological rehabilitation of patients with acute stroke. Asian Pacific Journal of Tropical Medicine. 2012;**5**(11):914-916. DOI: 10.1016/S1995-7645(12)60171-0

[38] Wang S, Blazer DG. Depression and cognition in the elderly. Annual Review of Clinical Psychology. 2015;**11**:331-360. DOI: 10.1146/annurev-clinpsy-032814-112828

[39] Routledge library editions: Sociology of religion. Aging and Health: A Global Perspective: Compiled by the World Health Organization. 1st ed. London: Routledge; 1989. DOI: 10.4324/9780429020568

[40] Rainer C, Nasrouei S, Tschofen S, Bliem H, Wilhelm F, Marksteiner J. Fear acquisition and extinction in elderly patients with depression. Journal of Affective Disorders. 2020;**276**:197-204. DOI: 10.1016/j.jad.2020.06.044

[41] Aziz R, Steffens DC. What are the causes of late-life depression? Psychiatric Clinics of North America. 2013;**36**(4):497-516. DOI: 10.1016/j.psc.2013.08.001

[42] Jiang X, Wang J. The causal relationship between envy and depression: A cross-lagged regression analysis. Social Behavior and Personality: An International Journal. 2020;**48**(12):e9444

[43] Malhi GS, Mann JJ. Depression. Lancet. 2018;**392**(10161):2299-2312. DOI: 10.1016/S0140-6736(18)31948-2

[44] Borges C et al. The Role of Sleep Effort as a Mediator Between Anxiety and Depression. Psychological Reports. 3 Jan 2023:332941221149181. DOI: 10.1177/00332941221149181

[45] Nie Y, Hu Z, Zhu T, Xu H. A cross-sectional study of the prevalence of and risk factors for suicidal ideation among the elderly in nursing homes in Hunan Province, China. Frontiers in Psychiatry. 2020;**11**:339. DOI: 10.3389/fpsyt.2020.00339

[46] Deng X, Zhang X, Li W, Feng R-X, Li L, Yi G-R, et al. Chronic liver injuries induce the conversion of CK19+ biliary epithelial cells to Hepatocytes. Cell Stem Cell. 2018;**23**:114-122

[47] Li J, Vestergaard M, Cnattingius S, Gissler M, Bech BH, Obel C, et al. Mortality after parental death in childhood: A nationwide cohort study from three Nordic countries. Plos Medicine. 2014;**11**(7):13. DOI: 10.1371/journal.pmed.1001679

[48] Kim SH. Suicidal ideation and suicide attempts in older adults: Influences of chronic illness, functional limitations, and pain. Geriatric Nursing. 2016;**37**(1):9-12

[49] Conejero I, Olié E, Courtet P, Calati R. Suicide in older adults: Current perspectives. Clinical Interventions in Aging. 2018;**13**:691-699. DOI: 10.2147/CIA.S130670

[50] Deng Y, Cherian J, Khan NUN, Kumari K, Sial MS, Comite U, et al. Family and academic stress and their impact on students' depression level and academic performance. Frontiers in Psychiatry. 2022;**16**(13):869337. DOI: 10.3389/fpsyt.2022.869337

[51] Qiao L, Lan C, Capriotti L, Ah-Fong A, Nino Sanchez J, Hamby R, et al. Spray-induced gene silencing for disease control is dependent on the efficiency of pathogen RNA uptake. Plant Biotechnology Journal. 2021;**19**(9):1756-1768. DOI: 10.1111/pbi.13589

[52] Luo J, Du J, Tao C, Xu H, Zhang Y. Exploring temporal suicidal behavior patterns on social media: Insight from twitter analytics. Health Informatics Journal. 2020;**26**(2):738-752. DOI: 10.1177/1460458219832043

[53] Herrmann T, Isa J, Kai-Uwe L. The Role Concept as a Basis for Designing Community Systems. Cooperative Systems Design. 2004;**4**:163-178

[54] Jia J, Zhao T, Liu Z, Liang Y, Li F, Li Y, et al. Association between healthy lifestyle and memory decline in older adults: 10 year, population based, prospective cohort study. BMJ. 2023;**25**(380):e072691. DOI: 10.1136/bmj-2022-072691

[55] De Leo D, Giannotti AV. Suicide in late life: A viewpoint. Preventive

Medicine. 2021;**152**(Pt. 1):106735. DOI: 10.1016/j.ypmed.2021.106735

[56] Laflamme L, Vaez M, Lundin K, Sengoelge M. Prevention of suicidal behavior in older people: A systematic review of reviews. PLoS One. 2022;**17**(1):e0262889. DOI: 10.1371/journal.pone.0262889

[57] Bonnewyn A, Shah A, Demyttenaere K. Suicidality and suicide in older people. Clinical Gerontologist. 2009;**19**(4):271-294. DOI: 10.1017/S0959259809990347

[58] Bonnewyn A, Katona C, Bruffaerts R, Haro JM, de Graaf R, Alonso J, et al. Pain and depression in older people: Comorbidity and patterns of help seeking. Journal of Affective Disorders. 2009;**117**(3):193-196. DOI: 10.1016/j.jad.2009.01.012

[59] Corna LM, Cairney J, Streiner DL. Suicide ideation in older adults: Relationship to mental health problems and service use. The Gerontologist. 2010;**50**(6):785-797. DOI: 10.1093/geront/gnq048

[60] Devita M, De Salvo R, Ravelli A, De Rui M, Coin A, Sergi G, et al. Recognizing depression in the elderly: Practical guidance and challenges for clinical management. Neuropsychiatric Disease and Treatment. 2022;**18**:2867-2880. DOI: 10.2147/NDT.S347356

[61] Patten SB, Williams JV, Lavorato DH, Wang JL, McDonald K, Bulloch AG. Descriptive epidemiology of major depressive disorder in Canada in 2012. Canadian Journal of Psychiatry. 2015;**60**(1):23-30. DOI: 10.1177/070674371506000106

[62] Vafaei A, Ahmed T, Freire Ado N, Zunzunegui MV, Guerra RO. Depression, sex and gender roles in older adult populations: The international mobility in aging study (IMIAS). PLoS One. 2016;**11**(1):e0146867. DOI: 10.1371/journal.pone.0146867

[63] Alvarado BE, Zunzunegui MV, Beland F, Sicotte M, Tellechea L. Social and gender inequalities in depressive symptoms among urban older adults of Latin America and the Caribbean. Journals of Gerontology. 2007;**62**:S226-S236

[64] Li CE, DiGiuseppe R, Froh J. The roles of sex, gender, and coping in adolescent depression. Adolescence. 2006;**41**:409-415

[65] Lutz J, Mackin RS, Otero MC, Morin R, Bickford D, Tosun D, et al. Improvements in functional disability after psychotherapy for depression are associated with reduced suicide ideation among older adults. American Journal of Geriatric Psychiatry. 2021;**29**:557-561

[66] Arslanoglou E, Banerjee S, Pantelides J, Evans L, Kiosses DN. Negative emotions and the course of depression during psychotherapy in suicidal older adults with depression and cognitive impairment. American Journal of Geriatric Psychiatry. 2019;**27**:1287-1295

[67] Oliveira A, Spinola V, Garrido D, Teixeira MM, Salles C, Haddad AE. Influence of learning styles on student performance in self-instructional courses. PLoS One. 2023;**18**(7):e0289036. DOI: 10.1371/journal.pone.0289036

[68] Awata S, Seki T, Koizumi Y, Sato S, Hozawa A, Omori K, et al. Factors associated with suicidal ideation in an elderly urban Japanese population: A community-based, cross-sectional study. Psychiatry and Clinical Neurosciences. 2005;**59**:327-336

[69] Lohman MC, Raue PJ, Greenberg RL, Bruce ML. Reducing suicidal ideation in home health care: Results from the CAREPATH depression care management trial. International Journal of Geriatric Psychiatry. 2016;**31**:708-715

[70] Barnow S, Linden M, Freyberger HJ. The relation between suicidal feelings and mental disorders in the elderly: Results from the Berlin aging study (BASE). Psychological Medicine. 2004;**34**:741-746

[71] Meeks TW, Dunn LB, Kim DS, Golshan S, Sewell DD, Atkinson JH, et al. Chronic pain and depression among geriatric psychiatry inpatients. International Journal of Geriatric Psychiatry. 2008;**23**:637-642

[72] Nishida N, Hata Y, Yoshida K, Kinoshita K. Neuropathologic features of suicide victims who presented with acute poststroke depression: Significance of association with neurodegenerative disorders. Journal of Neuropathology & Experimental Neurology. 2015;**74**:401-410

[73] Jang MH, Kim YH. The relationship of stress, depression, and suicidal ideation in the elderly. Journal of Korean Academy of Psychiatric and Mental Health Nursing. 2005;**14**(1):33-42

[74] Waern M, Rubenowitz E, Wilhelmson K. Predictors of suicide in the old elderly. Gerontology. 2003;**49**(5):328-334. DOI: 10.1159/000071715

[75] Kim HS. A study on epistemology of Korean elders' suicidal thought. Journal of Korean Gerontological Nursing Society. 2002;**22**(1):159-172

[76] Kim BJ, Kihl T. Suicidal ideation associated with depression and social support: A survey-based analysis of older adults in South Korea. BMC Psychiatry. 2021;**21**(1):409. DOI: 10.1186/s12888-021-03423-8

[77] Suominen K, Isometsä E, Suokas J, Haukka J, Achte K, Lönnqvist J. Completed suicide after a suicide attempt: A 37-year follow-up study. American Journal of Psychiatry. 2004;**161**(3):562-563. DOI: 10.1176/appi.ajp.161.3.562

[78] Alexopoulos GS. Mechanisms and treatment of late-life depression. Translational Psychiatry. 2019;**9**(1):188

[79] Blazer DG. Depression and social support in late life: A clear but not obvious relationship. Aging & Mental Health. 2005;**9**(6):497-499. DOI: 10.1080/13607860500294266

[80] Tengku Mohd TAM, Yunus RM, Hairi F, Hairi NN, Choo WY. Social support and depression among community dwelling older adults in Asia: A systematic review. BMJ Open. 2019;**9**(7):e026667. DOI: 10.1136/bmjopen-2018-026667

[81] Okoye EC, Onwuakagba IU, Akile CC, Okonkwo UP, Akosile CO, Mgbeojedo UG, et al. Social support, general self-efficacy, fear of falling, and physical activity among older adults in a middle-income country. Gerontology and Geriatric Medicine. 2022;**8**:1-13. DOI: 10.1177/2333721422 10977 50

[82] Uchino BN. Understanding the links between social support and physical health. A life-span perspective with emphasis on the separability of perceived and received support. Psychological Science. 2009;**4**:236-255

[83] Li LW, Liu J, Xu H, Zhang Z. Understanding rural-urban differences in depressive symptoms among older adults in China. Journal of Aging

and Health. 2016;**28**(2):341-362. DOI: 10.1177/0898264315591003

[84] Tsuboi H, Hirai H, Kondo K. Giving social support to outside family may be a desirable buffer against depressive symptoms in community-dwelling older adults: Japan gerontological evaluation study. Biopsychosocial Medicine. 2016;**10**:18. DOI: 10.1186/s13030-016-0064-6

[85] Yoo JS, Chang SJ, Kim HS. Prevalence and predictive factors of depression in community-dwelling older adults in South Korea. Research and Theory for Nursing Practice. 2016;**30**:200-211. DOI: 10.1891/1541-6577.30.3.200

[86] Ng CW, Tan WS, Gunapal PP, Wong LY, Heng BH. Association of Socioeconomic Status (SES) and social support with depressive symptoms among the elderly in Singapore. Annals of the Academy of Medicine, Singapore. 2014;**43**(12):576-587

[87] Chen S, Conwell Y, Vanorden K, Lu N, Fang Y, Ma Y, et al. Prevalence and natural course of late-life depression in China primary care: A population based study from an urban community. Journal of Affective Disorders. 2012;**141**(1):86-93. DOI: 10.1016/j.jad.2012.02.027

[88] Wang J, Zhao X. Family functioning and social support for older patients with depression in an urban area of Shanghai, China. Archives of Gerontology and Geriatrics. 2012;**55**(3):574-579. DOI: 10.1016/j.archger.2012.06.011

[89] Tiedt AD. The gender gap in depressive symptoms among Japanese elders: Evaluating social support and health as mediating factors. Journal of Cross-cultural Gerontology. 2010;**25**(3):239-256. DOI: 10.1007/s10823-010-9122-x

[90] Akosile CO, Onyekwuluje C, Mgbeojedo UG, Okoye EC, Fabunmi AA, Mong EU, et al. Social support, social participation, and life accomplishment of older adult residents of assisted living facilities and their adjoining communities. Gerontology and Geriatric Medicine. 2023;**9**:1-8. DOI: 10.1177/23337214231218797

[91] Chao SF. Assessing social support and depressive symptoms in older Chinese adults: A longitudinal perspective. Aging Mental Health. 2011;**15**:765-774. DOI: 10.1080/13607863.2011.562182

[92] Chou KL, Chi I. Reciprocal relationship between social support and depressive symptoms among Chinese elderly. Aging Mental Health. 2003;**7**:224-231. DOI: 10.1080/136031000101210

[93] Gong Y, Wen X, Guan C, Wang Z, Liang Y. The associations between family characteristics and depressive symptoms in older adults: A community-based survey in rural China. International Psychogeriatrics. 2012;**24**(8):1226-1234. DOI: 10.1017/S1041610211002663

[94] Suttajit S, Punpuing S, Jirapramukpitak T, et al. Impairment, disability, social support and depression among older parents in rural Thailand. Psychological Medicine. 2010;**40**:1711-1721. DOI: 10.1017/S003329170999208X

[95] Gariépy G, Honkaniemi H, Quesnel-Vallée A. Social support and protection from depression: Systematic review of current findings in Western countries. The British Journal of Psychiatry. 2016;**209**(4):284-293. DOI: 10.1192/bjp.bp.115.169094

[96] Agnew R. Pressured into Crime: An Overview of General Strain Theory. Boston, MA: Roxbury; 2006

[97] Gottfries CG. Late life depression. European Archives of Psychiatry and Clinical Neuroscience. 2001;**251**:57-61

[98] Johnson KJ, Mutchler JE. The emergence of a positive gerontology: From disengagement to social involvement. The Gerontologist. 2014;**54**(1):93-100

[99] Park NS, Jang Y, Lee BS, Haley WE, Chiriboga DA. The mediating role of loneliness in the relation between social engagement and depressive symptoms among older Korean Americans: Do men and women differ? Journals of Gerontology Series B: Psychological Sciences and Social Sciences. 2013;**68**(2):193-201

[100] Adams KB, Leibbrandt S, Moon H. A critical review of the literature on social and leisure activity and wellbeing in later life. Ageing & Society. 2011;**31**(4):683-712

[101] Coyle CE, Dugan E. Social isolation, loneliness and health among older adults. Journal of Aging and Health. 2012;**24**(8):1346-1363

[102] Thoits PA. Mechanisms linking social ties and support to physical and mental health. Journal of Health and Social Behavior. 2011;**52**(2):145-161

[103] Berkman LF, Glass T, Brissette I, Seeman TE. From social integration to health: Durkheim in the new millennium. Social Science & Medicine. 2000;**51**(6):843-857

[104] Chen YY, Wong GH, Lum TY, Lou VW, Ho AH, Luo H, et al. Neighborhood support network, perceived proximity to community facilities and depressive symptoms among low socioeconomic status Chinese elders. Aging & Mental Health. 2016;**20**(4):423-431. DOI: 10.1080/13607863.2015.1018867

[105] Ross CE, Jang SJ. Neighborhood disorder, fear, and mistrust: The buffering role of social ties with neighbors. American Journal of Community Psychology. 2000;**28**:401-420

[106] Krämer LV, Helmes AW, Bengel J. Understanding activity limitations in depression: Integrating the concepts of motivation and volition from health psychology into clinical psychology. European Psychologist. 2014;**19**(4):278-288. DOI: 10.1027/1016-9040/a000205

[107] Mancini AD, Bonanno GA. Marital closeness, functional disability, and adjustment in late life. Psychology and Aging. 2006;**21**(3):600

[108] Takahashi T, Ishida K, Yamamoto H, Takata J, Nishinaga M, Doi Y, et al. Modification of the functional reach test: Analysis of lateral and anterior functional reach in community-dwelling older people. Archives of Gerontology and Geriatrics. 2006;**42**(2):167-173

[109] Gureje O, Ogunniyi A, Kola L, Afolabi E. Functional disability in elderly Nigerians: Results from the Ibadan study of aging. Journal of the American Geriatrics Society. 2006;**54**(11):1784-1789

[110] Conn VS. Depressive symptom outcomes of physical activity interventions: Meta-analysis findings. Annals of Behavioral Medicine : A Publication of the Society of Behavioral Medicine. 2010;**39**(2):128-138. DOI: 10.1007/s12160-010-9172-x

[111] Deslandes A, Moraes H, Ferreira C, Veiga H, Silveira H, Mouta R, et al. Exercise and mental health: Many reasons to move. Neuropsychobiology. 2009;**59**(4):191-198

[112] Daley A. Exercise and depression: A review of reviews. Journal of Clinical Psychology in Medical Settings. 2008;**15**:140-147

[113] Lawlor DA, Hopker SW. The effectiveness of exercise as an intervention in the management of depression: Systematic review and meta-regression analysis of randomised controlled trials. BMJ. 2001;**322**(7289):763

[114] Martinsen EW. Physical activity in the prevention and treatment of anxiety and depression. Nordic Journal of Psychiatry. 2008;**62**(Suppl. 47):25-29

Chapter 4

Fostering Healthy Growth of Sexual and Gender Diverse Young People: The Role of Parents/ Caregivers and Social-Emotional Learning

Chiaki Konishi and Julia Tesolin

Abstract

There is a growing understanding and attention that strong support is critical for the well-being and mental health of sexual and gender diverse (SGD) young people, especially given the increasing research evidence indicating that they are experiencing greater rates of discrimination and bullying, which in turn is likely to contribute to their mental health problems, such as emotional distress and suicidality. However, limited knowledge remains about how we, as adults, can foster the healthy development of SGD young people. This chapter focuses on the roles of parents/caregivers and families and the great potential they have to contribute to the healthier development of SGD young people. In particular, we address the powerful benefits of incorporating a social-emotional learning perspective into the practical implications and recommendations of "what we can do as parents/caregivers and families."

Keywords: sexual and gender diverse young people, family, social-emotional learning, healthy growth, mental health

1. Introduction

There have been notable social and political as well as research movements, particularly throughout the 2000s, which were expected to offer a belief that health- and behavior-related risks for youth who (historically) identify as lesbian, gay, bisexual, transgender, queer, or questioning (LGBTQ+) would be reduced alongside social progress. This movement has promoted their greater visibility and rights and has helped youth recognize and acknowledge diverse sexual and gender identities earlier in their life [1]. Despite the advancement of societal and legal as well as research efforts suggesting affirmation and acceptance, sexual and gender diverse (SGD) youth still continue to experience greater levels of discrimination and bullying [2, 3], and mental health problems, such as depression [4] and suicidality [5], due to the stigmatized and marginalized experiences.

In the meantime, an increasing number of recent studies suggest that many people are understanding and claiming a sexual minority or gender identity (i.e., identity disclosure or "coming out") at relatively younger ages than in previous generations [1, 6]. Importantly, youth who disclose their sexual or gender identity to their families and peers are more susceptible to discrimination and bullying, and that disclosure is more strongly associated with mental health problems (e.g., depression) at younger ages [7]. Coming out is often challenging for youth, and the experience may be even more complicated by cultural factors such as beliefs and values or family living patterns (e.g., co-residence with parents into adulthood) [8, 9]. A study shows that validating responses to coming out from parents were more common in recent cohorts of LGB youth (teens in the 2010s compared to those who were teens in the 1990s or 1970s), consistent with increasing societal attitudes of support and acceptance [10]. However, at the same time, invalidating responses were equally frequent across cohorts [10]. Thus, although there have been increasing opportunities for visibility and support, experiences of stigma and discrimination have not declined.

Adolescence is a critical period of vulnerability for risks to mental and behavioral health. Given earlier recognition of gender or sexual minority identity in recent cohorts, a deeper understanding of sexual or gender identity development during adolescence is necessary. Strong support is critical for the well-being and mental health of SGD young people [11, 12].

In this chapter, we address the roles of parents/caregivers and families and the great potential they have to contribute to the healthier development of SGD young people. In particular, we consider the powerful benefits of incorporating a social-emotional learning (SEL) perspective into the practical implications and recommendations of "what we can do as parents/caregivers and families."

2. Sexual and gender diverse young people and mental health

Throughout childhood and adolescence, young people learn about themselves as they explore different aspects of their identities, including their sexual and gender identities. Young people's gender identity development is influenced by a multitude of individual (i.e., cognitive, emotional) and social (i.e., family, peer, and community relations) level factors [13], all of which contribute to the way they understand their own and others' genders. It is important to note that an individual's gender identity is internal, and is not necessarily visible to others [14]; it refers to a person's inherent sense of being male, female, or an alternative gender (e.g., genderqueer, gender non-conforming), which may or may not correspond to the sex the person was assigned at birth [14]. Specifically, transgender young people have a gender identity that is different from their sex assigned at birth [14, 15], whereas gender-diverse youth have gender identities (e.g., nonbinary, genderfluid, and agender) that exist outside the female/male gender binary [16, 17]. The term gender non-conforming is often used as an umbrella term to describe individuals whose gender identity differs from gender norms associated with their assigned birth sex [14, 18]. Research has demonstrated that some children may begin to feel a sense of "mismatch" between their assigned sex and gender identity as early as 2–3 years of age [19, 20], whereas, for others, this may appear during puberty or beyond [19, 21, 22].

With regards to sexual identity, monosexual identity labels, such as gay, lesbian, and bisexual (LGB) refer to a singular direction in which one's sexual attractions are oriented, while plurisexual identity labels, such as bisexual, pansexual, and queer, typically signify attraction to multiple genders when referring to sexual identity [23–25]. Relatedly, while the label "queer" may signify attraction to multiple genders, it may also refer to a gender identity that is intended to challenge sexual or gender normativity [23, 26]. It is also important to consider gender-questioning youth, who represent a multifaceted group within the spectrum of gender diversity. Questioning youth are typically unsure of or exploring their sexual identity because they may have experienced some sort of attraction or behavior and are now questioning whether heteronormative assumptions apply to them [27]. It is also possible that questioning youth are in fact certain that they are not heterosexual, but are still unsure which of the many non-heterosexual identity labels they might wish to adopt [27]. Adolescence is an especially crucial time for many SGD young people, as puberty is the onset of bodily and hormonal changes, which have the potential to increase the distress and emergence of mental health difficulties for these individuals with minoritized identities [28–30].

2.1 Common mental health issues

In comparison to their cisgender and heterosexual peers, SGD young people are more likely to experience poor mental health due to stigma and marginalization [31]. Research has demonstrated that internalizing mental health disorders, such as depression and anxiety, are elevated in both SGD young people [31–36], with transgender and gender diverse young people twice to three times more likely to report depression and anxiety than cisgender young people [37–41]. Furthermore, the increased incidence of internalizing disorders has also been well documented among SGD adolescents from various racial and ethnic groups (e.g., Black and Latinx youth), highlighting the fact that these results are not limited to the Western context [42–44]. Sexual minority adolescents, including those who identify as lesbian, gay, bisexual, or queer (LGBQ), are at greater risk for experiencing psychopathology and suicidal thoughts and behaviors (STBs), such as suicide ideation and suicide attempts [31]. A recent 2022 nationally representative population-based study of youth in Canada, which included 6800 adolescents aged 15–17 years, found that transgender adolescents showed 5 times the risk of suicidal ideation and 7.6 times the risk of suicide attempt, compared with cisgender, heterosexual adolescents [45]. In addition to STBs, SGD youth are more likely to experience self-harm or non-suicidal self-injury than their heterosexual and cisgender peers [46]. In a 2019 U.K. population-based study, sexual minority youth aged between 16 and 21, were 4–4.5 times more likely to report self-harm behaviors than their heterosexual peers [47].

While a number of studies have compared the mental health of SGD young people to their cisgender peers [32–41], less is known about how gender-diverse youth fair in comparison to their LGBQ cisgender peers. In a 2020 study conducted with 25,396 young people in the U.S. aged between 13 and 24 years of age, 83% of transgender and nonbinary youth reported experiencing a depressive mood in the past 12 months, 54% considered suicide in the past 12 months, and 29% attempted suicide in the past 12 months [37]. After adjusting for age, family income, and race/ethnicity, transgender, and nonbinary youth remained two times more likely to report depressive mood, seriously consider suicide, and attempt suicide than their cisgender LGBQ peers. The study also found that among transgender and nonbinary young people, transgender males reported the highest rates of depressive mood, seriously considering suicide, and attempted suicide across all gender identities. In line with the growing literature [48–50], these findings suggest that gender-diverse youth may be at an even higher risk for poor mental health outcomes than their cisgender LGBQ peers [42].

2.2 Contributing factors to mental health disparities

The disparities in mental health outcomes among SGD young people have been attributed to the chronic and pervasive stress associated with their minoritized identities, which is also known as minority stress [14, 51–55]. Based on the foundations of minority stress theory [56], the gender minority stress (GMS) model proposes that in addition to the stressors that all individuals experience, gender diverse young people, as members of a minoritized identity group, experience a host of distal (e.g., peer victimization, discrimination, and family rejection) and proximal (e.g., internalized stigma) stressors, which can contribute to their poor mental health [51, 52, 57, 58].

Peer victimization and discrimination are two of the most salient distal stressors that are relatively common among SGD young people. The high rates of peer victimization among SGD young people are often related to the ways in which they identify with their gender (e.g., their behaviors, their appearance, etc.) [59–61], as well as biased-based harassment based on their sexual orientation [62]. In comparison to heterosexual and cisgender high school students, SGD students are more likely to be bullied [49, 63–65], be threatened or injured with a weapon at school [49, 64], to be sexually assaulted [49, 66, 67] and to experience physical and sexual dating violence [49, 64, 66]. Further, the higher levels of peer victimization are notably associated with poorer mental health outcomes (e.g., depression, anxiety, suicidal ideation, and non-suicidal self-injury) [60, 68, 69]. Research has demonstrated that gender diverse young people may feel less of a sense of belonging to their school as a result of being victimized by their peers, which in turn indirectly influences their mental health [39, 60, 70]. In addition to being victimized and bullied for their sexual orientation and gender identity and expression, many SGD young people report that they have experienced gender-related discriminatory policies and practices at their school [71]. According to the 2019 National School Climate Survey, conducted by the Gay, Lesbian, and Straight Education Network (GLSEN), students reported being commonly restricted from expressing themselves as gender diverse at school, and these discriminatory policies included being disciplined for public displays of affection that are not disciplined among non-LGBTQ students, prevented from discussing or writing about gender diverse or LGBTQ topics in assignments, and being disciplined unfairly simply because they were LGBTQ [71]. Discriminatory school policies and practices that censor expressions of sexual and gender-diverse identities and enforce traditional gender norms have been shown to have important negative effects on SGD young people's well-being and mental health, such as higher rates of depressive mood, suicidal ideation, and suicide attempts than their heterosexual and cisgender peers [37, 46].

Beyond the school context, SGD young people also experience higher rates of family rejection than their heterosexual and cisgender peers, which may be another contributing factor to their poor mental health outcomes [37, 72–74]. In a sample of 54 U.S. transgender youth, researchers found that lower family acceptance from parents and primary caregivers, was significantly related to youth's negative psychosocial outcomes (e.g., depressive symptoms, internalizing problems, and externalizing problems) [75]. This finding has been supported by reports from qualitative studies with gender-diverse adolescents who have shared that parental rejection based on their gender identity (e.g., misgendering, criticism, and cutting them off from crucial resources) [76, 77] was psychologically detrimental and contributed to their existing mental health issues [76]. Caregivers may express indifference in a number of ways, such as ignoring their child's gender identity, deferring to the other caregiver on sex- and gender-related issues, and not seeking out information to increase their own understanding of such issues [75]. Relatedly, the less understanding, supportive, open, communicative, and accepting a family is, the more emotional and behavioral problems SGD children and adolescents experience [74, 78, 79]. Further, parental and caregiver rejection has also been found to contribute to negative beliefs and feelings about one's own sexual orientation [80]. When families reject or ignore a child's sexuality, the negative messages they convey (e.g., being gay is unacceptable) become internalized and can lead to a negative lesbian, gay, or bisexual (LGB) identity [79]. This negative LGB identity may then lead to greater psychological and behavioral problems, such as anxiety, sadness, withdrawal, and substance use behaviors [81]. Additionally, in more extreme cases of family rejection, parental abuse has been linked to negative mental health outcomes, such as suicide attempts, among SGD young people [82, 83].

While distal stressors may appear to be more prominent as they are evident in many of the social environments that SGD young people find themselves in, research suggests that proximal stressors can negatively affect these young people's mental health through as they affect their thoughts and beliefs about themselves [74, 84]. Internalized transphobia is one of the proximal stressors that many transgender young people experience, whereby they feel a sense of discomfort with their gender identity as a result of internalizing society's negative attitudes toward gender-diverse people [85, 86]. The internalized stigma that SGD young people experience also leads to feelings of emotional distress and negative self-perceptions, as they often expect rejection from others in a variety of social settings [87–89]. As previously addressed, SGD young people are more likely to be bullied and physically harmed by another person than their heterosexual and cisgender peers, but they are also more likely to report being afraid that someone at school would hurt or bother them [33, 90]. Notably, the gender minority stress (GMS) model suggests that proximal stressors, such as internalized stigma or transphobia, can act as mediators between distal stressors and gender diverse young people's poor mental health outcomes [52–55, 62].

Although much of the research has identified many of the important and relevant risk factors for SGD young people's mental health, it is equally as important to attend to the protective factors that are present in their lives [41, 91, 92]. Supportive relationships with the adults in their lives can buffer against the impact of the stressors that gender-diverse young people face [93–95], and as such it is critical to examine the important role that parents and caregivers play in supporting these young people.

3. Adult support as a protective factor

There is a growing understanding and attention that strong support is critical for the well-being and mental health of gender-diverse young people [11, 12], especially given the increasing research evidence indicating that they are facing greater levels of stigmatized experiences, including peer victimization and discrimination [2, 3]. These experiences are then likely to contribute to their poor mental health, such as emotional distress [4] and suicidality [5].

3.1 Perceived social support

According to Cohen and colleagues [96], social support has been defined as a "psychological and material resources intended to benefit someone's ability to cope with stress" (p. 676). A number of researchers have suggested the role of social support as a buffer against adverse effects from stressful situations since the mid-1970s [97–99]. For example, Cohen and McKay [100], Gore [101], and House [102] have argued that social support could function as a moderator buffering the negative effects of stressful life events on physical or psychological symptoms (i.e., the buffering hypothesis). Although definitions vary across research, Cobb [97] has distinguished three main elements of social support as one of the earliest understandings of the concept (i.e., information that an individual is cared for and loved, information that an individual is recognized and valued, and information that an individual belongs to a network or a group membership). Considering a behavioral perspective, House [102] has proposed four classifications of the concept: emotional support in the form of affective behaviors, such as love and caring; appraisal support (e.g., positive feedback); instrumental support such as time and resources provided; and informational support (e.g., suggestions, recommendations).

The subjective nature or the nature of the perception of social support has been widely used in the literature and research [103]. One of the many commonly used measures to examine the nature of perception is Zimet and colleagues' *Multidimensional Scale of Perceived Social Support* [104]. This assessment tool includes three subscales measuring perceived social support from family, friends, and significant others. This measure has been showing its sound psychometric evidence in various populations, including university students in an international sample [105], African-American adolescents living in urban areas [106], and Mexican-American adolescents [107]. The role of perceived social support has also been explored in LGBT adolescents [108]. Thus, the role of perceived social support has been studied for many years, at least five decades since the 1970s, in multiple populations.

3.2 Highlighting the roles of parents/caregivers and families in relation to social support

Social support from family members and adults at school (e.g., teachers, administrators, and counselors) has been shown to contribute to the well-being and adjustment of adolescents. For instance, adult support has been associated with several positive outcomes, including higher levels of school attendance, engagement, satisfaction, and self-efficacy [109, 110]. More importantly, research has also shown that such adult support is particularly important to youth who are socially stigmatized [111].

Previous studies have examined the buffering role of adult support for youth who were victims of sexual orientation discrimination [112–115]. For victims of sexual orientation discrimination, adult support at home and school could play a significant protective role. Darwich et al. [116] found that LGBQ youth reported lower feelings of school belonging and were more likely to skip school and experience sexual orientation discrimination compared to their heterosexual peers. However, both heterosexual and LGBQ youth who reported having at least one adult at school who supported them reported much lower rates of skipping school and being discriminated against compared to those without a supportive adult at school. Similarly, LGBQ youth with support from an adult at school reported higher rates of school belonging compared to those with no support at school. More recently, Konishi and Saewyc [113] examined the role of having caring adult support from both parents and teachers as a protective factor in reducing the risk for high levels of distress among high school students. Results identified the critical roles of caring adult support in reducing greater risk for social-emotional problems and educational concerns among all victimized adolescents, whether LGB, mostly heterosexual, or exclusively heterosexual. Both sources of caring support—from parents and teachers—were significantly effective in buffering the increased risk. Importantly, the benefits of having a supportive adult were apparent for all youth, regardless of how they identified their sexual orientation.

Schools are an important part of young people's microsystem, and in some cases, schools may be a place where SGD students can live as their authentic sexual or gender selves. However, as indicated in the earlier section, most generally, schools continue to remain largely detrimental places for SGD students. Given this reality, teachers have been encouraged to create and provide a safe place for all students, including SGD students [117]. Teachers play an important role in creating, maintaining, and influencing a school climate [118, 119]. Indeed, existing research reinforces the positive role of supportive adults in schools for LGBTQ students. LGBTQ students who identify the presence of supportive teachers and staff report more positive mental well-being and better academic outcomes [120–123]. In addition, when teachers and school staff intervene effectively in incidents of anti-LGBTQ bullying and harassment, LGBTQ students report fewer experiences of harassment and assault at school and lower rates of absenteeism [124].

Without a doubt, support from family is also key and the significance of family support is well documented in research [115, 125]. Families are a very important source of support for minority adolescents and remain essential for their adjustment even when adult support at school is insufficient [126]. Research clearly indicates that parental support served as the protective factor against mental health problems, such as emotional distress [127], depression [128], and suicidality [129]. On the other hand, when adolescents are not supported by their parents regarding their gender identities and expressions, they are likely at greater risk of having increased psychological distress [130, 131], including greater levels of depression [132] and suicidality [82].

While schools play a role in students' safety and learning, the foundation often starts at home. It is within this context that the role of home support becomes even more pronounced, serving as a critical buffer against the adverse effects of discrimination when school support may not suffice. This is particularly important for adolescents, who experience high levels of discrimination given that adult support at school has a limited role in protecting against school adjustment outcomes. When SGD students come home after facing such adverse challenges in school, it is important to consider how the home environment could represent a place where SGD students are supported.

Support and acceptance are important; however, how can we move forward and encourage parents and caregivers of SGD young people to engage in supportive ways, and moreover, to cultivate a sense of pride about who they are for their children? How can parents/caregivers show their children that they are unconditionally supportive of who they are? For example, it is common for parents to go into shock when they become aware of their children's sexual or gender diverse identities and expressions [133–135]. This initial shock often serves as a starting point for the parents to begin their own journey toward acceptance of their child [136, 137]. An SGD youth's experiences, therefore, cannot be understood in isolation but needs to be explored from a family perspective. In the following section, we share the powerful benefits of incorporating an SEL perspective into the practical implications and recommendations of "what we can do as parents/caregivers and families."

4. A social-emotional learning (SEL) perspective into practical implementations and recommendations

Supporting the social-emotional development of SGD young people is crucial, and parents and caregivers play a vital role in fostering an inclusive and affirming environment that nurtures their child's well-being. Social-emotional learning (SEL) has been defined by the Collaborative for Academic, Social and Emotional Learning (CASEL), as "the process through which all young people and adults acquire and apply the knowledge, skills, and attitudes to develop healthy identities, manage emotions, and achieve personal and collective goals, feel and show empathy for others, establish and maintain supportive relationships, and make responsible and caring decisions" [138]. One of the most prominent frameworks in SEL research was developed by CASEL and addresses the five core competencies of SEL, which include (a) self-awareness, (b) self-management, (c) social awareness, (d) relationship skills, and (e) responsible decision-making. Self-awareness includes the ability to understand one's own emotions and thoughts and how they influence behavior (e.g., the capacity to recognize one's own strengths and limitations, as well as the ability to develop interests and demonstrate a growth mindset). Self-management includes the ability to manage one's emotions, thoughts, and behaviors effectively in different situations and to achieve goals and aspirations (e.g., identifying and using stress management strategies). Social awareness includes the ability to empathize and understand the perspectives of others (e.g., the ability to feel compassion for others, understand broader norms, and recognize family, school, and community resources and supports). Relationship skills include the ability to establish and maintain healthy and supportive relationships with diverse individuals and groups (e.g., the capacity to communicate clearly, listen actively, cooperate, resolve conflict, and navigate settings with differing social and cultural settings). Responsible decision-making includes the ability to make caring and constructive choices about personal behavior and social interactions (e.g., the capacity to evaluate the benefits and consequences of various actions for personal, social, and collective well-being). The development of social and emotional competencies is important for young people, as these competencies have the potential to contribute to fostering healthy functioning by helping young people to form positive relationships with others, which can in turn foster positive developmental pathways throughout the life course [139–141]. However, this development is also crucial for parents or caregivers to acquire in order to provide caring relationships and create safe and supportive environments where young people can learn to develop the essential SEL competencies, which can also lead to improved mental health outcomes and well-being. Research has demonstrated that people who participated in SEL-based programs reported a decrease in emotional distress [142], increased positive attitudes about themselves and others, and enhanced coping skills, resiliency, and emotion identification, all of which can help reduce symptoms of depression and anxiety in the short term [143].

4.1 How SEL benefits sexual and gender diverse young people

With regards to SGD young people, the core SEL competencies, such as self-awareness and self-management, are especially relevant to the decisions that they are making about their sexual and gender identities, as well as their actions and behaviors in relation to others of the same or different sexual orientations and/or genders. Identity construction is an especially important social process whereby SGD young people are developing their self-identities [141], not only individually, but also in conjunction with information that is being conveyed to them from a variety of social influences (e.g., peers, families, and caregivers). The SEL competencies, especially regarding social awareness and relationship building, are also important for parents or caregivers of SGD young people to help foster the healthy growth of their children. While research about the ways in which SGD young people and their parents or caregivers develop SEL competencies is limited, there is some indication that they may both experience more challenges with social-emotional competencies, such as self-management, in comparison to their cisgender and heterosexual peers [144, 145]. Given the prevalence of mental health issues (e.g., depression and anxiety) in SGD young people, it is critical that they learn how to identify the emotions that they are experiencing (i.e., self-awareness) in order to manage those emotions, thoughts, and behaviors effectively (i.e., self-management). Currently, there are a growing number of studies that aim to explore how interventions targeting the domains of both SEL and gender equity contribute to the beliefs and norms that young people hold about gender diversity [146–148]. One of which aimed to evaluate the impacts of an SEL intervention designed for very young adolescents (i.e., 10–11 years old) in the low-income setting of Tanzania as a way to promote positive gender transformative SEL mindsets and skills to foster healthy developmental trajectories during the transition from childhood into adolescence [146]. The *Discover* program was implemented in four primary schools over a 6-week period. Results from the study revealed that the integration of gender-transformative content with SEL content promoted increased gender-equitable norms, beliefs, and behaviors among adolescents. The success of many SEL programs, such as the *Discover* program, has been credited to the implementation of experiential learning in the classroom, which is one of the key settings for social-emotional learning to take place [138].

Notably, when schools and families (e.g., parents and caregivers) form authentic partnerships with one another, they can help build strong connections that reinforce students' social and emotional development [138]. Research suggests that evidence-based SEL programs are even more successful when they include strategies for collaborating and working with young people's families [149]. Efforts to engage parents and caregivers in understanding and supporting SGD young people are essential to fostering their social and emotional development.

4.2 What parents and caregivers can do to support sexual and gender diverse young people

Given that the family context is considered to be a key setting for the SEL of both young people [138] and their parents or caregivers, it is essential to address some of the practical implementations and recommendations for families and caregivers of SGD young people. Firstly, in order to develop the SEL competencies, it is essential that they have a supportive environment to do so [149]. As such, parents and caregivers should ensure that they are putting efforts into creating a supportive and safe home environment for their young people, where they feel accepted and their sexual and gender identity is affirmed. This can be done in a variety of ways, such as making sure that the young person is being by maintaining communication and encouraging honest and open discussion for the young person to share their thoughts and feelings about their sexual and gender identity exploration. Relatedly, it is essential for parents and caregivers to listen actively and empathetically to what the young person has to say when having discussions on more sensitive topics. In creating a space where SGD young people can feel that they are valued and cared for, parents and caregivers can then help foster their core SEL competencies.

In order to foster *self-awareness*, parents and caregivers can talk with the young person about their sexual and/or gender-diverse identity, encouraging them to be open and honest about their emotions regarding how they feel, especially if they have recently begun exploring or transitioning into a new gender identity [150]. It is also imperative that parents and caregivers take the time to listen and understand what the sexual and/or gender-diverse young person's identity means to them, even if they themselves may feel uncomfortable or unfamiliar with sexual or gender diversity. With regards to young people who may be questioning their sexuality or gender identity, being supportive does not mean that they are "encouraging" or "pushing" a child into a specific sexual orientation or gender identity, but rather they are giving the young person the space to explore what it might be like to live in another gender role or explore their sexuality, which helps the young person to discover their authentic self [27, 151].

Helping SGD young people to develop *self-management* competency could involve parents and caregivers offering support to the young person who may be a victim of discriminatory or biased-based bullying [12]. Together, the parent or caregiver and the young person can work to identify coping strategies to help them effectively manage their emotions of stress and anxiety. It is also important that families establish a relationship with the school staff (i.e., school counselor or psychologist) to ensure that the young person has the support available if/when a situation may occur in the classroom.

The competency of *social awareness* is more for parents or caregivers to cultivate for themselves. Listening actively and understanding for others' perspectives would be a way to start. It is critical for parents or caregivers to share and understand the feelings of others, as well as respecting for others (in our case, their SGD children) with an open mind. A common saying associated with this area (i.e., self-awareness) is "putting yourself in the shoes" of another. Connecting and talking to other parents or caregivers of SGD young people could also be helpful to offer further opportunities to develop better understanding of the role of recognition and acceptance of others' uniqueness and views on their children's growth.

The *relationship competency* is another area for parents or caregivers to cultivate for themselves. Becoming one whom people can rely on and/or want to talk to when needed is an *ingredient* for building trust. Then in turn, that trust contributes to establishing a healthy relationship or a secure base where people feel comfortable to share and voice. It is also important that in their relationships with their SGD children, that parents or caregivers encourage the young person to seek support and mental health services when expressing feelings of depression, anxiety, or suicide related to gender-based victimization or discrimination.

Fostering *responsible decision-making* could involve parents or caregivers respecting the young person to involve them in making decisions about their lives. Helping the SGD young person develops a sense of autonomy over their choices and options by involving them in decision-making can also encourage them to help themselves and prepares them for adult life [152]. When parents and caregivers listen to and apply their suggestions it communicates to the young person that their family values their abilities, strengths, and resources.

The aforementioned recommendations are just a few examples of ways in which SGD young people can be supported by their parents and caregivers. Parents and caregivers should seek out resources and tools (e.g., support groups for families of gender-diverse children), and professional help when needed (e.g., gender-affirming therapists and counselors). Parents of SGD young people have explained that being in contact with other parents of SGD children, either online or in-person community groups, helped with the process of accepting and supporting their child's sexual or/

and gender identity [83]. These spaces offer an opportunity for parents and caregivers to share personal stories with other people who are going through the same thing, while also getting support from people in similar situations [135, 136]. By speaking to other families and sharing information about available resources, parents can learn how to better understand sexual and gender-diverse identities, while acquiring the tools to help them navigate many aspects of their young person's journey.

5. Conclusion

Sexual and gender diversity has been obtaining increasing societal awareness of sexual and gender possibilities, especially considering the growing numbers of young adults reporting their affiliation or membership with broader terms reflecting sexual or/and gender diversity (e.g., genderqueer, nonbinary). These shifts draw new awareness that everyone has a sexual or/and gender identity. The terms cisgender (often shortened as *cis*) and heterosexual are becoming (in fact, have always been) part of the diversity and among the broadened continuum of sexuality or gender; no longer just the dominant and unnamed majority groups. Our intention in this chapter was to provide an opportunity to consider "how we, as parents or caregivers, can support our children's healthy identity development, especially regarding sexuality and gender." We believe in the strong benefits of integrating SEL into the nurturing process.

Conflict of interest

The authors declare no conflict of interest.

Author details

Chiaki Konishi* and Julia Tesolin
Department of Educational and Counselling Psychology, McGill University, Montreal, QC, Canada

*Address all correspondence to: chiaki.konishi@mcgill.ca

References

[1] Bishop MD, Fish JN, Hammack PL, Russell ST. Sexual identity development milestones in three generations of sexual minority people: A national probability sample. Developmental Psychology. 2020;**56**:2177-2193. DOI: 10.1037/dev0001105

[2] Bishop A, Overcash F, McGuire J, Reicks M. Diet and physical activity behaviors among adolescent transgender students: School survey results. Journal of Adolescent Health. 2020;**66**:484-490. DOI: 10.1016/j.jadohealth.2019.10.026

[3] Heino E, Ellonen N, Kaltiala R. Transgender identity is associated with bullying involvement among Finnish adolescents. Frontiers in Psychology. 2020;**11**:1-11. DOI: 10.3389/fpsyg.2020.612424

[4] Waller CR, Méndez Leal AS, Silvers JA. Disparities in depression and anxiety that impact self-identified sexual minority people affect a broader group of same-gender attracted young adults. The Journal of Adolescent Health. 2023;**73**:739745. DOI: 10.1016/j.jadohealth.2023.05.024

[5] Williams AJ, Jones C, Arcelus J, Townsend E, Lazaridou A, Michail M, et al. A systematic review and meta-analysis of victimisation and mental health prevalence among LGBTQ young people with experiences of self-harm and suicide. PLoS One. 2021;**16**:1-26. DOI: 10.1371/journal.pone.0245268

[6] Puckett JA, Tornello S, Mustanski B, Newcomb ME. Gender variations, generational effects, and mental health of transgender people in relation to timing and status of gender identity milestones. Psychology of Sexual Orientation and Gender Diversity. 2022;**9**:165-178. DOI: 10.1037/sgd0000391

[7] Mallory AB, Pollitt AM, Bishop MD, Russell ST. Changes in disclosure stress and depression symptoms in a sample of lesbian, gay, and bisexual youth. Developmental Psychology. 2021;**57**:570-583. DOI: 10.1037/dev0001168

[8] Gattamorta KA, Salerno J, Quidley-Rodriguez N. Hispanic parental experiences of learning a child identifies as a sexual minority. Journal of GLBT Family Studies. 2019;**15**:151-164. DOI: 10.1080/1550428X.2018.1518740

[9] Huebner DM, Roche KM, Rith KA. Effects of family demographics and the passage of time on parents' difficulty with their lesbian, gay, or bisexual youth's sexual orientation. Archives of Sexual Behavior. 2019;**48**:1581-1588. DOI: 10.1007/s10508-019-1430-9

[10] van Bergen DD, Wilson BDM, Russell ST, Gordon AG, Rothblum ED. Parental responses to coming out by lesbian, gay, bisexual, queer, pansexual, or two-spirited people across three age cohorts. Journal of Marriage and the Family. 2021;**83**:1116-1133. DOI: 10.1111/jomf.12731

[11] Belmont N, Cronin TJ, Pepping CA. Affirmation-support, parental conflict, and mental health outcomes of transgender and gender diverse youth. International Journal of Transgender Health. 2024;**25**:50-62. DOI: 10.1080/26895269.2023.2252418

[12] Pullen-Sansfaçon A, Kirichenko V, Holmes C, Feder S, Lawson ML, Ghosh S, et al. Parents' journeys to acceptance and support of gender-diverse and trans children and youth. Journal of

Family Issues. 2020;**41**:1214-1236. DOI: 10.1177/0192513X19888779

[13] Mezzalira S, Scandurra C, Mezza F, Miscioscia M, Innamorati M, Bochicchio V. Gender felt pressure, affective domains, and mental health outcomes among transgender and gender diverse (TGD) children and adolescents: A systematic review with developmental and clinical implications. International Journal of Environmental Research and Public Health. 2022;**785**:1-25. DOI: 10.3390/ijerph20010785

[14] American Psychological Association. Key Terms and Concepts in Understanding Gender Diversity and Sexual Orientation among Students. 2015. pp. 1-6. Available from: https://www.apa.org/pi/lgbt/programs/safe-supportive/lgbt/key-terms.pdf

[15] Gainor K. Including transgender issues in lesbian, gay and bisexual psychology: Implications for clinical practice and training. In: Greene B, Croom G, editors. Psychological Perspectives on Lesbian and Gay Issues: Education, Research, and Practice in Lesbian, Gay, Bisexual, and Transgendered Psychology: A Resource Manual. Thousand Oaks: SAGE Publications; 2000. pp. 131-161. DOI: 10.4135/9781452233697

[16] Gordon AR, Krieger N, Okechukwu CA, Haneuse S, Samnaliev M, Charlton BM, et al. Decrements in health-related quality of life associated with gender nonconformity among US adolescents and young adults. Quality of Life Research. 2017;**26**:2129-2138. DOI: 10.1007/s11136-017-1545-1

[17] Lowry R, Johns MM, Gordon AR, Austin SB, Robin LE, Kann LK. Nonconforming gender expression and associated mental distress and substance use among high school students. JAMA Pediatrics. 2018;**172**(11):1020-1028. DOI: 10.1001/jamapediatrics.2018.2140

[18] Guss C, Shumer D, Katz-Wise SL. Transgender and gender nonconforming adolescent care: Psychosocial and medical considerations. Current Opinion in Pediatrics. 2015;**27**(4):421-426. DOI: 10.1097/MOP.0000000000000240

[19] Steensma TD, Kreukels BP, de Vries AL, Cohen-Kettenis PT. Gender identity development in adolescence. Hormones and Behavior. 2013;**64**(2):288-297. DOI: 10.1016/j.yhbeh.2013.02.020

[20] Reilly M, Desousa V, Garza-Flores A, Perrin EC. Young children with gender nonconforming behaviors and preferences. Journal of Developmental Behavioral Pediatrics. 2019;**40**(1):60-71. DOI: 10.1097/DBP.0000000000000612

[21] Mahfouda S, Moore JK, Siafarikas A, Zepf FD, Lin A. Puberty suppression in transgender children and adolescents. The Lancet Diabetes and Endocrinology. 2017;**5**(10):816-826. DOI: 10.1016/S2213-8587(17)30099-2

[22] Vandermorris A, Metzger D. An affirming approach to caring for transgender and gender-diverse youth. Paediatrics & Child Health. 2023;**28**(7):437-448. DOI: 10.1093/pch/pxad045

[23] Hammack PL, Hughes SD, Atwood JM, Cohen EM, Clark RC. Gender and sexual identity in adolescence: A mixed-methods study of labeling in diverse community settings. Journal Adolescent Research. 2022;**37**(2):167-220. DOI: 10.1177/07435584211000315

[24] Hammack PL, Frost DM, Hughes SD. Queer intimacies: A new paradigm for the study of relationship

diversity. The Journal of Sex Research. 2019;**56**(4-5):556-592. DOI: 10.1080/00224499.2018.1531281

[25] Galupo MP, Ramirez JL, Pulice-Farrow L. "Regardless of their gender": Descriptions of sexual identity among bisexual, pansexual, and queer identified individuals. In: Under the Bisexual Umbrella. New York: Routledge; 2018. pp. 108-124

[26] Morandini JS, Blaszczynski A, Dar-Nimrod I. Who adopts queer and pansexual sexual identities? The Journal of Sex Research. 2017;**54**(7):911-922. DOI: 10.1080/00224499.2016.1249332

[27] Price-Feeney M, Green AE, Dorison SH. Suicidality among youth who are questioning, unsure of, or exploring their sexual identity. The Journal of Sex Research. 2021;**58**:581-588. DOI: 10.1080/00224499.2020.1832184

[28] Steensma TD, Biemond R, de Boer F, Cohen-Kettenis PT. Desisting and persisting gender dysphoria after childhood: A qualitative follow-up study. Clinical Child Psychology and Psychiatry. 2011;**4**:499-516. DOI: 10.1177/1359104510378303

[29] Hunter J, Butler C, Cooper K. Gender minority stress in trans and gender diverse adolescents and young people. Clinical Child Psychology and Psychiatry. 2021;**26**:1182-1195. DOI: 10.1177/1359104520988419

[30] Kessler RC, Amminger GP, Aguilar-Gaxiola S, Alonso J, Lee S, Üstün TB. Age of onset of mental disorders: A review of recent literature. Current Opinion in Psychiatry. 2007;**20**:359-364. DOI: 10.1097/YCO.0b013e32816ebc8c

[31] Wittlin NM, Kuper LE, Olson KR. Mental health of transgender and gender diverse youth. Annual Review of Clinical Psychology. 2023;**19**:207-232. DOI: 10.1146/annurev-clinpsy-070221-041445

[32] Kotov R, Krueger RF, Watson D, Achenbach TM, Althoff RR, et al. The hierarchical taxonomy of psychopathology (HiTOP): A dimensional alternative to traditional nosologies. Journal of Abnormal Psychology. 2017;**126**:454-477. DOI: 10.1037/abn0000258

[33] Clark TC, Lucassen MFG, Bullen P, Denny SJ, Fleming TM, et al. The health and well-being of transgender high school students: Results from the New Zealand adolescent health survey (Youth'12). Journal of Adolescent Health. 2014;**55**:193-199. DOI: 10.1016/j.jadohealth.2013.11.008

[34] Eisenberg ME, Gower AL, McMorris BJ, Rider GN, Shea G, Coleman E. Risk and protective factors in the lives of transgender/gender nonconforming adolescents. Journal of Adolescent Health. 2017;**61**:521-526. DOI: 10.1016/j.jadohealth.2017.04.014

[35] Guz S, Kattari SK, Atteberry-Ash B, Klemmer CL, Call J, Kattari L. Depression and suicide risk at the cross-section of sexual orientation and gender identity for youth. Journal of Adolescent Health. 2021;**68**:317-323. DOI: 10.1016/j.jadohealth.2020.06.015

[36] Chodzen G, Hidalgo MA, Chen D, Garofalo R. Minority stress factors associated with depression and anxiety among transgender and gender-nonconforming youth. Journal of Adolescent Health. 2019;**64**:467-471. DOI: 10.1016/j.jadohealth.2018.07.006

[37] Price-Feeney M, Green AE, Dorison S. Understanding the mental health of transgender and nonbinary

youth. Journal of Adolescent Health. 2020;**66**:684-690. DOI: 10.1016/j.jadohealth.2019.11.314

[38] Russell ST, Pollitt AM, Li G, Grossman AH. Chosen name use is linked to reduced depressive symptoms, suicidal ideation, and suicidal behavior among transgender youth. Journal of Adolescent Health. 2018;**63**:503-505. DOI: 10.1016/j.jadohealth.2018.02.003

[39] Price-Feeney M, Green AE, Dorison SH. Impact of bathroom discrimination on mental health among transgender and nonbinary youth. Journal of Adolescent Health. 2021;**68**:1142-1147. DOI: 10.1016/j.jadohealth.2020.10.001

[40] Toomey RB, Syvertsen AK, Shramko M. Transgender adolescent suicide behavior. Pediatrics. 2018;**142**:4. DOI: 10.1542/peds.2017-4218

[41] Parodi KB, Holt MK, Green JG, Katz-Wise SL, Shah TN, Kraus AD, et al. Associations between school-related factors and mental health among transgender and gender diverse youth. Journal of School Psychology. 2022;**90**:135-149. DOI: 10.1016/j.jsp.2021.12.001

[42] Vance SR, Boyer CB, Glidden DV, Sevelius J. Mental health and psychosocial risk and protective factors among black and Latinx transgender youth compared with peers. JAMA Network Open. 2021;**4**(3):1-12. DOI: 10.1001/jamanetworkopen.2021.3256

[43] Wang Y, Yu H, Yang Y, Drescher J, Li R, et al. Mental health status of cisgender and gender-diverse secondary school students in China. JAMA Psychiatry. 2020;**3**(10):1-13. DOI: 10.1001/jamanetworkopen.2020.22796

[44] Toomey RB, Huynh VW, Jones SK, Lee S, Revels-Macalinao M. Sexual minority youth of color: A content analysis and critical review of the literature. Journal of Gay & Lesbian Mental Health. 2017;**21**(1):3-31. DOI: 10.1080/19359705.2016.1217499

[45] Kingsbury M, Hammond NG, Johnstone F, Colman I. Suicidality among sexual minority and transgender adolescents: A nationally representative population-based study of youth in Canada. CMAJ. 2022;**194**(22):767-773. DOI: 10.1503/cmaj.212054

[46] Fish JN, Baams L, McGuire JK. Sexual and gender minority mental health among children and youth. In: The Oxford Handbook of Sexual and Gender Minority Mental Health. Oxford: Oxford University Press; 2020. p. 229

[47] Irish M, Solmi F, Mars B, King M, Lewis G, Pearson RM, et al. Depression and self-harm from adolescence to young adulthood in sexual minorities compared with heterosexuals in the UK: A population-based cohort study. The Lancet Child & Adolescent Health. 2019;**3**:91-98. DOI: 10.1016/S2352-4642(18)30343-2

[48] Russell ST, Fish JN. Mental health in lesbian, gay, bisexual, and transgender (LGBT) youth. Annual Review of Clinical Psychology. 2016;**12**:465-487. DOI: 10.1146/annurev-clinpsy-021815-093153

[49] Johns MM. Transgender identity and experiences of violence victimization, substance use, suicide risk, and sexual risk behaviors among high school students—19 states and large urban school districts, 2017. Morbidity and Mortality Weekly Report. 2019;**68**(3):67-71. DOI: 10.15585/mmwr.mm6803a3

[50] Reisner SL, Vetters R, Leclerc M, Zaslow S, Wolfrum S, Shumer D, et al. Mental health of transgender youth in care at an adolescent urban community health center: A matched retrospective cohort study. Journal of Adolescent Health. 2015;**56**(3):274-279. DOI: 10.1016/j.jadohealth.2014.10.264

[51] Conn BM, Chen D, Olson-Kennedy J, Chan YM, Ehrensaft D, Garofalo R, et al. High internalized transphobia and low gender identity pride are associated with depression symptoms among transgender and gender-diverse youth. Journal of Adolescent Health. 2023;**72**(6):877-884. DOI: 10.1016/j.jadohealth.2022.12.011

[52] Lefevor GT, Boyd-Rogers CC, Sprague BM, Janis RA. Health disparities between genderqueer, transgender, and cisgender individuals: An extension of minority stress theory. Journal of Counseling Psychology. 2019;**66**(4):385. DOI: 10.1037/cou0000339

[53] Hendricks ML, Testa RJ. A conceptual framework for clinical work with transgender and gender nonconforming clients: An adaptation of the minority stress model. Professional Psychology: Research and Practice. 2012;**43**(5):460. DOI: 10.1037/a0029597

[54] Valentine SE, Shipherd JC. A systematic review of social stress and mental health among transgender and gender non-conforming people in the United States. Clinical Psychology Review. 2018;**66**:24-38. DOI: 10.1016/j.cpr.2018.03.003

[55] Testa RJ, Habarth J, Peta J, Balsam K, Bockting W. Development of the gender minority stress and resilience measure. Psychology of Sexual Orientation and Gender Diversity. 2015;**2**(1):65. DOI: 10.1037/sgd0000081

[56] Meyer IH. Prejudice, social stress, and mental health in lesbian, gay, and bisexual populations: Conceptual issues and research evidence. Psychological Bulletin. 2003;**129**(5):674. DOI: 10.1037/0033-2909.129.5.674

[57] Surace T, Fusar-Poli L, Vozza L, Cavone V, Arcidiacono C, Mammano R, et al. Lifetime prevalence of suicidal ideation and suicidal behaviors in gender non-conforming youths: A meta-analysis. European Child & Adolescent Psychiatry. 2021;**30**(8):1147-1161. DOI: 10.1007/s00787-020-01508-5

[58] Trujillo MA, Perrin PB, Sutter M, Tabaac A, Benotsch EG. The buffering role of social support on the associations among discrimination, mental health, and suicidality in a transgender sample. International Journal of Transgenderism. 2017;**18**(1):39-52. DOI: 10.1080/15532739.2016.1247405

[59] Chavanduka TM, Gamarel KE, Todd KP, Stephenson R. Responses to the gender minority stress and resilience scales among transgender and nonbinary youth. Journal of LGBT Youth. 2021;**18**(2):135-154. DOI: 10.1080/19361653.2020.1828395

[60] Hatchel T, Valido A, De Pedro KT, Huang Y, Espelage DL. Minority stress among transgender adolescents: The role of peer victimization, school belonging, and ethnicity. Journal of Child and Family Studies. 2019;**28**:2467-2476. DOI: 10.1007/s10826-018-1168-3

[61] Peng K, Zhu X, Gillespie A, Wang Y, Gao Y, Xin Y, et al. Self-reported rates of abuse, neglect, and bullying experienced by transgender and gender-nonbinary adolescents in China. JAMA Network Open. 2019;**2**(9):e1911058. DOI: 10.1001/jamanetworkopen.2019.11058

[62] Atzenbuehler ML. How does sexual minority stigma “get under the skin”? A psychological mediation framework. Psychological Bulletin. 2009;**135**(5):707. DOI: 10.1037/a0016441

[63] Wang Y, Yu H, Yang Y, Drescher J, Li R, Yin W, et al. Mental health status of cisgender and gender-diverse secondary school students in China. JAMA Network Open. 2020;**3**(10):e2022796. DOI: 10.1001/jamanetworkopen.2020.22796

[64] Jackman KB, Caceres BA, Kreuze EJ, Bockting WO. Suicidality among gender minority youth: Analysis of 2017 youth risk behavior survey data. Archives of Suicide Research. 2021;**25**(2):208-223. DOI: 10.1080/13811118.2019.1664458

[65] Sinnott JD. Identity Flexibility during Adulthood. New York: Springer Verlag; 2017

[66] Ross-Reed DE, Reno J, Peñaloza L, Green D, FitzGerald C. Family, school, and peer support are associated with rates of violence victimization and self-harm among gender minority and cisgender youth. Journal of Adolescent Health. 2019;**65**(6):776-783. DOI: 10.1016/j.jadohealth.2019.06.006

[67] Norris AL, Orchowski LM. Peer victimization of sexual minority and transgender youth: A cross-sectional study of high school students. Psychology of Violence. 2020 Mar;**10**(2):201. DOI: 10.1037/vio0000260

[68] Taliaferro LA, McMorris BJ, Eisenberg ME. Connections that moderate risk of non-suicidal self-injury among transgender and gender non-conforming youth. Psychiatry Research. 2018;**268**:65-67. DOI: 10.1016/j.psychres.2018.07.010

[69] Witcomb GL, Claes L, Bouman WP, Nixon E, Motmans J, Arcelus J. Experiences and psychological wellbeing outcomes associated with bullying in treatment-seeking transgender and gender-diverse youth. LGBT Health. 2019;**6**(5):216-226. DOI: 10.1089/lgbt.2018.0179

[70] Austin A, Craig SL, D’Souza S, McInroy LB. Suicidality among transgender youth: Elucidating the role of interpersonal risk factors. Journal of Interpersonal Violence. 2022;**37**(5-6):NP2696-718. DOI: 10.1177/0886260519843723

[71] Kosciw JG, Clark CM, Truong NL, Zongrone AD. The 2019 National School Climate Survey: The Experiences of Lesbian, Gay, Bisexual, Transgender, and Queer Youth in our Nation's Schools. A Report from GLSEN. New York, NY: Gay, Lesbian and Straight Education Network (GLSEN); 2020. Available from: https://www.glsen.org/research/2019-national-school-climate-survey

[72] Röder M, Barkmann C, Richter-Appelt H, Schulte-Markwort M, Ravens-Sieberer U, Becker I. Health-related quality of life in transgender adolescents: Associations with body image and emotional and behavioral problems. International Journal of Transgenderism. 2018;**19**(1):78-91. DOI: 10.1080/15532739.2017.1399496

[73] Drydakis N. Social rejection, family acceptance, economic recession, and physical and mental health of sexual minorities. Sexuality Research and Social Policy. 2021;**19**(10):1-23. DOI: 10.1007/s13178-021-00640-4

[74] Willoughby BL, Doty ND, Malik NM. Victimization, family rejection, and outcomes of gay, lesbian, and bisexual young people: The role of negative GLB identity. Journal of GLBT

Family Studies. 2010;**6**(4):403-424. DOI: 10.1080/1550428X.2010.511085

[75] Pariseau EM, Chevalier L, Long KA, Clapham R, Edwards-Leeper L, Tishelman AC. The relationship between family acceptance-rejection and transgender youth psychosocial functioning. Clinical Practice in Pediatric Psychology. 2019;**7**(3):267. DOI: 10.1037/cpp0000306

[76] Johnson KC, LeBlanc AJ, Sterzing PR, Deardorff J, Antin T, Bockting WO. Trans adolescents' perceptions and experiences of their parents' supportive and rejecting behaviors. Journal of Counseling Psychology. 2020;**67**(2):156. DOI: 10.1037/cou0000400

[77] Newhook JT, Benson K, Bridger T, Crowther C, Sinnott R. The TransKidsNL study: Healthcare and support needs of transgender children, youth, and families on the island of Newfoundland. Canadian Journal of Community Mental Health. 2019;**37**(2):13-28. DOI: 10.7870/cjcmh-2018-033

[78] Sievert ED, Schweizer K, Barkmann C, Fahrenkrug S, Becker-Hebly I. Not social transition status, but peer relations and family functioning predict psychological functioning in a German clinical sample of children with gender dysphoria. Clinical Child Psychology and Psychiatry. 2021;**26**(1):79-95. DOI: 10.1177/1359104520964530

[79] Levitan N, Barkmann C, Richter-Appelt H, Schulte-Markwort M, Becker-Hebly I. Risk factors for psychological functioning in German adolescents with gender dysphoria: Poor peer relations and general family functioning. European Child & Adolescent Psychiatry. 2019;**28**:1487-1498. DOI: 10.1007/s00787-019-01315-6

[80] Mohr J, Fassinger R. Measuring dimensions of lesbian and gay male experience. Measurement and Evaluation in Counseling and Development. 2000;**33**(2):66-90. DOI: 10.1080/07481756.2000.12068999

[81] Carastathis GS, Cohen L, Kaczmarek E, Chang P. Rejected by family for being gay or lesbian: Portrayals, perceptions, and resilience. Journal of Homosexuality. 2017;**64**(3):289-320. DOI: 10.1080/00918369.2016.1179035

[82] Grossman AH, D'Augelli AR. Transgender youth and life-threatening behaviors. Suicide and Life-threatening Behavior. 2007;**37**(5):527-537. DOI: 10.1521/suli.2007.37.5.527

[83] Salerno JP, Gattamorta KA, Williams ND. Impact of family rejection and racism on sexual and gender minority stress among LGBTQ young people of color during COVID-19. Psychological Trauma: Theory, Research, Practice, and Policy. 2023;**15**(4):637. DOI: 10.1037/tra0001254

[84] Toomey RB. Advancing research on minority stress and resilience in trans children and adolescents in the 21st century. Child Development Perspectives. 2021;**15**(2):96-102. DOI: 10.1111/cdep.12404

[85] Pellicane MJ, Ciesla JA. Associations between minority stress, depression, and suicidal ideation and attempts in transgender and gender diverse (TGD) individuals: Systematic review and meta-analysis. Clinical Psychology Review. 2022;**91**:102113. DOI: 10.1016/j.cpr.2021.102113

[86] Bockting WO, Miner MH, Swinburne Romine RE, Dolezal C, Robinson BB, Rosser BS, et al. The transgender identity survey: A measure of internalized transphobia. LGBT Health. 2020;**7**(1):15-27. DOI: 10.1089/lgbt.2018.0221

[87] Rood BA, Reisner SL, Puckett JA, Surace FI, Berman AK, Pantalone DW. Internalized transphobia: Exploring perceptions of social messages in transgender and gender-nonconforming adults. International Journal of Transgenderism. 2017;**18**(4):411-426. DOI: 10.1080/15532739.2017.1329048

[88] Rood BA, Reisner SL, Surace FI, Puckett JA, Maroney MR, Pantalone DW. Expecting rejection: Understanding the minority stress experiences of transgender and gender-nonconforming individuals. Transgender Health. 2016;**1**(1):151-164. DOI: 10.1089/trgh.2016.0012

[89] Baams L, Kiekens WJ, Fish JN. The rejection sensitivity model: Sexual minority adolescents in context. Archives of Sexual Behavior. 2020;**49**:2259-2263. DOI: 10.1007/s10508-019-01572-2

[90] Cénat JM, Blais M, Hébert M, Lavoie F, Guerrier M. Correlates of bullying in Quebec high school students: The vulnerability of sexual-minority youth. Journal of Affective Disorders. 2015;**183**:315-321. DOI: 10.1016/j.jad.2015.05.011

[91] Hendricks ML, Bockting WO. Innovations in research with transgender and gender nonconforming people and their communities. Psychology of Sexual Orientation and Gender Diversity. 2016;**3**(2):187. DOI: 10.1037/sgd0000162

[92] Duong J, Bradshaw C. Associations between bullying and engaging in aggressive and suicidal behaviors among sexual minority youth: The moderating role of connectedness. Journal of School Health. 2014;**84**(10):636-645. DOI: 10.1111/josh.12196

[93] Gibson DJ, Glazier JJ, Olson KR. Evaluation of anxiety and depression in a community sample of transgender youth. JAMA Network Open. 2021;**4**(4):e214739. DOI: 10.1001/jamanetworkopen.2021.4739

[94] Kuvalanka KA, Weiner JL, Munroe C, Goldberg AE, Gardner M. Trans and gender-nonconforming children and their caregivers: Gender presentations, peer relations, and well-being at baseline. Journal of Family Psychology. 2017;**31**(7):889. DOI: 10.1037/fam0000346

[95] Mintz S, Valido A, Rivas-Koehl M, Kuehl T, Espelage DL, Woolweaver A, et al. Supporting sexual minority youth: Protective factors of adverse health outcomes and implications for public health. Journal of Adolescent Health. 2021;**69**(6):983-990. DOI: 10.1016/j.jadohealth.2021.05.021

[96] Cohen S. Social relationships and health. American Psychologist. 2024;**59**:676-684. DOI: 10.1037/0003-066x.59.8.676

[97] Cobb S. Social support as a moderator of life stress. Psychosomatic Medicine. 1976;**38**:300-314. DOI: 10.1097/00006842-197609000-00003

[98] Cohen SE, Syme S. Social Support and Health. San Francisco: Academic Press; 1985. 390 p

[99] Cohen S, Wills TA. Stress, social support, and the buffering hypothesis. Psychological Bulletin. 1985;**98**:310-357. DOI: 10.1037//0033-2909.98.2.310

[100] Cohen S, McKay G. Social support, stress and the buffering hypothesis: A theoretical analysis. In: Baum A, Singer JE, Taylor SE, editors. Handbook of Psychology and Health. Hillsdale: Lawrence Erlbaum Associates Inc; 1984. pp. 253-267

[101] Gore S. Stress-buffering functions of social supports: An appraisal and

clarification of research models. In: Dohrenwend BS, Dohrenwend BP, editors. Stressful Life Events and their Contexts. New York: Prodist; 1981. pp. 202-222

[102] House JS. Work Stress and Social Support. Reading: Addison-Wesley; 1981. 156 p

[103] Barrera M Jr. Distinctions between social support concepts, measures, and models. American Journal of Community Psychology. 1986;**14**:413-445. DOI: 10.1007/BF00922627

[104] Zimet GD, Dahlem NW, Zimet SG, Farley GK. The multidimensional scale of perceived social support. Journal of Personality Assessment. 1988;**52**:30-41. DOI: 10.1207/s15327752jpa5201_2

[105] Duru E. Re-examination of the psychometric characteristics of the multidimensional scale of perceived social support among Turkish university students. Social Behavior and Personality: An International Journal. 2007;**35**:443-452. DOI: 10.2224/sbp.2007.35.4.443

[106] Canty-Mitchell J, Zimet GD. Psychometric properties of the multidimensional scale of perceived social support in urban adolescents. American Journal of Community Psychology. 2000;**28**:391-400. DOI: 10.1023/a:1005109522457

[107] Edwards LM. Measuring perceived social support in Mexican American adolescents: Psychometric properties of the multidimensional scale of perceived social support. Hispanic Journal of Behavioral Sciences. 2004;**26**:187-194. DOI: 10.1177/0739986304264374

[108] McConnell EA, Birkett M, Mustanski B. Families matter: Social support and mental health trajectories among lesbian, gay, bisexual, and transgender adolescents. Journal of Adolescent Health. 2016;**59**:674-680. DOI: 10.1016/j.jadohealth.2016.07.026

[109] Conner JO, Miles SB, Pope DC. How many teachers does it take to support a student?: Examining the relationship between teacher support and adverse health outcomes in high-performing, pressure-cooker high schools. The High School Journal. 2014;**98**:22-42. DOI: 10.1353/hsj.2014.0012

[110] Rosenfeld LB, Richman JM, Bowen GL. Social support networks and school outcomes: The centrality of the teacher. Child and Adolescent Social Work Journal. 2000;**17**:205-226. DOI: 10.1023/A:1007535930286

[111] Lesesne CA, Rasberry CN, Kroupa E, Topete P, Carver LH, Morris E, et al. Communicating with school staff about sexual identity, health and safety: An exploratory study of the experiences and preferences of black and Latino teen young men who have sex with men. LGBT Health. 2015;**2**:258-264. DOI: 10.1089/lgbt.2014.0087

[112] Darwich L, Hymel S, Waterhouse T. School avoidance and substance use among lesbian, gay, bisexual, and questioning youths: The impact of peer victimization and adult support. Journal of Educational Psychology. 2012;**104**:381-392. DOI: 10.1037/a0026684

[113] Konishi C, Saewyc E. Still a target: Sexual diversity and power of caring. School Psychology International. 2014;**35**:504-515. DOI: 10.1177/0143034313512407

[114] Murdock TB, Bolch MB. Risk and protective factors for poor school adjustment in lesbian, gay, and bisexual (LGB) high school youth: Variable and person-centered analyses. Psychology

in the Schools. 2005;**42**:159-172. DOI: 10.1002/pits.20054

[115] Poteat VP, Mereish EH, DiGiovanni CD, Koenig BW. The effects of general and homophobic victimization on adolescents' psychosocial and educational concerns: The importance of intersecting identities and parent support. Journal of Counseling Psychology. 2011;**58**:597-609. DOI: 10.1037/a0025095

[116] Darwich L, Hymel S, Waterhouse T, Prevost A. Adult support at school: Does it make a difference for LGBQ youth? In: Poster Presented at the Safe Schools Survey Research Symposium. Abbotsford, BC, Canada; 2009

[117] Dessel AB, Kulick A, Wernick LJ, Sullivan D. The importance of teacher support: Differential impacts by gender and sexuality. Journal of Adolescence. 2017;**56**:136-144. DOI: 10.1016/j.adolescence.2017.02.002

[118] Garnett BR, Masyn KE, Austin SB, Miller M, Williams DR, Viswanath K. The intersectionality of discrimination attributes and bullying among youth: An applied latent class analysis. Journal of Youth and Adolescence. 2014;**43**:1225-1239. DOI: 10.1007/s10964-013-0073-8

[119] Poteat VP, Vecho O. Who intervenes against homophobic behavior? Attributes that distinguish active bystanders. Journal of School Psychology. 2016;**54**:17-28. DOI: 10.1016/j.jsp.2015.10.002

[120] Russell ST, Kosciw J, Horn S, Saewyc E. Social policy report: Safe schools policy for LGBTQ students. Child Development. 2010;**24**:1-25. DOI: 10.1002/j.2379-3988.2010.tb00065.x

[121] Kosciw JG, Palmer NA, Kull RM, Greytak EA. The effect of negative school climate on academic outcomes for LGBT youth and the role of in-school supports. Journal of School Violence. 2013;**12**:45-63. DOI: 10.1080/15388220.2012.732546

[122] Russell ST, Seif H, Truong NL. School outcomes of sexual minority youth in the United States: Evidence from a national study. Journal of Adolescence. 2001;**24**:111-127. DOI: 10.1006/jado.2000.0365

[123] Goodenow C, Szalacha L, Westheimer K. School support groups, other school factors, and the safety of sexual minority adolescents. Psychology in the Schools. 2006;**43**:573-589. DOI: 10.1002/pits.20173

[124] Kosciw JG, Greytak EA, Giga NM, et al. The 2015 National School Climate Survey: The Experiences of Lesbian, Gay, Bisexual, Transgender, and Queer Youth in our Nation's Schools. New York: GLSEN; 2016. 220 p

[125] Leung E, Kassel-Gomez G, Sullivan S, Murahara F, Flanagan T. Social support in schools and related outcomes for LGBTQ youth: A scoping review. Discover Education. 2022;**1**:18. DOI: 10.1007/s44217-022-00016-9

[126] Mueller C, Haines RT. Adolescent perceptions of family connectedness and school belonging: Links with self-concept and depressive symptoms among gifted African American and Hispanic youth. Gifted Children. 2012;**5**:3. Available from: http://docs.lib.purdue.edu/giftedchildren/vol5/iss2/3

[127] Gower AL, Rider GN, Brown C, McMorris BJ, Coleman E, Taliaferro LA, et al. Supporting transgender and gender diverse youth: Protection against emotional distress and substance use. American Journal of Preventive Medicine. 2018;**55**:787-794. DOI: 10.1016/j.amepre.2018.06.030

[128] Birkett M, Newcomb ME, Mustanski B. Does it get better? A longitudinal analysis of psychological distress and victimization in lesbian, gay, bisexual, transgender, and questioning youth. Journal of Adolescent Health. 2015;**56**:280-285. DOI: 10.1016/j.jadohealth.2014.10.275

[129] Grossman AH, D'augelli AR, Frank JA. Aspects of psychological resilience among transgender youth. Journal of LGBT Youth. 2011;**8**:103-115. DOI: 10.1080/19361653.2011.541347

[130] Le V, Arayasirikul S, Chen YH, Jin H, Wilson EC. Types of social support and parental acceptance among transfemale youth and their impact on mental health, sexual debut, history of sex work and condomless anal intercourse. Journal of the International AIDS Society. 2016;**19**:20781. DOI: 10.7448/IAS.19.3.20781

[131] McConnell EA, Birkett M, Mustanski B. Families matter: Social support and mental health trajectories among lesbian, gay, bisexual, and transgender youth. Journal of Adolescent Health. 2016;**59**:674-680. DOI: 10.1016/j.jadohealth.2016.07.026

[132] Yadegarfard M, Meinhold-Bergmann ME, Ho R. Family rejection, social isolation, and loneliness as predictors of negative health outcomes (depression, suicidal ideation, and sexual risk behavior) among Thai male-to-female transgender adolescents. Journal of LGBT Youth. 2014;**11**:347-363. DOI: 10.1080/19361653.2014.910483

[133] Ellis KM, Eriksen K. Transsexual and transgenderist experiences and treatment options. The Family Journal. 2002;**10**:289-299. DOI: 10.1177/10680702010003005

[134] Lev AI. Transgender Emergence: Therapeutic Guidelines for Working with Gender-Variant People and their Families. New York: Routledge; 2013. p. 500

[135] Pullen Sansfaçon A, Robichaud MJ, Dumais-Michaud AA. The experience of parents who support their children's gender variance. Journal of LGBT Youth. 2015;**12**:39-63. DOI: 10.1080/19361653.2014.935555

[136] Gray SA, Sweeney KK, Randazzo R, Levitt HM. "Am I doing the right thing?": Pathways to parenting a gender variant child. Family Process. 2016;**55**:123-138. DOI: 10.1111/famp.12128

[137] Rahilly EP. The gender binary meets the gender-variant child: Parents' negotiations with childhood gender variance. Gender & Society. 2015;**29**:338-361. DOI: 10.1177/0192513X1988877

[138] Collaborative for academic, social, and emotional learning (CASEL). Core SEL Competencies 2022. Available from: https://casel.org/core-competencies/

[139] Graber JA, Brooks-Gunn J. Transitions and turning points: Navigating the passage from childhood through adolescence. Developmental Psychology. 1996;**32**(4):768-776. DOI: 10.1037/0012-1649.32.4.768

[140] McLaughlin C, Clarke B. Relational matters: A review of the impact of school experience on mental health in early adolescence. Educational and Child Psychology. 2010;**27**:91-103. DOI: 10.53841/bpsecp.2010.27.1.91

[141] Oberle E, Schonert-Reichl KA, Hertzman C, Zumbo BD. Social-emotional competencies make the grade: Predicting academic success in early adolescence. Journal of Applied Developmental Psychology.

2014;**35**(3):138-147. DOI: 10.1016/j.appdev.2014.02.004

[142] Durlak JA, Mahoney JL, Boyle AE. What we know, and what we need to find out about universal, school-based social and emotional learning programs for children and adolescents: A review of meta-analyses and directions for future research. Psychological Bulletin. 2022;**148**(11-12):765-782. DOI: 10.1037/bul0000383

[143] Clarke A, Sorgenfrei M, Mulcahy J, Davie P, Friedrich C, McBride T. Adolescent mental health: A systematic review on the effectiveness of school-based interventions. Early Intervention Foundation. 2021:1-79. Available from: https://www.eif.org.uk/report/adolescent-mental-healtha-systematic-review-on-the-effectiveness-of-schoolbased-interventions

[144] Ramos Carranza P, Boat A, Hsieh TY. School-based discrimination and social-emotional learning among Latinx youth: The moderating role of school commitment to diversity, equity, and inclusion. Youth & Society. 2024;**56**:387-410

[145] Stettler NM, Katz LF. Minority stress, emotion regulation, and the parenting of sexual-minority youth. Journal of GLBT Family Studies. 2017;**13**:380-400. DOI: 10.1080/1550428X.2016.1273152

[146] Cahill H, Kern ML, Dadvand B, Cruickshank EW, Midford R, Smith C, et al. An integrative approach to evaluating the implementation of social and emotional learning and gender-based violence prevention education. International Journal of Emotional Education. 2019;**11**(1):135-152

[147] Cherewick M, Lebu S, Su C, Richards L, Njau PF, Dahl RE. Adolescent, caregiver and community experiences with a gender transformative, social emotional learning intervention. International Journal for Equity in Health. 2021;**20**(55):1-17. DOI: 10.1186/s12939-021-01395-5

[148] Malhotra N, Ayele ZE, Zheng D, Ben AY. Improving social and emotional learning for schoolgirls: An impact study of curriculum-based socio-emotional education in rural Uganda. International Journal of Educational Research. 2021;**108**:1-10. DOI: 10.1016/j.ijer.2021.101778

[149] Albright MI, Weissberg RP. School-family partnerships to promote social and emotional learning. In: Christenson SL, Reschly AL, editors. Handbook of School-Family Partnerships. New York: Routledge; 2010. pp. 246-265

[150] Ryan C. Engaging families to support lesbian, gay, bisexual, and transgender youth: The family acceptance project. Prevention Researcher. 2010;**17**(4):11-13

[151] Buckloh LM, Poquiz JL, Alioto A, Moyer DN, Axelrad ME. Best practices in working with parents and caregivers of transgender and gender diverse youth. Clinical Practice in Pediatric Psychology. 2022;**10**:325. DOI: 10.1037/cpp0000398

[152] Laursen EK, Birmingham SM. Caring relationships as a protective factor for at-risk youth: An ethnographic study. Families in Society. 2003;**84**:240-246. DOI: 10.1606/1044-3894.101

Chapter 5

Loneliness, Depression, Suicide

Nuray Simsek and Handan Zincir

Abstract

Traditionally, the phenomenon of loneliness was viewed as a painful feeling or a chronic affliction, whereas today it is seen as a signal to change behavior. There are many emotional distresses that accompany loneliness, but it is not clear whether they are a cause or a consequence of loneliness. Emotional states associated with loneliness include low self-esteem, shyness, anxiety, anger and tension, neuroticism and introversion, hypersensitivity, self-blame, and feelings of worthlessness. Loneliness is known to trigger depressive symptoms and suicidal thoughts and behaviors. Loneliness and depression are related concepts, yet they are distinct from each other. Loneliness has also been associated with suicide, with or without depression. Durkheim's suicide theory can be a guide in understanding the relationship between loneliness and suicide. Durkheim considered suicide as a social phenomenon. In a study analyzing comparative and longitudinal studies on loneliness, depressive symptoms, and suicidal ideation in adolescents, it was reported that it was not fully understood whether loneliness had a specific relationship with suicidal ideation and that studies gave mixed findings in this regard. As a result, loneliness is a concept associated with depression and suicide. It is possible to see this relationship in every age stage.

Keywords: loneliness, depression, suicide, behavior, social interaction, suicidal behaviors

1. Introduction

Loneliness is a universal emotion that can carry positive meanings for some and negative, frightening meanings for others. The reflections of this emotion can be seen anywhere in life, from art to philosophy, and from literature to health. Although loneliness, which is the subject of many works, is seen by some writers as a source that nourishes literature and poetry, it can sometimes be experienced as a challenging mental state for individuals.

With the intensification of living conditions today, people have increasingly begun to distance themselves from one another. Additionally, conducting many activities such as entertainment, shopping, and research via the internet has led individuals to withdraw from society, limit their social interactions, and become isolated. Traditionally, the phenomenon of loneliness was viewed as a painful feeling or a chronic affliction, whereas today it is seen as a signal to change behavior. In other words, loneliness, in one aspect, is a motivating signal for the individual to be sensitive to potential social threats and to renew the connections necessary for survival and development. However, the other aspect of loneliness reflects a perceived inconsistency between social needs and their presence in the environment. In the literature, it is associated with many negative conditions such as depression, suicidal tendencies, a decrease in positive emotions, poor sleep quality, and deterioration in overall health.

In this section, the concept of loneliness will be discussed and then the relationship between loneliness, depression, and suicide will be discussed.

2. The concept of loneliness

Loneliness is one of the most difficult concepts to define and measure, despite the fact that it can be experienced anywhere in the world, in any culture. Initial definitions have changed over time. According to the Oxford Universal Dictionary (1964), in the medieval period, being alone was used in the sense of completeness in one's singular existence. Therefore, the risks or negative consequences of being alone (and therefore of loneliness) were not perceived in the same way as they are today.

Systematic research on loneliness first emerged in England in 1938. Until the 1970s, the concept of loneliness was considered part of mental distress, such as depression and anxiety. However, in the 1980s, it began to be identified as a distinct clinical problem. Loneliness was a research focus until the 1980s, and in the 1990s, it continued to exist as both a therapeutic and research subject in the field of psychological counseling. From past to present, explanations regarding loneliness can be found in the literature of many disciplines.

Summarizing the dictionary definitions of the term "loneliness," D'Aboy noted that although loneliness is a familiar experience for most people, it lacks a consistent definition. The Oxford Dictionary lists only three sentences in its definition of loneliness that include its psychological context. The first definition describes loneliness as a quality or state, the second refers to a lack of society or friends, and the third includes the word "desolateness," which means desolation, solitude, or being deserted, to define the concept. In his study, D'Aboy listed synonyms used in different dictionaries to define loneliness, such as alienation, mental alienation, alone, estrangement, isolation, separation, and solitude [1, 2]. In the literature, the concepts used to define loneliness are noted to reflect both positive and negative connotations, as well as voluntary or involuntary states. The positive or negative meanings of loneliness are shaped by societal perceptions. Killeen explains the effect of the social perception process on the feeling of loneliness along a changing linear spectrum. At the negative end of this spectrum is alienation, while at the positive end is connectedness. Loneliness, social isolation, aloneness, and solitude are states that fall between these two extremes [3].

Loneliness can carry different meanings in different cultures, either positive or negative. For instance, while seclusion, defined as the act of withdrawing into oneself to merge with God by cutting off all ties with the external world, may be perceived as unbearable for someone in Western society, it can be viewed as a stage of purification and maturation in Eastern cultures. Similarly, in Mediterranean cultures where relationships are close-knit, loneliness generally evokes feelings of abandonment and isolation, whereas in Western societies, it can signify individuation and standing on one's own feet [4]. In this context, it can be said that the meaning of loneliness may vary from society to society and even within the same society over time.

Loneliness has been approached in different ways in various disciplines. While philosophers depict the individual's experience of loneliness in different manners,

DOI: http://dx.doi.org/10.5772/intechopen.1006101

there is a common ground among them. These common grounds include the understanding that loneliness is a fundamental element of human existence, a motivating force for the search for truth and meaning, a way for individuals to discover themselves, and a bridge to new possibilities. Additionally, critical life transitions are seen as a vital aspect of loneliness from a philosophical perspective, along with an individual's awareness of their own isolation [5]. In psychology, loneliness is associated with various phenomena such as individuals finding their inner world more appealing, avoiding relationships with others as a way to cope with fundamental anxiety, attachment issues during childhood, or the fundamental task of collaborating with others [2, 5–7]. Psychological theorists generally accept that loneliness is sometimes a result of individuals' own choices and is associated with childhood experiences that may contribute to feelings of loneliness in future years.

In Erikson's psychosocial development theory, the sixth stage is the intimacy versus isolation stage. In this stage, which covers the average age of twenty to thirty, the individual is expected to establish and maintain close relationships with other people. While the individual tends towards close relationships on the one hand, on the other hand, he/she tends to limit the relationships that he/she thinks will harm him/herself. This selectivity may also cause the individual to experience anxiety about being alone. When an individual is unable to establish and develop healthy relationships, loneliness becomes an important crisis for the individual [8].

3. Types of loneliness

In classifications of loneliness, attention is drawn to the emotional and social aspects of the concept. Loneliness is perceived as an unpleasant emotion, stemming from a sense of inadequacy or deficiency in social interactions [2, 7]. This deficiency in social domain can be attributed to the individual's perception and evaluations of themselves. Indeed, Peplau and Perlman listed these points in their definition of loneliness as follows:

1. Loneliness stems from inadequacy in an individual's social relationships.

2. Loneliness is a subjective experience that varies according to one's perception. Unlike social isolation, a person can also feel lonely in a crowd.

3. Loneliness is an unpleasant, distressing experience.

In general, it can be said that loneliness is related to the quality of relationships rather than their quantity. In their daily lives, people need not only the presence of others but also the presence of others who value them, whom they can trust and with whom they can communicate, plan, and work together to survive, thrive, and protect their own children. According to Frankl, the fundamental motivation that directs human behavior is finding meaning in life. He considers love as one of the significant values that add meaning to human life. Loving another person and engaging in interactions with them are expressed as ways to find meaning in life. Frankl emphasizes that individuals who experience a loss of meaning in life often struggle with detachment from daily life, introversion, and intense feelings of loneliness [2, 6].

4. Loneliness according to developmental phases

Loneliness is an emotion that can be experienced in every stage of life. However, its causes or accompanying circumstances may vary. Prolonged hospitalizations or physical barriers that restrict social activities can cause loneliness in individuals of all age groups. In addition to these, characteristics according to different stages of life are discussed below.

4.1 Childhood

It is observed that studies on loneliness are mainly conducted during adolescence and beyond, focusing on the relationship between loneliness experienced during these periods and early life experiences. According to Horney, children whose need for love is not met during childhood experience insecurity and anxiety. Children with anxiety develop unhealthy methods to cope with their feelings of loneliness and helplessness and use them in adulthood. For example, in order to gain people's love and closeness, they may pity themselves or try to put pressure on others. Furthermore, Bowlby's attachment theory suggests that early attachment styles are related to feelings of loneliness in adulthood. Additionally, experiences of childhood trauma are closely associated with loneliness observed during adolescence and beyond [2]. Rokach conducted a study examining loneliness during childhood and reported that the family serves as a protective factor against loneliness during this period [9].

In general, the family plays a significant role in childhood loneliness. A baby, who grows up with warm relationships and whose needs are met in a timely manner, gradually becomes aware of himself/herself and others and establishes relationships knowing that others are different individuals with different needs. However, in the opposite situation, the baby keeps the love environment he/she needs in his/her dreams and thus becomes lonely. If he/she cannot get out of this imaginary world in childhood, he/she may become more and more lonely and experience relationship problems. Negative parental attitudes, losses such as divorce and death, and introverted or aggressive personality traits are reported as risk factors for loneliness in childhood.

4.2 Adolescence

Adolescence is a period of estrangement from the family and peer relationships gain importance. This period between childhood and adulthood is one of the riskiest developmental periods in terms of loneliness. In studies related to loneliness, it is noteworthy that loneliness in young people is associated with parental loneliness, parental attitudes, childhood traumas, perceptions of inadequacy towards themselves and peer bullying. It has been reported that adolescents who perceive their parents' attitudes as democratic feel less lonely, their perception of social support from family and friends is higher, the level of loneliness increases as the perception of inadequacy increases, and adolescents with high levels of self-esteem and trust in people and secure attachment style feel less lonely [10–16].

Belonging to a group is one of the important needs of adolescents. Kavaklı reported that adolescents who experienced psychological or social exclusion felt lonelier, had a weaker sense of belonging, and had lower self-worth. In the same study, it was also noteworthy that psychological exclusion had a stronger effect than social exclusion [17].

In recent times, especially among adolescents, the use of communication technologies has rapidly increased, leading to many needs such as information, entertainment, and social interaction being fulfilled through the internet. It is observed that loneliness during this period also poses a risk for harmful use of communication technologies. Studies report that adolescents with high levels of loneliness also have high levels of smartphone and internet addiction [18–22].

4.3 Adulthood

It is known that negative life experiences such as parental divorce, neglect, and abuse in childhood have an impact on adult loneliness, as well as individual factors such as low self-esteem and lack of social skills. Again, moving, status changes, and changes in expectations for social interactions can be effective in the emergence of the feeling of loneliness. In addition, the feeling of loneliness may also be effective on the life satisfaction of individuals, and it has been reported that there is a positive relationship between loneliness and life satisfaction [23].

We can see that individuals who experience loneliness are accompanied by various emotional and behavioral reactions. Emotionally, they may feel worthlessness, exclusion, lack of love, isolation, sadness, anger, and depressive feelings. In behavioral reactions, behaviors such as introversion, avoiding social contact, and spending more time working and studying can be observed.

4.4 Old age

Loneliness in old age is a significant health problem that can arise from various factors. During this period, many individual and environmental factors such as retirement, loss of spouse, sensory losses, sociocultural limitations, economic losses, and low self-esteem, among others, can cause the elderly to feel lonely. The weakening of social interactions and loneliness in old age are associated with decreased life satisfaction, cognitive decline, depression, increased incidence of various diseases, and mortality [8, 24, 25]. Multiple chronic diseases, weakening of support systems, and dependency experienced by the elderly while performing their daily activities can also bring death anxiety.

5. Loneliness, depression and suicide

There is a multifaceted relationship between loneliness and physical and mental health. Illness and treatment processes often cause individuals to feel lonely [26–28]. Sometimes negative interpersonal relationships and loneliness can lead to an increase in symptoms. Here, the individual's feeling of loneliness may be related to many factors such as the vital threat posed by the disease, obstacles, stigma, isolation required for treatment, and the length of the disease and treatment process. As disease processes are effective in the emergence of feelings of loneliness in individuals, various physical and mental health problems may arise as a result of loneliness [29–31].

There are many emotional distresses that accompany loneliness, but it is not clear whether they are a cause or a consequence of loneliness. Emotional states associated with loneliness include low self-esteem, shyness, anxiety, anger and tension, neuroticism and introversion, hypersensitivity, self-blame, and feelings of worthlessness. Loneliness is known to trigger depressive symptoms and suicidal thoughts and behaviors. Individuals who feel lonely may perceive themselves as being utterly alone in the world, believing that no one can help them, and may consequently choose suicide as a way out [14, 18, 28, 32, 33].

Loneliness and depression are related concepts, yet they are distinct from each other [34, 35]. Initiating and maintaining social relationships is important for life satisfaction. It is reported that loneliness, a condition in which social interaction cannot be achieved at the desired level, is associated with depressive symptoms [36]. On the other hand, depression is associated with social withdrawal and negative evaluation of social relationships, which may increase the risk of loneliness [37].

There are many studies showing the relationship between loneliness and depression. In one study, it was reported that loneliness levels of adolescents were at a moderate level and there was a positive significant relationship between loneliness and depression [38]. Beutel et al. in their study examining the relationship between loneliness and mental health in the general population, reported that the rate of loneliness in the population was 10.5% and more than half of the loneliest participants were also depressed, and more than 40% of this group had anxiety and suicidal thoughts [34]. One of the most comprehensive studies examining the relationship between loneliness and depression is the longitudinal study by Cacioppo and colleagues. In this two-stage study, it was reported that there was a mutual interaction between loneliness and depressive symptoms in individuals over the age of 50 [39].

Another topic of interest is whether childhood loneliness is associated with depression in adulthood. Xerxa et al. have conducted a study that may shed light on this issue. In this study, which examined loneliness as a specific risk factor for psychiatric disorders in adults, 1420 participants aged 9, 11, and 13 were assessed and followed up. The initial assessments were completed by the age of 16. Subsequently, these individuals were reassessed at ages 19, 21, 25, and 30. All assessments were completed for 83% of the participants. In this study, childhood loneliness was found to be associated with anxiety and depression in both childhood and adulthood [40].

Loneliness has also been associated with suicide, with or without depression. Durkheim's suicide theory can be a guide in understanding the relationship between loneliness and suicide. Durkheim considered suicide as a social phenomenon. In his theory, he mentioned two main dimensions of suicide: social integration and social regulation. He stated that in selfish suicides, which is the first of the four types of suicide he has defined, the weakening of the ties of the individual with the community in which he is in starts the process of loneliness, and with this, the level of social integration begins to decrease [41].

Another approach that sheds light on the relationship between loneliness and suicide is the interpersonal theory of suicide. This theory focuses on thwarted belonging. It is stated that the absence of belongingness includes loneliness and the absence of relationships based on mutual compassion. In the integrated motivational-volitional model of suicidal behavior, it is suggested that factors such as thwarted belongingness and perceived burdensomeness direct the transition from suicidal ideation to suicide attempts [42]. In the literature, there is information suggesting that the sense of belongingness has a protective role against loneliness [43, 44]. Zhou et al. in a study conducted with university students, suggested that school belonging acts as a buffer against depression and suicide by reducing the negative effects of loneliness. In their study, they found a strong positive relationship between suicidal behavior and loneliness and depression, but a negative relationship between school belonging and suicidal behavior. They have indicated that depression and suicide levels are high among those with low levels of belongingness, whereas depression and suicidal behavior decrease with high levels of belongingness [45].

The feelings of loneliness and suicide rates vary according to age groups. Adolescents are a group with a high suicide rate. In studies conducted among adolescents, there are findings pointing to a relationship between loneliness and suicide. In one study, 65% of adolescents reported that there were times in their lives when they felt very lonely; 33.3% of adolescents in this group reported that they had thought about killing themselves in the last year, and 6.1% reported attempting suicide. Furthermore, found that these youths the likelihood of losing their lives due to suicide in the future higher than those who did not experience loneliness [33]. Park et al. who put forward similar results to this study, found a significant relationship between loneliness and depression and suicidal thoughts in their study conducted with the participation of 2668 adolescents. In this study, the rate of depression was 32.9% in adolescents who felt less lonely, while this rate was 71.9% in those who felt very lonely. The same difference was also valid for suicidal ideations, plans, and attempts. These rates increased from 10.3 to 39.3% in suicidal ideation, from 2.5 to 13.5% in suicide planning and from 1.7 to 8.9% in suicide attempts [46].

In a study analyzing comparative and longitudinal studies on loneliness, depressive symptoms, and suicidal ideation in adolescents, it was reported that it was not fully understood whether loneliness had a specific relationship with suicidal ideation and that studies gave mixed findings in this regard. One of the findings of this study is that loneliness is a predictor of suicidal ideation while trying to adapt to the changes that occur in early adolescence. In some of the studies, it was reported that loneliness predicted suicidal ideation independently of depression and negative life events, whereas in some other studies, loneliness did not predict suicidal ideation when problems such as depression, hopelessness and substance abuse could be managed. These different findings suggest the need for further research [37]. Additionally, it has been reported that anxiety in adolescents is related to both depression and loneliness; therefore, it should be considered as a control variable in the relationship between loneliness and depression. [37, 46]. In this regard, the study of Yang et al. in which depression, anxiety, and loneliness were examined in a network model contains important findings. In this study, unhappiness, one of the sub-dimensions of loneliness, was found to be associated with the sub-dimensions of depression such as anhedonia, sad mood, and suicide. Furthermore, a strong correlation was found between anhedonia and not feeling together with others. In the model, the relationship between suicide and various factors such as psychomotor agitation, has feelings of worthlessness, unhappiness, being excluded, and lack of someone to seek help from has been established. When examining the relationship between loneliness and anxiety, the relationship between isolation and a high level of anxiety symptoms is particularly noteworthy [47].

Another group with a high suicide rate is the elderly, and loneliness is reported to be among the risk factors for suicide in elderly individuals [44, 48]. Lapane et al. conducted a systematic review of studies examining the effects of loneliness and social isolation on health in elderly individuals residing in long-term care facilities. In this study, while there were studies indicating the relationship between loneliness and suicidal ideation, it was emphasized in the two studies examined that loneliness indirectly affected suicidal ideation through depression [35]. Niu and colleagues compared loneliness, hopelessness, and depression between elderly individuals who died by suicide and healthy elderly individuals in a rural area of China. The elderly individuals who died by suicide were examined through psychological autopsy. The study concluded that suicide cases had higher levels of loneliness, hopelessness, and depression, as well as lower levels of social support compared to the living comparison group [44].

Another important aspect that needs to be addressed in the relationship between loneliness, depression, and suicide is the loneliness experienced after sudden losses and its relationship with depression and suicide. Sudden losses can cause a person to feel lonely in relation to the sudden loss of a trusted person. Possible accusatory approaches and negative criticism after sudden losses can lead to more stigmatization, guilt, shame, and social isolation. Loneliness and inadequacy in social support systems experienced during this process are reported as risk factors for suicide attempts. Pitman and colleagues' study is noteworthy in this regard. In their study conducted with 3193 individuals who experienced sudden loss, they found a strong relationship between loneliness scores and the likelihood of suicidal ideation or suicide attempt after loss [42]. Spino et al. also emphasized the importance of social support systems in reducing loneliness and depression experienced after suicide. In their study, they noted that as personal network and relationship scores increased among bereaved individuals, depression and loneliness scores decreased [49].

6. Solution proposals

In this section, the relationship between loneliness and depression and suicide is discussed in the light of the literature. As a result, it can be said that loneliness is a concept closely related to depression and suicide. In this context, it is thought that interventions aimed at preventing loneliness or coping with loneliness will contribute to the prevention of depression and suicide.

Perlman and Peplau, in accordance with their definitions of loneliness, have proposed three groups of strategies to cope with loneliness. These strategies are altering the desired level of social contact to cope with loneliness, increasing the achieved level of social contact, and changing the importance and/or perceived magnitude of the discrepancy between the desired and achieved levels of social interaction. Perlman and Peplau have suggested recommendations such as identifying activities that are enjoyable alone, changing standards for selecting friends, forming new social relationships, or improving existing ones in order to achieve these goals [50].

Rokach, who has also provided recommendations for coping with loneliness, conceptualizes coping with loneliness within three overarching categories. These include increasing awareness of one's thoughts and feelings and sometimes connecting to a higher power in the universe and exploring the meaning of life, making efforts to build social bridges that can reconnect with others, and involve distancing and denial [51]. In studies on loneliness, it is necessary to distinguish between social isolation and loneliness. While social isolation is an objective situation that can be seen by others, loneliness is a subjective feeling experienced within oneself. Social isolation is considered to be among the etiology or risk factors of loneliness. Loneliness, on the other hand, mostly describes the emotional reaction of being alone, which is not desired by the person. It is reported that physical and social isolation and emotional deprivation are risk factors for loneliness in individuals.

Therefore, the assessment to social isolation and attempts to reduce etc., it can be counted among the interventions to prevent loneliness. At this point, the individual should be encouraged to establish and maintain a meaningful relationship with at least one person; to establish a balance between emotional dependence and independence in the established relationship; to participate in social activities and get satisfaction from this; to use effective interpersonal communication skills such as self-disclosure, assertiveness, sensitivity, cooperation, and sincerity; to volunteer to ask for help from others; and to verbally express that they can receive adequate social support. It is also important to make evaluations in different age groups depending on their age characteristics in studies on combating loneliness. While evaluating loneliness in an adolescent, especially the evaluation of peer relationships has an important place. In adolescence, it may be useful to encourage participation in peer relationships and sports activities, and to direct them to activities such as keeping pets. In elderly individuals, the evaluation of sensory functions and how losses in these areas are reflected in interaction with others should be addressed [7, 52, 53]. Additionally, whether elderly individuals live in a care facility or in their own homes, regular visits and frequent contact via phone or other means significantly reduce feelings of loneliness in the elderly.

Loneliness has been particularly highlighted in studies related to depression and suicide, especially during the Covid-19 pandemic. Therefore, we believe it would be beneficial to include recommendations from studies conducted during the pandemic. For instance, Rabasco et al. examined the relationship between social distancing measures during the pandemic and loneliness, depression, and suicide. They found no association between them. On the other hand, in the same study, it was concluded that social interaction, especially electronic social contact, reduced loneliness, depression, and suicide. The study emphasized the importance of social contact that individuals establish with others, suggesting that it does not necessarily have to be face-to-face; interaction electronically is recommended [54]. In another study during the period, Xiao et al. evaluated the impact of loneliness on depression in adolescents along with multiple variables. They determined that loneliness had a significant effect on depression. In multiple models, they proposed that goal orientation and psychological resilience mediate the relationship between loneliness and depression. Indeed, according to this, loneliness can be said to increase depression by negatively affecting both goal orientation and resilience. Based on this finding, the authors recommended interventions aimed at enhancing goal orientation and psychological resilience in adolescents. Additionally, this study suggests that cognitive restructuring reduces the feeling of loneliness and therefore can be used as a strategy to reduce depression [55]. In recent years, loneliness has been seen as a public health problem and reflected in the policies of countries. In 2018, the UK appointed the world's first ever "Minister for Loneliness." In launching the first cross-government strategy to tackle loneliness, Prime Minister Theresa May said that loneliness is one of the biggest public health challenges of our time. In this coping strategy for dealing with loneliness, the primary goals are to establish organizations that support and enhance relationships, build community infrastructure that strengthens social connections, and create a culture that supports the connections within communities.

In line with this, activities such as the government collaborating with local authorities, voluntary community organizations, and employers, as well as organizing mobile support services like "rural café caravans" that promote social cohesion, have been planned [56]. Furthermore, in Japan, the increasing suicide rates have led the government to focus on individuals living alone. In order to reduce social loneliness and isolation among single individuals and to strengthen connections between people, a Minister of Loneliness has been appointed [57]. In our country and in many other countries, coping with loneliness has been included in the scope of work of governments, and work for lonely individuals has been included within the Ministry of Family and Social Services.

As a result, loneliness is a concept associated with depression and suicide. It is possible to see this relationship in every age stage. Health threats such as pandemics have been associated with loneliness and an increase in depression and suicidal tendencies. In this context, interventions to prevent loneliness are considered important at both individual and societal levels.

Author details

Nuray Simsek and Handan Zincir*
Faculty of Health Sciences, Department of Nursing, Erciyes University, Kayseri, Türkiye

*Address all correspondence to: handanzincir@gmail.com

References

[1] D'Aboy JE. Loneliness: An investigation of terminology. Dissertation Abstracts International. 1972;**33**(7-B):3281. Available from: https://www.proquest.com/docview/288428802?pq-origsite=gscholar&fromopenview=true

[2] Rosedale M. Loneliness: An exploration of meaning. Journal of the American Psychiatric Nurses Association. 2007;**13**(4):201-209

[3] Ulutaş E, Gökçen A. Toplum tipleri ve yalnızlık halleri. OPUS–Uluslararası Toplum Araştırmaları Dergisi. 2019;**10**(17):1809-1835

[4] Yaşar MR. Yalnızlık. F.Ü. Sosyal Bilimler Dergisi. 2007;**17**(1):237-260

[5] Karnick PM. Feeling lonely: Theoretical perspectives. Nursing Science Quarterly. 2005;**18**(1):7-12

[6] Karahan TF, Sardoğan ME. Psikolojik danışma ve psikoterapide kuramlar. 4. Basım ed. Ankara: Nobel Akademik Yayıncılık; 2016

[7] Öz F. Yalnızlık. In: İçn: Sağlık Alanında Temel Kavramlar. Yenilenmiş 2. Baskı ed. Ankara: Mattek Matbaacılık; 2010. pp. 149-170

[8] Engin E, Uğuryol M, Kaçmaz ED. Yalnızlık kavramı ve sağlıklı yaşam üzerine etkileri: gözden geçirme. Uluslararası Sosyal Araştırmalar Dergisi. 2016;**9**(42):1101-1105

[9] Rokach A. Loneliness updated: An introduction. The Journal of Psychology. 2012;**146**(1):1-6

[10] Çeçen AR. Öğrencilerinin cinsiyetlerine ve ana baba tutum algılarına göre yalnızlık ve sosyal destek düzeylerinin incelenmesi. Türk Eğitim Bilimleri Dergisi. 2008;**6**(3):415-431

[11] Çimşir E, Akdoğan R. Yalnızlık ve yetersizlik duygusu arasındaki ilişkide kendini saklamanın aracı rolü. Anadolu Journal of Educational Sciences International. 2019;**9**(1):111-128

[12] Duyan V, ve ark. Lisede okuyan öğrencilerin yalnızlık durumlarına etki eden değişkenlerin incelenmesi. Eğitim ve Bilim. 2008;**33**(150):28-41

[13] Erdoğdu MY, Gündoğmuş G. Yalnızlık düzeyinin yordanmasında anne baba tutumları ve okul tükenmişliğinin rolü. Mehmet Akif Ersoy Üniversitesi Sosyal Bilimler Enstitüsü Dergisi. 2020;**31**:159-168

[14] Karahan TF, Sardoğan ME, Şar AH, ve ark. Üniversite öğrencilerinin yalnızlık düzeyleri ile benlik saygısı düzeyleri arasındaki ilişkiler. Ondokuz Mayıs Üniversitesi Eğitim Fakültesi Dergisi. 2004;**18**:27-39

[15] Karakuş Ö. Ergenlerde bağlanma stilleri ve yalnızlık arasındaki ilişki. Toplum ve Sosyal Hizmet. 2012;**23**(2):33-46

[16] Türkkan T, Odacı H. Lise öğrencilerinin çocukluk çağı örselenme yaşantıları ile bilişsel çarpıtma ve yalnızlık eğilimleri arasındaki ilişki. Klinik Psikiyatri. 2019;**22**:93-103

[17] Kavaklı M. Psikolojik dışlanma ve sosyal dışlanma arasındaki farklılık: Benlik değeri, yalnızlık ve genel aidiyet duygusu üzerindeki etkileri. Black Sea Journal of Social Sciences. 2019;**11**(20):45-55

[18] Aktaş H, Yılmaz N. Üniversite gençlerinin yalnızlık ve utangaçlık unsurları açısından akıllı telefon bağımlılığı. International Journal of Social Sciences and Education Research. 2017;**3**(1):85-100

[19] Çakır Ö, Oğuz E. Lise öğrencilerinin yalnızlık düzeyleri ile akıllı telefon bağımlılığı arasındaki ilişki. Mersin Üniversitesi Eğitim Fakültesi Dergisi. 2017;**13**(1):418-429

[20] Çakır V, Çakır V. Yalnızlık ve televizyon kullanımı. Selçuk İletişim. 2011;**7**(1):131-147

[21] Durak Batıgün A, Hasta D. İnternet bağımlılığı: Yalnızlık ve kişilerarası ilişki tarzları açısından bir değerlendirme. Anadolu Psikiyatri Dergisi. 2010;**11**:213-219

[22] Oktan V. Üniversite öğrencilerinde problemli internet kullanımı, yalnızlık ve algılanan sosyal destek. Kastamonu Eğitim Dergisi. 2015;**23**(1):281-292

[23] Avşaroğlu S, Hudaynazarova A, Nurkoyuncu S, ve ark. Yetişkinlerin yaşam doyumu, yalnızlık ve öz-tiksinme düzeyleri arasındaki ilişkinin incelenmesi. MANAS Sosyal Araştırmalar Dergisi. 2021;**10**(1):183-198

[24] Kapıkıran Ş. Yaşlılarda yalnızlık ile yaşam doyumu arasındaki ilişki: Sosyal desteğin aracılık rolünün sınanması. Yaşlı Sorunları Araştırma Dergisi. 2016;**9**:13-25

[25] Şimşek N, Küçük Öztürk G, Yüceler KH. Yaşlılık ve yalnızlık. Uluslararası Sosyal Araştırmalar Dergisi. 2018;**11**(58):496-499

[26] Bal Yılmaz H, Işık Esenay F, Karayağız MG. Kanserli çocuklarda yalnızlık. Ege Pediatri Bülteni. 2007;**14**(3):171-175

[27] Kavlak O, Saruhan A. İnfertil kadınlarda yalnızlık düzeyi ve bunu etkileyen faktörlerin incelenmesi. Ege Tıp Dergisi. 2002;**41**(4):229-232

[28] Pritchard ME, Yalch KL. Relationships among loneliness, interpersonal dependency, and disordered eating in young adults. Personality and Individual Differences. 2009;**46**(3):341-346

[29] Hawkley LC, Cacioppo JT. Loneliness matters: A theoretical and empirical review of consequences and mechanisms. Annals of Behavioral Medicine. 2010;**40**(2):1-14

[30] Masi MC, Chen HY, Hawkley LC, et al. Meta-analysis of interventions to reduce loneliness. Personality and Social Psychology Review. 2011;**15**(3):219-266

[31] Yanguas J, Pinazo-Henandis S, Tarazona-Santabalbina FJ. The complexity of loneliness. Acta Bio-Medica. 2018;**89**(2):302-314

[32] Durak BA. İntihar olasılığı ve cinsiyet: İletişim becerileri, yaşamı sürdürme nedenleri, yalnızlık ve umutsuzluk açısından bir inceleme. Türk Psikoloji Dergisi. 2008;**23**(62):65-75

[33] Eskin M. Ergenlikte yalnızlık, başetme yöntemleri ve yalnızlığın intihar davranışı ile ilişkisi. Klinik Psikiyatri. 2001;**4**:5-11

[34] Beutel ME, Klein EM, Brähler E, et al. Loneliness in the general population: Prevalence, determinants and relations to mental health. BMC Psychiatry. 2017;**17**(1):97. DOI: 10.1186/s12888-017-1262-x

[35] Lapane KL, Lim E, McPhillips E, Barooah A, Yuan Y, Dube CE. Health effects of loneliness and social isolation in older adults living in congregate long

term care settings: A systematic review of quantitative and qualitative evidence. Archives of Gerontology and Geriatrics. 2022;**102**:104728. DOI: 10.1016/j.archger.2022.104728

[36] Heinrich LM, Gullone E. The clinical significance of loneliness: A literature review. Clinical Psychology Review. 2006;**26**(6):695-718. DOI: 10.1016/j.cpr.2006.04.002

[37] Lasgaard M, Goossens L, Elklit A. Loneliness, depressive symptomatology, and suicide ideation in adolescence: Cross-sectional and longitudinal analyses. Journal of Abnormal Child Psychology. 2011;**39**(1):137-150. DOI: 10.1007/s10802-010-9442-x

[38] Ceyhan E, Ceyhan AA. Üniversite psikolojik danışma merkezine başvuran öğrencilerin yalnızlık ve depresyon düzeyleri. Eğitim ve Bilim. 2011;**36**(160):81-92

[39] Cacioppo JT, Hughes ME, Waite LJ, Hawkley LC, Thisted RA. Loneliness as a specific risk factor for depressive symptoms: Cross-sectional and longitudinal analyses. Psychology and Aging. 2006;**21**(1):140-151. DOI: 10.1037/0882-7974.21.1.140

[40] Xerxa Y, Rescorla LA, Shanahan L, Tiemeier H, Copeland WE. Childhood loneliness as a specific risk factor for adult psychiatric disorders. Psychological Medicine. 2023;**53**(1):227-235. DOI: 10.1017/S0033291721001422

[41] Kołodziej-Sarzyńska M, Majewska M, Juchnowicz D, Karakuła-Juchnowicz H. Risk factors of suicide with reference to the theory of social integration by Émile Durkheim. Psychiatria Polska. 2019;**53**(4):865-881. DOI: 10.12740/PP/92217

[42] Pitman AL, King MB, Marston L, Osborn DPJ. The association of loneliness after sudden bereavement with risk of suicide attempt: A nationwide survey of bereaved adults. Social Psychiatry and Psychiatric Epidemiology. 2020;**55**(8):1081-1092. DOI: 10.1007/s00127-020-01921

[43] Mellor D, Stokes M, Firth L, Hayashi Y, Cummins R. Need for belonging, relationship satisfaction, loneliness, and life satisfaction. Personality and Individual Differences. 2008;**45**:213-218

[44] Niu L, Jia C, Ma Z, Wang G, Sun B, Zhang D, et al. Loneliness, hopelessness and suicide in later life: A case-control psychological autopsy study in rural China. Epidemiology and Psychiatric Sciences. 2020;**24**:29. DOI: 10.1017/S2045796020000335

[45] Zhou C, Gao M, Shi X, Zhang Z. Suicidal behavior, depression and loneliness among college students: The role of school belonging. Psychology, Health & Medicine. 2023;**28**(6):1520-1526. DOI: 10.1080/13548506.2022.2113105

[46] Park HG, Jeong S, Kwon M. Factors related to depression according to the degree of loneliness in adolescents with severe friend-relationship stress. Healthcare (Basel). 2023;**11**(9):1354. DOI: 10.3390/healthcare11091354

[47] Yang M, Wei W, Ren L, Pu Z, Zhang Y, Li Y, et al. How loneliness linked to anxiety and depression: A network analysis based on Chinese university students. BMC Public Health. 2023;**23**(1):2499. DOI: 10.1186/s12889-023-17435-4

[48] De Leo D. Late-life suicide in an aging world. Nature Aging. 2022;**2**(1):7-12. DOI: 10.1038/s43587-021-00160-1

[49] Spino E, Kameg KM, Cline TW, Terhorst L, Mitchell AM. Impact of social

support on symptoms of depression and loneliness in survivors bereaved by suicide. Archives of Psychiatric Nursing. 2016;**30**(5):602-606. DOI: 10.1016/j.apnu.2016.02.001

[50] Perlman D, Peplau LA. Toward a social psychology of loneliness. In: Duck B, Gihour R, editors. Personal Relationships in Disorder. London: Academic Press; 1981. pp. 31-56

[51] Rokach A. Cultural background and coping with loneliness. The Journal of Psychology. 1999;**133**(2):217-229

[52] Hakverdioğlu Yönt G. Yalnızlık riski. İçn: Erkal İlhan S, Ançel G, Hakverdioğlu Yönt G, edt. Hemşirelik tanıları girişimleri sonuçları. Ankara: Andaç Yayınları, 2017; 648-650

[53] Wilkinson JM, Ahern NR. Prentice Hall Nursing Diagnosis Handbook with NIC Intervention and NOC Outcomes. 9th ed. New Jersey: Pearson Education, Upper Saddle River; 2009. pp. 391-394

[54] Rabasco A, Corcoran V, Andover M. Alone but not lonely: The relationship between COVID-19 social factors, loneliness, depression, and suicidal ideation. PLoS One. 2021;**16**(12):e0261867. DOI: 10.1371/journal.pone.0261867

[55] Xiao MQ, Liu XT, Huang QX, He SQ. The effect of loneliness on depression in young people: A multiple mediated effects model. European Review for Medical and Pharmacological Sciences. 2023;**27**(18):8614-8627. DOI: 10.26355/eurrev_202309_33786

[56] A connected society A strategy for tackling loneliness – laying the foundations for change. Available from: https://assets.publishing.service.gov.uk/government/uploads/system/uploads/attachment_data/file/936725/6.4882_DCMS_Loneliness_Strategy_web_Update_V2.pdf

[57] Japonya'da "Yalnızlık Bakanı" Atandı. Available from: https://www.trthaber.com/haber/dunya/japonyada-yalnizlik-bakani-atandi-559601.html

Chapter 6

The Influence of Big Five Personality Traits on Depression and Suicidal Behavior

Junting Chen and Hao Huang

Abstract

In our study, we investigated the interrelations and impact of the Big Five personality factors—neuroticism, extraversion, conscientiousness, agreeableness, openness—on depression and suicidal behavior. Neuroticism, being associated with emotional instability and sensitivity to stress, contributes substantially to increasing the risk of depression and ideation about suicide. Extraversion and conscientiousness have specific protective effects mediated by social support and efficient coping strategies. Whereas these roles of agreeableness and openness are more subtle and contribute to resilience in very context-dependent ways. Lastly, we also propose targeted interventions according to the characteristics of each Big Five personality trait, including cognitive behavioral therapy and mindfulness-based stress reduction for neuroticism, positive psychology interventions for extraversion, etc. Since then, future research directions shall be integrated into therapeutic approaches and comprehensive care models to reduce depression and suicidal behavior on an international scale.

Keywords: big five personality traits, depression, suicidal behavior, mental health, psychological interventions

1. Introduction

Depression is among the most prevalent mental illnesses in the world and forms a significant burden to the public health domain. Concerning the Global Burden of Disease (GBD) study, the global disability-adjusted life years (DALYs) for all causes, including depression, moved from 2.63 billion for the period ending in 2010 to 2.88 billion through the year 2021 [1]. This is why depression is called the "common cold" of psychology [2]. Synchronously, Suicide is a vital global public health issue, contributing notably to the burden of disease. Depression is a major risk factor for suicide, the most common psychiatric condition found in suicide decedents is Major Depressive Disorder [3].

Depression creates a significant risk of death by suicide [4]. In depressed patients, a higher risk of suicide is associated with the presence, duration, and severity of depressive symptoms [5]. Personality psychology can account for individual differences that may be influencing the outcome of mental health. The big five personality traits, in particular, are from a range of openness, conscientiousness, extraversion, agreeableness, and neuroticism, forming an excellent foundation on which to understand the differences in predicting mental health disorders, such as depression and suicidal behavior. Concluding from the previous study, neuroticism—characterized by emotional instability and negative affectivity—appears to be a robust risk factor not only for depression but also for suicidal ideation. High levels of neuroticism are related to increased stress vulnerability, depression, and suicidal ideation [6]. Conscientiousness and extraversion, however, in more general terms, play protective roles in these relations. Conscientiousness is related to well-developed, healthy ways of coping and tends to enhance perceived social support [7]. The earlier study also points out that there may be some effects of openness and agreeableness on mental conditions, but these outcomes may be easily influenced by external factors. Higher openness may be related positively to resilience under stress, while agreeableness may be related to more accessible access to social support networks, which serve as protective factors against depression and suicide [8].

Studies of Big Five personality traits provide significant information for prediction and further use in the treatment of depression and suicidal behavior. Therefore, the interaction of personality traits with mental health outcomes is essential in the context of prevention and intervention. This chapter discusses the relationship between Big Five personality traits and mental health disorders, particularly depression and suicide, from psychological and physiological perspectives. The second point will explore the interaction effects of different impactful personality traits on depression and suicidal behavior. The last part is about the strategies for prevention, directions of intervention, and policy recommendations according to the personality traits in depression treatment and suicide prevention guidelines to reduce the burden globally.

2. The association between big five personality traits and mental health disorder

The Big Five personality traits describe openness, conscientiousness, extraversion, agreeableness, and neuroticism, with which one can understand individual differences in behavior, emotion, and cognition. Openness is a high appreciation of art, feelings, adventure, unusual ideas, imagination, and curiosity. Conscientiousness deals with self-discipline, carefulness, and reliability, and people who have a high level of conscientiousness are organized, dependable, and goal-oriented. Extraversion refers to being energized, optimistic, outgoing, and gregarious, showing more activity and being reinforced positively by situational contexts than introverted people, who are stimulated by lower stimulation and solitary activities. Agreeableness generally pertains to social harmony and includes cooperation, trustworthy behavior, kindness, and consideration. Conversely, Neuroticism refers to negative affect and emotional instability [9, 10]. These personality dimensions can be measured by self-reports like the Big Five Inventory (BFI) or the NEO Personality Inventory (NEO-PI-R), which demand the individual to describe how much they engage in behavior typical of each trait. The reliability and validity of these instruments have been well established across a wide range of populations and contexts, making them valuable for research and clinical use in understanding personality and its impact on mental health [11].

Mental health disorders are generally described as a diverse range of conditions that impact mood, thinking, and behavior. Among these, depression plays a highly significant role as the single most common and disabling mental health condition and has a tremendous impact on an individual's functional efficiency in daily life.

It generates low moods, loss of interest, and diverse physical and emotional issues among individuals. There lies a great concern between depression and suicide. Depression is a major risk factor for suicide, with many individuals experiencing severe depressive symptoms contemplating or attempting suicide [12]. There is direct evidence that neuroticism is closely related to depression and suicidal behavior. High-level neuroticism reflects high emotional instability and an oversensitivity to stress. This trait is associated with an increase in the activity of the hypothalamic-pituitary-adrenal (HPA) axis, high cortisol levels, and a prolonged response to stress. Such physiological reactions make high-neuroticism individuals more susceptible to depressive symptoms and suicide ideation dysfunctional behavior [13]. One study showed the fact that neuroticism is positively related to the severity of depression and, therefore, its substantial risk factor for morbidity [14]. However, extraversion will generally go against the grain of depression and suicide behavior due to the management of positive affect, especially in social support, which is high and good social regulation. Extraverts are more likely to be engaged in social activities and have good relations, which is protective from the risk of depression [15]. It has been shown that extraversion is related to low levels of cortisol reactivity to stressors, giving additional weight to its protective status [16]. Yet another trait that is a contributory factor for lower depression and suicidal risk is conscientiousness. Conscientious individuals display mature and effective coping strategies, have greater impulse control, and are more responsible, with a lower level of neuroinflammation, which is a recognized factor in depression [17]. Agreeableness and openness should also be taken into account, but they are more complicated and context-dependent in their effects. High agreeableness has increased social support networks, and positive interpersonal relationships will reduce the risk of depression and suicide [18]. Although the highest openness is marked for highly creative minds and manifested through interests in many topics, the majority's findings were inconsistent. In a meta-analysis of 175 studies, it was found that agreeableness and openness were largely unrelated to depressive symptoms [19]. However, some studies have shown an inverse relationship between agreeableness and openness with depression [20, 21]. The different research results may be attributed to the differences in research samples, personality traits, depressive symptoms assessment methods, national cultural background as well as adjustment for potential confounding factors.

3. Impact of personality traits on depression and suicidal behavior

3.1 Neuroticism: a risk factor for depression and suicidal behavior

Neuroticism is the equivalent of emotional instability, anxiety, mood swings, worry, and sadness. High neurotic individuals are more likely to have strong negative emotions and easily be overwhelmed by any stressors; they are much more hopeful and desperate. Sensitivity to negative affect and stress can emerge as a potent mechanism in the emergence and severity of depressive symptoms and suicidal behaviors [22]. Neuroticism influences one's perceptions and responses to stress. High neuroticism would, in turn, lead to rumination, whereby individuals keep their minds centered on their agony and negative experiences. This rumination can lead to a vicious cycle of worsening mood and increased depressive symptoms. For example, neurotic people tend not to regulate their emotions effectively and are, therefore, more prone to depression [23]. High neuroticism is also linked to maladaptive coping strategies, such as avoidant behaviors and substance use, which may worsen mental health problems and increase the risk of suicidal behavior. For instance, neurotic patients often become addicted to alcohol or drugs to control their bad moods, and these forms of substance abuse transform into another stratified level of risks associated with depression and suicide estimations [24]. Importantly, neuroticism is the underlying factor that mediates adverse childhood experiences (ACEs) to adulthood with depressive disorder and suicidal behaviors. Thus, people who have developed increased neuroticism and have also experienced increased ACEs are highly predisposed to the development of depression and suicide ideation [25]. Emotional regulation, perception of stress, and coping strategies are the mediators in the neuroticism-depression relationship and suicidal behavior. In people with a high degree of neuroticism, increased emotional sensitivity, a ruminative nature, and maladaptive coping imply increased vulnerability to depressive symptoms and suicidal thoughts.

3.2 Extraversion: protective against depression and suicidal behavior

Extraversion is generally considered one of the protective factors for depression and suicidal behavior, as being positively associated with all desirable emotional experiences, sociability, and strong social support. Extraverted people have more contact with others, so their positive emotional experiences are more and have a buffering influence on well-being in terms of more stress or increased negative emotions. This trait is linked to greater positivity of affect and more robust resiliency, so the risk entailed by depression is reduced [26]. Another reason for high positive health effects can also be given to extraversion's association with affective positive regulation. High extraverts often manifest positive affect that culminates with more resistance to stress, which, in turn, reduces the propensity to depression. This proclivity toward positive emotionality is a pretty crucial protective factor against the development of depression and suicidal thoughts [27]. However, the protective influence of extraversion needs to be cautiously noted as it varies across different conditions. While extraversion has led to positive mental health in almost every situation, one research reported that its association with suicidal ideation appears paradoxical in conditions of sleep deprivation and insomnia. This reflects that the protective effects of extraversion are context-dependent, and in conditions of stress or physical tiring, extraverts might even feel more vulnerable [28]. For instance, in one study concerning the pandemic and its related consequences, it was observed in adolescents that higher levels of extraversion were associated with a steeper rise in feelings of depression and a third of this overall effect was mediated through an increase in loneliness. The findings would also not be consistent with earlier findings, which found that extraverted adolescents experienced reduced depressive feelings and that extraversion was only a protective factor. In situations where peer contact is low, extraversion could be a liability [29]. Extraversion protects against depression and suicidal behavior due to increased social support and positive emotional regulation. Extraverts would probably be more proactive in writing into their social networks, which would provide emotional support and protect them from stressors. However, the protective effects of extraversion can be context-dependent, as evidenced by increased vulnerability to suicidal ideation during sleep deprivation or severe insomnia.

3.3 Conscientiousness and its protective role against depression and suicidal behavior

Conscientiousness is a personality trait labeled as hardworking and diligent behavior that leads to orderliness, a sense of duty, purposefulness, and dependability.

High levels of conscientiousness protect against depression or suicidal behavior since highly conscientious individuals will have good coping strategies, impulse control, and a sense of duty, which prevent them from spiraling downwards in cases that typify depression. Conscientiousness is inversely associated with the indication of depressive symptoms, showing its protective role against mental issues [6, 30]. Highly conscientious individuals score highest on indices of good health. The tendency to practice healthy lifestyles, such as routine exercise, proper nutrition, and avoidance of dangerous behaviors, such as smoking and over-use of alcohol, increases well-being and lowers the risk of depression [31]. Furthermore, the presence of the moderation component that comes along with conscientiousness in this scenario is that which enables perceived stress in an individual to be positively correlated with depressive symptomatology. More conscientious individuals can handle increasing stress without necessarily plunging into depression. As such, conscientiousness buffers the positive relationship between perceived stress and depression, hinting at more excellent resiliency to the ill effects of stress for conscientious people [32]. However, not all the benefits of conscientiousness apply universally. Several studies speculated on a protective value lower against uncontrollable stress and a graded decrease in anxious-depressive morbidity across trait levels of conscientiousness over time. For instance, highly conscientious individuals faced with uncontrollable and genuinely stressful life circumstances might show an amplified response in brain stress-response systems involving the amygdala and insula, with a commensurate increase in output of the stress hormone cortisol. It implies that while conscientiousness has a general protective effect against vulnerability under stress, it is also able to predict susceptibility to specific adverse responses under conditions of stress. Hence, due diligence is achieved not only as a matter of a desirable quality but, instead as one tied in with costs or benefits according to the extent of control one has over the event [33].

3.4 The role of agreeableness in mitigating depression and suicidal behavior

Agreeableness is a personality domain characterized by attributes such as trust, altruism, kindness, affection, and other prosocial behaviors, which make agreeable people more likely to behave cooperatively in ways that lead to supportive social networks and lessened risks for depression or suicide. High agreeableness might lead to enhanced emotional resilience through relationship formation with support and a tendency for prosocial behaviors, which might be fundamental to mitigating stress and negative emotions [34]. Research conducted has shown high agreeableness to act as a protective factor, enacting more positive interactions with other people and hence reducing isolation feelings and loneliness, which are significant precursors of depression and suicidal ideation [35]. Meantime, interventions directed at making people more agreeable have included exercises in kind acts and compassionate behavior and are successful in considerably lowering the level of co-occurring depression and raising life satisfaction, particularly for those low in agreeableness at base rate [36]. This suggests that enhancing pro-social behaviors and social relations may be critical in interventions that are directed to mental health against depression and suicide.

3.5 Openness and its complex relationship with mental health

Openness to experience is a personality trait characterized by imagination, creativity, curiosity, and a preference for novelty and variety. High openness in individuals means being flexible and open to gaining new experiences, which is an excellent asset to positive mental health and resilience to stress and depressive symptoms [37]. However, the relationship between openness and mental health is complex and multifaceted. Studies indicate that openness can play both protective and risk roles in mental health. High openness is most related to the ability to create flexible minds and solve problems under any condition, which in turn supports adjusting stress more adaptively and preventing depression. They are generally more changeable and open to new kinds of coping strategies, which enable the reduction of the impacts of stressors and improve the general state of mental health [38]. On the other hand, high openness might relate to enhanced sensitivity toward emotional experiences that, in turn, at times, improve an individual's vulnerability in a situation. For instance, high openness introduces sensitivity to significant events in life that could create depression if not handled correctly. A study exploring the relationship between stressful life events and openness found that while it was related to more intellectual engagement, openness also mediated the relationship between stress and depression. This relationship was found to be complex [39]. Yet some studies suggest that the association of only modest strength is between openness and depressive episodes. And this relation changes to get lower, especially after controlling for the difference in educational levels. There are two possible explanations for this finding. First, the educational level might interact with openness and amplify the link between openness and depression. Alternatively, it may suggest that the aspect of openness correlated with educational level acts as a proxy for education [40, 41]. This implies that educational level might be an important moderating variable in the

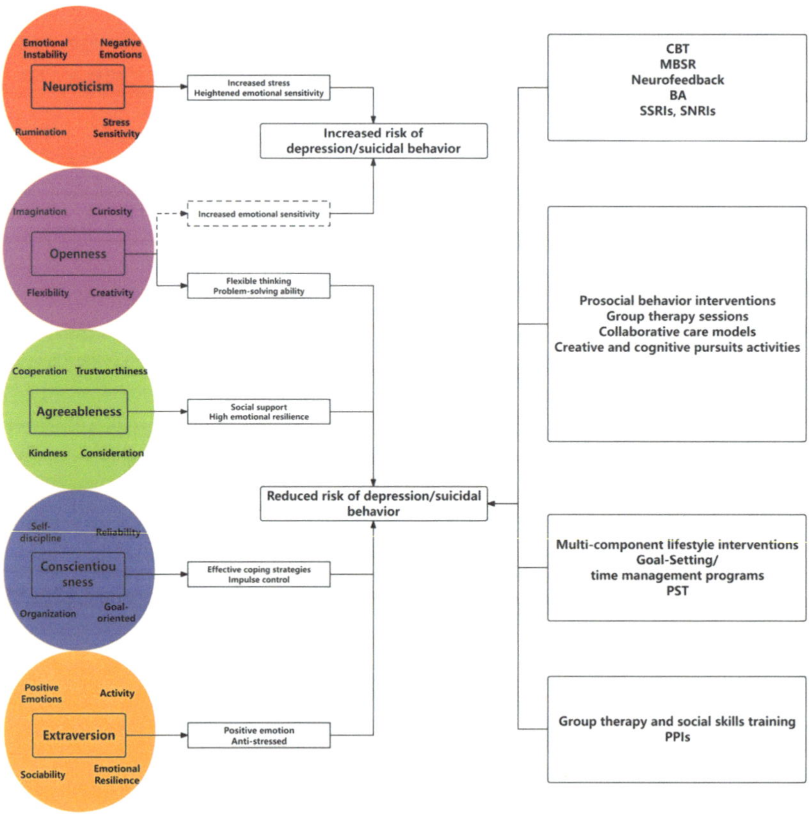

Figure 1.
The impact of big five personality traits on depression and suicidal behavior risk and interventions.

relationship between depression and openness. In other words, educational level itself is directly related to traits of openness and mental health status, potentially influencing how individuals experience and express depressive emotions. With regard to this case, the results prompt us to investigate further the social and educational variables of mental health problems. Furthermore, certain facets of openness, such as openness to esthetics and values, have shown distinct relationships with depression. Openness to esthetics, which involves an appreciation for art and beauty, has been found to positively predict depression, whereas openness to values, which reflects a readiness to re-evaluate values and accept new ones, negatively predicts depression and anhedonia [38]. **Figure 1** shows how each trait of the Big Five personality affects the risk of depression and suicidal behaviors and demonstrates various interventions that target these risks.

4. Practical applications and policy implications

With the link or relationship presented between the Big Five personality and mental health outcomes, several preventive strategies and psychological interventions are instituted to lessen the magnitude of depression and suicidal behavior. The value of specifying the application of such interventions to individual personality traits is increased. This would mean more personally attuned care in terms of mental health.

4.1 Neuroticism-focused interventions

Neuroticism is characterized by the effect of negativity, as well as high emotional instability. This situation calls for focused efforts to eliminate psychological and physiological aspects of mental well-being. Successful interventions for high levels of neuroticism significantly reduce the risk of depression and suicidal tendencies. The cornerstone management in neuroticism-induced issues remains Cognitive Behavioral Therapy (CBT), which is highly reliant on changing maladaptive thought patterns and behaviors. CBT teaches how to challenge and reframe negative thoughts; as a consequence, the level of anxiety and depressive symptoms is significantly decreased and more adaptive coping strategies appear [42].

The courses of Mindfulness-Based Stress Reduction (MBSR) are also successful in neuroticism. The subjects are advised to inculcate the practice of mindfulness that develops emotional regulation and a lower level of rumination, which is quite a common phenomenon among highly neurotic people [43]. Neurofeedback is another innovative approach that can be utilized. By training individuals to control their brain activity, particularly in areas related to emotional regulation, neurofeedback has shown promise in reducing symptoms of anxiety and depression, thereby improving overall emotional stability [44].

An improvement in the support of pharmacological treatment with Selective serotonin reuptake inhibitors (SSRIs) and Serotonin and norepinephrine reuptake inhibitors (SNRIs) improves the management of physiological symptoms from high neuroticism. These medications usually act on the modulation of mood and even modulate stress responses, which have significant improvement in results related to mental health [45]. Behavioral Activation (BA) therapy is also critical, as it encourages engagement in positive activities, countering the avoidance behaviors typical in highly neurotic individuals. This approach helps reduce depressive symptoms by promoting activity and reducing rumination [46]. Added to that, multi-component behavioral treatments, with exercise, diet, sleep management, and smoking cessation now part of mental health management, have reduced symptoms of depression among those high in neuroticism [47]. These interventions help address both the psychological and physiological aspects of neuroticism, providing a comprehensive treatment approach.

4.2 Extraversion-enhancing programs

A high extraversion score is characterized by a robust social network and more positive affect, which might reduce the effects of possible harmful effects of stress on emotional well-being. To harness these protective qualities, targeted interventions can be developed to enhance social connectedness and emotional resilience. Interventions aimed at increasing social engagement are particularly effective for extraverted individuals. Group therapy and social skills training will help patients use their inborn or natural proclivity for sociability to enhance a better support mechanism. These will provide a superior environment in which the extraverts can interact with other people on different issues and share experiences—thus elaborating the coping mechanisms under better group support. Social support, as studies would illustrate, is quite critical in the reduction of the stress effects and a luminary cause of depression [48]. There are also positive effects and emotional regulation-promoting interventions. Positive psychology interventions(PPIs) are designed to enhance well-being. They include practicing gratitude, identifying individuals' strengths, and engaging in activities that raise positive emotions. These interventions are particularly effective in improving the mental health of extraverted individuals, taking them to a higher level. These interventions help extraverts maintain their positive outlook and resilience in the face of stress [49]. The protective influence of extraversion is important in understanding how it may sometimes vary. For instance, in times of greater social restraint, such as the ongoing COVID-19 pandemic, extraverts, anticipated somewhat ironically, may feel lonelier and more depressed because they are unable to socialize. In such cases, interventions should focus on maintaining virtual social connections and providing platforms for remote social engagement [50].

4.3 Conscientiousness-based strategies

High levels of conscientiousness are identified with self-discipline, carefulness, thoroughness, and reliability, for which there are significant links to low depression and minimal suicidal behavior principally because such people have their forms of adaptive strategies, impulse control, and a sense of responsibility. Indeed, interventions that target trait enhancement in these attributes make significant strides in improving mental health outcomes [51]. People high in conscientiousness typically follow health practices and are good at stress-coping. Structured interventions based on such predispositions offer maximal utility. For instance, multi-component lifestyle interventions, including regular physical activity, balanced nutrition, and sufficient sleep, hold promise in reducing depressive symptoms [52]. They also reduce neuroinflammation associated with depression [53]. Goal-setting and time management programs may also have benefits on the protective factors of conscientiousness. In most cases, participants must set realistic goals and improve their organizational skills to become more experienced in their achievements and sense of control, all of which are important to mental well-being. Goal-setting interventions have provided evidence of levels where stress was reduced and motivation increased, linked with decreasing levels of depressive symptoms [54]. Problem-Solving Therapy (PST) aligns well with the traits of conscientious individuals. PST teaches systematic approaches to solving personal problems and coping with stress, enhancing problem-solving skills and resilience. This form of therapy has been shown to effectively reduce depressive symptoms and improve overall mental health [55].

4.4 Interventions for agreeableness and openness

Trait agreeableness and openness are different yet essential traits that can impact mental health and well-being. Both contribute to stress resilience and may permit the design of effective interventions toward the reduction of depression and suicidal behavior [56]. High agreeableness creates a supportive social network, essential for mental health. In this context, prosocial behavior interventions, such as ones focused on training in empathy or volunteer programs, can be very effective. These programs improve the person's social milieu and generate a sense of belonging, which is crucial for his health and prevents the development of mental disorders [57]. Openness, conversely, maintains cognitive flexibility and creative ability. High openness individuals will be more likely to seek new experiences to have innovative coping strategies. This trait may be beneficial when dealing with stress and depressive symptoms because individuals can view problems from multiple perspectives and generate novel solutions. Participation in creative and cognitive pursuits fosters psychological resiliency and flexibility, which are critical influences on good mental health [58]. Combining interventions for agreeableness and openness can lead to comprehensive mental health strategies. For example, group therapy sessions can simultaneously enhance social support networks (agreeableness) and provide opportunities for creative and reflective exercises (openness). Collaborative care models, which integrate mental and physical health care, can also be effective. These models involve coordinated efforts between healthcare providers to address both the psychological and physiological aspects of mental health, ensuring a holistic approach to treatment [47].

5. Conclusion and future directions

Among the various critical psychological factors determining the consequences on mental health or risk of depression and suicidal behavior are the Big Five personality traits: neuroticism, extraversion, conscientiousness, agreeableness, and openness. An appreciation of these traits gives insights that pertain to individual differences in the predisposition of mental health disorders. Neuroticism, as a disposition for emotional instability and negative affect, has been documented sufficiently as a risk factor for depression and suicidal ideation that calls for the need for directed prevention. On the other hand, extraversion and conscientiousness have been shown to protect through social support and effective coping, respectively. Agreeableness and openness are resilience factors to stress, yet more context-dependent, and they are synonymous with prosocial behaviors and cognitive flexibility to promote mental well-being.

Future study needs to be aimed at developing and delivering integrated interventions that take on their protective role and improve mental health prognosis. We need to focus on multimodal holistic interventions, which include CBT and MBSR, neurofeedback for affect dysregulation, and blue light intervention for depression. Furthermore, the efficacy of multi-component behavioral interventions incorporating these other health behaviors (physical exercise, diet, sleep management, and smoking cessation) for depression symptom reduction and health-related quality of life improvement should be evaluated. Positive psychology interventions and virtual platforms can be used to enhance social connectedness that may buffer emotional resilience. Strategies that focus on goals, reduction of stress, time management, and health-building behaviors play a key role in facilitating resilience and lowering distress-related psychological problems. Collaborative care models that blend physical and mental health can offer tailored support, bolstering intervention endeavors. Integrated strategies that aim to alter specific personality traits (agreeableness and openness, respectively) may enhance social support networks and cognitive flexibility, both critical for improved mental health outcomes. Such findings could deepen our understanding of how personality traits contribute to the risk for mental health problems and additionally inform more personalized prevention and intervention strategies, with an overall beneficial impact on the global burden of depression and suicidal behavior.

Funding

This study was supported by grants from the Zunyi City Bureau of Science, Technology, and Big Data, (No. Zunshi Kehe HZ Zi (2023) 211).

Conflict of interest

The authors declare no conflict of interest.

Author details

Junting Chen and Hao Huang*
Department of Neurology, Affiliated Hospital of Zunyi Medical University Guizhou, China

*Address all correspondence to: haohuang325@163.com

References

[1] Ferrari AJ, Santomauro DF, Aali A, et al. Global incidence, prevalence, years lived with disability (YLDs), disability-adjusted life-years (DALYs), and healthy life expectancy (HALE) for 371 diseases and injuries in 204 countries and territories and 811 subnational locations, 1990-2021: A systematic analysis for the global burden of disease study 2021. The Lancet. 2024;**403**(10440):2133-2161. DOI: 10.1016/S0140-6736(24)00757-8

[2] Goodwin GM. Major depression is sometimes described as the common cold of psychiatry. Journal of Psychopharmacology (Oxford, England). 2008;**22**(Suppl. 3):3. DOI: 10.1177/0269881108094716

[3] Overholser JC, Braden A, Dieter L. Understanding suicide risk: Identification of high-risk groups during high-risk times. Journal of Clinical Psychology. 2012;**68**(3):349-361. DOI: 10.1002/jclp.20859

[4] Conner K. Suicidal behavior: Links between alcohol use disorder and acute use of alcohol. ARCR. 2019;**40**(1):arcr.v40.1.02. DOI: 10.35946/arcr.v40.1.02

[5] Holma KM, Melartin TK, Haukka J, Holma IAK, Sokero TP, Isometsä ET. Incidence and predictors of suicide attempts in DSM–IV major depressive disorder: A five-year prospective study. AJP. 2010;**167**(7):801-808. DOI: 10.1176/appi.ajp.2010.09050627

[6] Lester D. Depression, suicidal ideation and the big five personality traits. Austin Journal of Psychiatry and Behavioral Sciences. (USA: Stockton University, School of Social and Behavioral Sciences). 2021;7(1). DOI: 10.26420/austinjpsychiatrybehavsci.2021.1077

[7] Allen TA, Carey BE, McBride C, Bagby RM, DeYoung CG, Quilty LC. Big five aspects of personality interact to predict depression. Journal of Personality. 2018;**86**(4):714-725. DOI: 10.1111/jopy.12352

[8] Flint J, Cohen L, Nath D, et al. The association between the suicide crisis syndrome and suicidal behaviors: The moderating role of personality traits. European Psychiatry. 2021;**64**(1):1-30. DOI: 10.1192/j.eurpsy.2021.2235

[9] Mammadov S. Big five personality traits and academic performance: A meta-analysis. Journal of Personality. 2022;**90**(2):222-255. DOI: 10.1111/jopy.12663

[10] Michikyan M, Subrahmanyam K, Dennis J. Can you tell who i am? Neuroticism, extraversion, and online self-presentation among young adults. Computers in Human Behavior. 2014;**33**:179-183. DOI: 10.1016/j.chb.2014.01.010

[11] Soto CJ, John OP. The next big five inventory (BFI-2): Developing and assessing a hierarchical model with 15 facets to enhance bandwidth, fidelity, and predictive power. Journal of Personality and Social Psychology. 2017;**113**(1):117-143. DOI: 10.1037/pspp0000096

[12] Souza LC, Galvão LP, Paiva HS, et al. Major depressive disorder as a risk factor for suicidal ideation for attendees of educational institutions: A meta-analysis and meta-regression. Revista Paulista de Pediatria. 2023;**41**:e2021344. DOI: 10.1590/1984-0462/2023/41/2021344

[13] Mikulska J, Juszczyk G, Gawrońska-Grzywacz M, Herbet M. HPA Axis in

the pathomechanism of depression and schizophrenia: New therapeutic strategies based on its participation. Brain Sciences. 2021;**11**(10):1298. DOI: 10.3390/brainsci11101298

[14] Fabbri C, Mutz J, Lewis CM, Serretti A. Depressive symptoms and neuroticism-related traits are the main factors associated with wellbeing independent of the history of lifetime depression in the UK biobank. Psychological Medicine. 2023;**53**(7):3000-3008. DOI: 10.1017/S003329172100502X

[15] Branje S, Morris AS. The impact of the COVID-19 pandemic on adolescent emotional, social, and academic adjustment. Journal of Research on Adolescence. 2021;**31**(3):486-499. DOI: 10.1111/jora.12668

[16] Nikčević AV, Marino C, Kolubinski DC, Leach D, Spada MM. Modelling the contribution of the big five personality traits, health anxiety, and COVID-19 psychological distress to generalised anxiety and depressive symptoms during the COVID-19 pandemic. Journal of Affective Disorders. 2021;**279**:578-584. DOI: 10.1016/j.jad.2020.10.053

[17] Bogg T, Roberts BW. The case for conscientiousness: Evidence and implications for a personality trait marker of health and longevity. Annals of Behavioral Medicine. 2013;**45**(3):278-288. DOI: 10.1007/s12160-012-9454-6

[18] Zhao H, Shi H, Ren Z, et al. The mediating role of extra-family social relationship between personality and depressive symptoms among Chinese adults. International Journal of Public Health. 2022;**67**:1604797. DOI: 10.3389/ijph.2022.1604797

[19] Kotov R, Gamez W, Schmidt F, Watson D. Linking "big" personality traits to anxiety, depressive, and substance use disorders: A meta-analysis. Psychological Bulletin. 2010;**136**(5):768-821. DOI: 10.1037/a0020327

[20] Shanahan MJ, Hill PL, Roberts BW, Eccles J, Friedman HS. Conscientiousness, health, and aging: The life course of personality model. Developmental Psychology. 2014;**50**(5):1407-1425. DOI: 10.1037/a0031130

[21] Terracciano A, Lobina M, Piras MG, et al. Neuroticism, depressive symptoms, and serum BDNF. Psychosomatic Medicine. 2011;**73**(8):638-642. DOI: 10.1097/PSY.0b013e3182306a4f

[22] Rappaport LM, Flint J, Kendler KS. Clarifying the role of neuroticism in suicidal ideation and suicide attempt among women with major depressive disorder. Psychological Medicine. 2017;**47**(13):2334-2344. DOI: 10.1017/S003329171700085X

[23] Vasupanrajit A, Maes M, Jirakran K, Tunvirachaisakul C. Brooding and neuroticism are strongly interrelated manifestations of the phenome of depression. Frontiers in Psychiatry. 2023;**14**:1249839. DOI: 10.3389/fpsyt.2023.1249839

[24] Gobbi G, Atkin T, Zytynski T, et al. Association of Cannabis use in adolescence and risk of depression, anxiety, and suicidality in young adulthood: A systematic review and meta-analysis. JAMA Psychiatry. 2019;**76**(4):426. DOI: 10.1001/jamapsychiatry.2018.4500

[25] Jirakran K, Vasupanrajit A, Tunvirachaisakul C, Maes M. The effects of adverse childhood experiences on depression and suicidal behaviors are partially mediated by neuroticism: A subclinical manifestation of major depression. Frontiers in Psychiatry.

2023;**14**:1158036. DOI: 10.3389/fpsyt.2023.1158036

[26] McDonnell S, Semkovska M. Resilience as mediator between extraversion, neuroticism, and depressive symptoms in university students. Journal of Positive School Psychology. 2020;**4**(1):26-40

[27] Yu T, Hu J. Extraversion and neuroticism on college freshmen's depressive symptoms during the COVID-19 pandemic: The mediating role of social support. Frontiers in Psychiatry. 2022;**13**:822699. DOI: 10.3389/fpsyt.2022.822699

[28] Killgore W, Capaldi V, Grandner M, Kamimori G. 786 trait extraversion is associated with increased suicidal ideation during total sleep deprivation and insomnia. Sleep. 2021;**44** (Suppl. 2):A306-A307. DOI: 10.1093/sleep/zsab072.783

[29] Alt P, Reim J, Walper S. Fall from grace: Increased loneliness and depressiveness among extraverted youth during the German COVID-19 lockdown. Journal of Research on Adolescence. 2021;**31**(3):678-691. DOI: 10.1111/jora.12648

[30] Farzaneh H, Mahmoud N, Ali MM. The relationship between the big five personality traits with depression: The mediating role of self-esteem and self-efficacy. Journal of Counseling Research. 2020;**18**(72):114-137

[31] Steptoe A, Easterlin E, Kirschbaum C. Conscientiousness, hair cortisol concentration, and health behaviour in older men and women. Psychoneuroendocrinology. 2017;**86**:122-127. DOI: 10.1016/j.psyneuen.2017.09.016

[32] Chen Y, Peng Y, Ma X, Dong X. Conscientiousness moderates the relationship between perceived stress and depressive symptoms among U.S. Chinese older adults. The Journals of Gerontology. Series A, Biological Sciences and Medical Sciences. 2017;**72**(Suppl. 1):S108-S112. DOI: 10.1093/gerona/glw172

[33] Dahm AS, Schmierer P, Veer IM, et al. The burden of conscientiousness? Examining brain activation and cortisol response during social evaluative stress. Psychoneuroendocrinology. 2017;**78**:48-56. DOI: 10.1016/j.psyneuen.2017.01.019

[34] Caprara GV, Luengo Kanacri BP, Zuffianò A, Gerbino M, Pastorelli C. Why and how to promote adolescents' prosocial behaviors: Direct, mediated and moderated effects of the CEPIDEA school-based program. Journal of Youth Adolescence. 2015;**44**(12):2211-2229. DOI: 10.1007/s10964-015-0293-1

[35] Zavala D, Munoz E, Sliwinski M, Scott S. Does discrimination attenuate age-benefits in emotional health? Innovation in Aging. 2020;**4**(Suppl. 1):456-456. DOI: 10.1093/geroni/igaa057.1475

[36] Mongrain M, Barnes C, Barnhart R, Zalan LB. Acts of kindness reduce depression in individuals low on agreeableness. Translational Issues in Psychological Science. 2018;**4**(3):323-334. DOI: 10.1037/tps0000168

[37] Forgeard M, Herzhoff K, Jayawickreme E, Tsukayama E, Beard C, Björgvinsson T. Changes in daily manifestations of openness to experience during intensive cognitive-behavioral treatment. Journal of Personality. 2019;**87**(4):856-870. DOI: 10.1111/jopy.12438

[38] Khoo S, Simms LJ. Links between depression and openness and its facets. Personality and Mental Health.

2018;**12**(3):203-215. DOI: 10.1002/pmh.1417

[39] Chiappelli J, Kvarta M, Bruce H, Chen S, Kochunov P, Hong LE. Stressful life events and openness to experience: Relevance to depression. Journal of Affective Disorders. 2021;**295**:711-716. DOI: 10.1016/j.jad.2021.08.112

[40] Koorevaar AML, Comijs HC, Dhondt ADF, et al. Big five personality and depression diagnosis, severity and age of onset in older adults. Journal of Affective Disorders. 2013;**151**(1):178-185. DOI: 10.1016/j.jad.2013.05.075

[41] Weber K, Giannakopoulos P, Bacchetta JP, et al. Personality traits are associated with acute major depression across the age spectrum. Aging and Mental Health. 2012;**16**(4):472-480. DOI: 10.1080/13607863.2011.630375

[42] Hofmann SG, Asnaani A, Vonk IJJ, Sawyer AT, Fang A. The efficacy of cognitive behavioral therapy: A review of meta-analyses. Cognitive Therapy and Research. 2012;**36**(5):427-440. DOI: 10.1007/s10608-012-9476-1

[43] Gu J, Strauss C, Bond R, Cavanagh K. How do mindfulness-based cognitive therapy and mindfulness-based stress reduction improve mental health and wellbeing? A systematic review and meta-analysis of mediation studies. Clinical Psychology Review. 2015;**37**:1-12. DOI: 10.1016/j.cpr.2015.01.006

[44] Hammond DC. Neurofeedback treatment of depression and anxiety. Journal of Adult Development. 2005;**12**(2-3):131-137. DOI: 10.1007/s10804-005-7029-5

[45] Driessen E, Dekker JJM, Peen J, et al. The efficacy of adding short-term psychodynamic psychotherapy to antidepressants in the treatment of depression: A systematic review and meta-analysis of individual participant data. Clinical Psychology Review. 2020;**80**:101886. DOI: 10.1016/j.cpr.2020.101886

[46] Richards DA, Ekers D, McMillan D, et al. Cost and outcome of behavioural activation versus cognitive behavioural therapy for depression (COBRA): A randomised, controlled, non-inferiority trial. The Lancet. 2016;**388**(10047):871-880. DOI: 10.1016/S0140-6736(16)31140-0

[47] Patel V, Saxena S, Lund C, et al. Transforming mental health systems globally: Principles and policy recommendations. The Lancet. 2023;**402**(10402):656-666. DOI: 10.1016/S0140-6736(23)00918-2

[48] Cuijpers P, Noma H, Karyotaki E, Cipriani A, Furukawa TA. Effectiveness and acceptability of cognitive behavior therapy delivery formats in adults with depression: A network meta-analysis. JAMA Psychiatry. 2019;**76**(7):700. DOI: 10.1001/jamapsychiatry.2019.0268

[49] Seligman MEP, Steen TA, Park N, Peterson C. Positive psychology progress: Empirical validation of interventions. American Psychologist. 2005;**60**(5):410-421. DOI: 10.1037/0003-066X.60.5.410

[50] Killgore WDS, Cloonan SA, Taylor EC, Miller MA, Dailey NS. Three months of loneliness during the COVID-19 lockdown. Psychiatry Research. 2020;**293**:113392. DOI: 10.1016/j.psychres.2020.113392

[51] Bogg T, Roberts BW. Duel or diversion? Conscientiousness and executive function in the prediction of health and longevity. Annals of Behavioral Medicine. 2013;**45**(3):400-401. DOI: 10.1007/s12160-013-9468-8

[52] Kiecolt-Glaser JK, Habash DL, Fagundes CP, et al. Daily stressors, past depression, and metabolic responses to high-fat meals: A novel path to obesity. Biological Psychiatry. 2015;**77**(7):653-660. DOI: 10.1016/j.biopsych.2014.05.018

[53] Kiecolt-Glaser JK, Derry HM, Fagundes CP. Inflammation: Depression fans the flames and feasts on the heat. AJP. 2015;**172**(11):1075-1091. DOI: 10.1176/appi.ajp.2015.15020152

[54] Brunstein JC. Personal goals and subjective well-being: A longitudinal study. Journal of Personality and Social Psychology. 1993;**65**(5):1061-1070. DOI: 10.1037/0022-3514.65.5.1061

[55] Nezu AM. Problem solving and behavior therapy revisited. Behavior Therapy. 2004;**35**(1):1-33. DOI: 10.1016/S0005-7894(04)80002-9

[56] Widiger TA, Oltmanns JR. The general factor of psychopathology and personality. Clinical Psychological Science. 2017;**5**(1):182-183. DOI: 10.1177/2167702616657042

[57] Wickramaratne PJ, Yangchen T, Lepow L, et al. Social connectedness as a determinant of mental health: A scoping review. PLoS One. 2022;**17**(10):e0275004. DOI: 10.1371/journal.pone.0275004

[58] Jin X, Ye Y. Impact of fine arts education on psychological wellbeing of higher education students through moderating role of creativity and self-efficacy. Frontiers in Psychology. 2022;**13**:957578. DOI: 10.3389/fpsyg.2022.957578

Chapter 7

The Relationship between Depression and Suicide

Fatih Kara and Arzu Gülbahçe

Abstract

Suicide is the voluntary ending of one's life. It is a state of aggression directed toward the person's self. Suicidal ideation can be considered in three dimensions: suicidal behavior, suicide attempt, and completed suicide. It is thought that, for every completed suicide, there are an average of 30 suicide attempts. While suicide attempts are 1.5–3 times more common in women than men, completed suicides are 2–3 times more common in men. According to the data of the World Health Organization, 800,000 people die every year due to suicide in the world. Therefore, this situation can be considered a public health problem. Suicide occurs throughout the lifespan and was the fourth leading cause of death among 15–29-year-olds globally in 2019. Suicide is a serious public health problem; however, suicides are preventable with timely, evidence-based, and often low-cost interventions. For national responses to be effective, a comprehensive multisectoral suicide prevention strategy is needed. Depression is the condition with the highest risk of suicide. A depressed patient sometimes has a higher risk of suicide during the recovery period. Because while vegetative symptoms improve in a shorter time with antidepressant treatment, it takes a little longer for depressive thoughts to improve.

Keywords: depression, suicide, relationship, health problem, increase

1. Introduction

The World Health Organization (WHO) defines health not only as the absence of disease and disability but also as a state of complete physical, mental, and social well-being [1]. Therefore, it is necessary to carefully evaluate mental health as an important criterion of being healthy. Mental health is a general state of well-being in which an individual is aware of his/her own potential, can cope with the stress of daily life, is productive and works efficiently, and can contribute to the society in which he/she lives [2].

On the other hand, mental disorders can be defined as the presence of unusual deviations and anomalies in a person's feelings, thoughts, and behaviors [2]. Mental disorders are among the health problems frequently encountered in society. The World Health Organization has announced the prevalence of mental disorders as 24% and stated that one in every four people struggles with a mental disorder at some point in their lives [3]. In the "Turkey Mental Health Profile" study, one of the largest epidemiological studies conducted in Turkey, it was reported that 18% of the population in Turkey has a mental illness throughout their life, and the same study found that the prevalence of mental illness in adults is 17.2% [4].

Neuropsychiatric disorders account for 13% of global disability-adjusted life years lost to disease and injury. Estimates suggest that this figure could rise to 15% by 2020, with depression alone contributing to 5.7% loss [5]. About 5 of the 10 diseases that most frequently cause disability and premature death in the world are psychiatric diseases, including depression, schizophrenia, bipolar disorder, alcoholism, and compulsive disorder [6]. Depression is one of the most common psychological problems that negatively affect the individual, such as reduction in daily and professional work, loss of productivity, financial difficulties, and damage to interpersonal relationships or marriages [2]. Depression is considered a major public health problem that has a significant impact on individuals and society. Depressive disorders are common in the general population [3]. It causes serious difficulties for the individual to cope with the problems of daily life [3]. In addition, depression is a common disease with a high rate of chronicity and recurrence [3]. One in every ten men or one in every four women experiences a depressive disorder during their lifetime. There is a possibility of recurrence of the disease in 70% of patients diagnosed with depression [2].

When it is considered that depression can cause suicide and that 11–17% of suicide cases end their lives this way, the seriousness of the situation becomes clearer.

The most serious consequence of depression is suicide [4]. Approximately 800,000 suicide cases per year are associated with depression [7]. In 1974, the World Health Organization defined suicide as "a person's conscious and varying degrees of self-harm with the aim of death" [7]. Again, according to the definition of the World Health Organization, actions that result in death are called suicide, and those that are not suicidal (for example, to communicate distress, to temporarily reduce unpleasant feelings) are called "suicide attempts" [5].

60–70% of those who commit suicide are patients with significant depression in their past. Depression is associated not only with completed suicides but also with suicide attempts. As the severity of depression increases, the seriousness of the suicide attempt and the intent to die also increase [6].

When examining the level of suicidal ideation in patients with depression, it is necessary to evaluate childhood traumas and coping strategies together. Childhood traumas are defined as a child experiencing an event that causes emotional pain or distress and often has long-term mental and physical effects. These experiences can be major natural events, terror, migration, war, domestic violence, neglect, or abuse [8]. Behaviors that negatively affect the child's development, cause some restrictions, and hurt them mentally, and are inappropriate are described as child neglect and abuse [9]. The concept of neglect is classified as emotional neglect and physical neglect; abuse is classified as physical abuse, emotional abuse, and sexual abuse [10]. According to the report published by the World Health Organization in 2014, approximately 23% of adults were exposed to physical abuse during childhood, 16.3% to physical neglect, and 36.3% to emotional abuse. It has been reported that the lifetime rate of exposure to abuse does not differ greatly between genders, but women experience sexual abuse at a higher rate [11].

Having traumatic experiences in childhood, when coping skills are not yet sufficiently developed, negatively affects mental health. Using a coping attitude to alleviate or eliminate stressful situations is a common situation [12]. Coping is a complex and difficult process to understand. While some methods used in this process remain passive, active solutions can sometimes be produced to eliminate the current negative situation. Coping attitudes have been classified in various ways by different studies, but Carver and his colleagues have developed the Coping Attitudes Assessment Scale, which has shaped coping attitudes and their classification in detail. This classification is as follows:

Problem-focused coping, emotion-focused coping, and dysfunctional coping. Each of these three subgroups has five subscales and a total of fifteen subscales are mentioned [12, 13]. Depression has been linked to emotion-focused coping attitudes. According to a study, individuals reporting depressive symptoms tend to use emotion-oriented coping more than problem-focused coping attitudes. The use of dysfunctional coping attitudes also plays an important role in the development of psychopathological symptoms [14].

Psychiatric nurses have important responsibilities in the prevention, care, and rehabilitation of depression, which is a significant mental health problem. Psychiatric nurses should monitor the level of depressive symptoms in the patient with the knowledge and skills they have, support the patient in developing effective coping skills, evaluate the risk of suicide, and take the necessary precautions. In addition, examining the existence of childhood traumas as one of the factors that can be involved in the etiology of depression and interpreting the effect of this negative experience on the present are important in terms of providing qualified nursing care [15]. Therefore, the study was conducted to evaluate the level of suicidal ideation in depressed patients and to examine the relationship between them.

2. Suicide

The concept of suicide cannot be considered separately from life because it is related to death. As a common feature of all living things, wherever there is life, there is also death. Despite this, the feelings, thoughts, and behaviors regarding the end of life may differ depending on the way of death. In its most general form, the end of human life is defined in five different ways. These are classified as natural means, accidents, being killed by others, destruction caused by natural disasters, and suicide. Among the ways of ending life, the concept of suicide is the most difficult to understand and define due to its multifactorial etiology, the interaction and intertwining of many different factors [16].

It is reported that the word "suicide" was first used in the book "Religio Medici," designed by the Englishman Sir Thomas Browne and published in 1643 [17]. The Latin word origin is derived from the suffixes "sui" meaning "self" and "caedere" meaning "killing" [18], and the word "suicide," which has preserved its meaning to this day, was thus defined.

The most well-known definition of the concept of suicide, which is still frequently used today, was made by the French sociologist Émile Durkheim [19] in his work titled "Le SuicideEtude Sociolocique" (Suicide-Social Scientific Study). Durkheim's definition was summarized by Cuhadaroğlu and Sonuvar [20] as "Every death caused directly or indirectly by a negative action taken by the victim of the event, knowing that it will lead to death, is called suicide" [19]. According to Durkheim [21], suicide is a disorder that occurs as a result of a pathological development and, like all other disorders, it occurs within a development process, therefore, it has a slow development course. When this pathological development process is completed, the individual's psychological well-being becomes one of the symptoms of suicide and is defined as "presuicidal syndrome [21]." Jacobson [22], similar to Durkheim [21], first defined the concept of suicide as a psychopathological development and then stated that it was a psychopathology showing symptoms of depression [22].

There are different views among suicidologists regarding the definition and classification of suicide. However, it is a common view that the concept of suicide is considered a "behavior." The use of many concepts in the literature related to suicide interchangeably and the lack of clear definitions create difficulties in terms of definition and understanding [23]. In the following sections, the definitions of other concepts related to the concept of suicide will be made and the points regarding how these concepts can be distinguished from each other will be discussed.

2.1 Suicidal thoughts

There are many different views on the definition and content of suicidal thoughts, just like the concept of suicide. The American Psychiatric Association (APA) defines suicidal thoughts in its simplest form as "thoughts of wanting to die."

However, this definition is not detailed enough to provide information on the purpose, scope, and source of suicidal thoughts. According to Alptekin and Duyan, suicidal thoughts are thoughts that an individual cannot get out of their mind and are related to death [24].

A similar definition was made by Spirito and Lewander, who stated that it means "not only thoughts of death, but also thoughts about having a detailed plan for suicide (e.g., which method to use, how to access these tools, etc.) [25]." On the other hand, according to the views that define suicidal thoughts in two categories as "active" and "passive" thoughts, "active suicidal thoughts" are thoughts about having a plan to kill oneself and putting this plan into action, while thoughts that are not accompanied by any preparation and plan but are accompanied by a desire to die are evaluated as "passive suicidal thoughts" [26].

2.2 Suicidal behavior

When the literature is examined, different views on the definition and classification of suicidal behavior are striking. Following the meetings held by the National Institute of Mental Health and the Center for Suicide Prevention in the United States in the early 1970s, opinions on the classification of suicidal behavior were presented [24]. Following these meetings and committees, Aaron Beck, who was the chairman of the Beck Committee, and his committee presented their views that are still widely accepted today. According to this view, suicidal behaviors are classified as "completed suicide," "suicide attempt," and "suicidal ideation" [27]. It is noteworthy that suicidal thoughts are also defined as behaviors within this classification.

Lester [28], who emphasized the importance of suicidal intention in his studies in the field of suicide and discussed the importance of suicidal intention for classification, conducted studies on the final part of suicidal behavior. Lester's [28] classification of suicidal behavior mentions five parts. Accordingly, all suicidal behaviors should be separated as "completed suicide," "suicide attempt," "suicidal threat," "suicidal ideation," and "suicide that was not previously considered planned." However, the concept of "completed suicide," which means a suicidal behavior that ends in death, is often referred to in the literature as "suicide" [24]. Another explanation similar to Lester's [28] classification was made by Bauer et al. Accordingly, this approach divided suicidal behaviors into two main classes: "verbal suicidal behavior" and "non-verbal suicidal behavior," and did not accept Lester's classification of "unthought-unplanned suicide" in the fourth category, and preferred the concept of "repeated suicide attempt" [28].

2.3 Suicide attempt

Suicide attempts are defined in the simplest terms as suicidal behaviors that do not result in death. The definition of suicide and suicide-related concepts interchangeably or with different concepts is also valid for suicide attempts [29]. While the term "attempted suicide" is used in our country when talking about incomplete suicides in the American literature, it is seen that the terms "deliberate self-harm" or "parasuicide," which are used in our country as deliberate self-harm, are preferred in European publications [30].

The definition of the concept of suicide attempt made by the WHO in the study conducted in 1986 under the name "European Multicenter Suicidal Behavior Study" is one of the most important definitions made. De Leo summarizes this definition as follows: "It is an unconventional, intentional behavior that will harm oneself or a drug taken in a dose greater than the prescribed/applied treatment, with the aim of making changes in one's environment without the intervention of others and thus achieving certain concrete results that one desires, and it is a non-fatal action that takes place [18]." According to this definition, all voluntary behaviors in which an individual aims to kill himself/herself, but which do not end in death, are considered suicidal behavior [18].

2.4 Suicide in the world

The epidemiological characteristics of suicide attempts are not as well known as those of completed suicides. According to the World Health Organization, suicides are one of the 10 leading causes of death in developed countries. As of 2000, 815,000 people in the world have committed suicide. In other words, one person commits suicide every 40 seconds. Suicide attempts are expressed as 10–20 times this rate. According to the World Health Organization, 13 out of every 100,000 young people between the ages of 15 and 24 end their own lives [5].

In the United States (US), suicide is the eighth leading cause of death, accounting for approximately 30,000 deaths per year. The suicide rate in the US is 11/100,000 per year. At least 31,000 people in the US die from suicide each year. This accounts for 1.4% of all deaths. More than 1500 Americans attempt suicide each day, with approximately 86 of them dying. This rate is the third leading cause of death among those aged 15–24, after accidents and homicide [31].

Suicide rates vary greatly from country to country and culture to culture. In West Germany, the suicide rate was 36/100,000, in Lithuania 34.4/100,000, and in Ireland 3/100,000. In Spain in 2002, the suicide rate for 10–14 year olds was 0.38:100,000, while for 15–19 year olds, the rate was 2.7:100,000 [31]. A study in China estimated that suicide deaths accounted for 3.6% of all deaths [32].

According to the National Crime Records Bureau in India, suicide is among the top 10 causes of death. Again, suicide is among the top three causes of death in the 16–35 age group in India. The number of suicides in India increased from 40,000 in 1968 to 110,000 in 1999; the national incidence is 11:100,000 per year [33].

The average annual suicide rate in England and Wales is around 10:100,000. The annual number of deaths is around 5000 [13].

Japan has one of the highest suicide rates in the world. According to the national police agency, in 1998, there were 32,863 suicides (26,100,000). In 2001, according to data from the same sources, the number of suicides in Japan was 31,042 and 24.4:100,000 [15].

In Lithuania, although the suicide mortality rate has been stable since 1995, it is still among the highest in Europe. The rate, which was 44:100,000 in 2002, is four times higher than the European Union rate and three times higher than the Scandinavian countries [17].

In Hong Kong, suicide rates have also increased significantly in recent years. The ratio, which was 13.2:100,000 in 1998, became 18.6:100,000 in 2003. It is stated that the major increase in suicide deaths in Hong Kong was in men between the ages of 25 and 39 [15].

3. Depression

Depression is a symptom cluster that can occur in a wide range from normal sadness to severe psychotic symptoms. This sadness, which can be experienced by every person, occurs when it is severe, intense, and long-lasting, and a major depression picture emerges.

Major depression is distinguished from the normal depressed mood by a significant deterioration in physical functions, decrease in functionality, the occurrence of suicidal thoughts or attempts, and deterioration in reality evaluation [34]. Sleep disturbances, changes in appetite and body weight, lack of sexual interest and desire, physical complaints, vegetative symptoms such as fatigue and lack of energy, depressed mood, loss of interest and pleasure, slowed thinking speed, cognitive symptoms such as decreased attention and concentration skills, thoughts of guilt and worthlessness that may reach a psychotic level, and recurrent thoughts of death and suicide are the core symptoms of major depression [35]. Major depression is seen with different frequencies in different populations, but its prevalence in the general population varies between 3.5 and 6.5% [36]. Being a woman, being an adolescent and elderly, having a low socioeconomic level, being divorced or widowed, having a positive family history, and experiencing stressful life events are significant risk factors for the development of major depression [37].

Neuropsychiatric diseases are responsible for 13% of the life years lost due to disability due to illness and injury worldwide, and it is estimated that this rate will reach 15% by 2020, with depression alone causing 5.7% loss [38]. About 5 of the 10 diseases that most frequently cause disability and premature death in the world are psychiatric diseases, including depression, schizophrenia, bipolar disorder, alcoholism, and compulsive disorder [6].

Depression is one of the most common psychological problems that negatively affect individuals, such as reduction in daily and professional work, loss of productivity, financial difficulties, damage to interpersonal relationships or marriages [2]. Depression is considered a major public health problem that has a significant impact on individuals and society. Depressive disorders are common in the general population. It causes serious difficulties for individuals to cope with the problems of daily life. In addition, depression is a common, chronic, and recurrent disease [3]. One in every 10 men or one in every four women will experience a depressive disorder during their lifetime. 70% of patients diagnosed with depression have a possibility of recurrence of the disease [2].

When it is considered that depression can cause suicide and that 11–17% of suicide cases end their lives this way, the seriousness of the situation becomes clearer. The most serious consequence of depression is suicide [4]. Approximately 800,000 suicide cases per year are associated with depression [7]. In 1974, the World Health Organization defined suicide as "a person's conscious and varying degrees of self-harm with the aim of death" [7]. Again, according to the definition of the World Health Organization, actions that result in death are called suicide, and those that are not suicidal (for example, to communicate distress, to temporarily reduce unpleasant feelings) are called "suicide attempts." 60–70% of those who commit suicide are patients with significant depression in their past. Depression is associated not only with completed suicides but also with suicide attempts. As the severity of depression increases, the seriousness of the suicide attempt and the intent to die also increase [6].

4. The relationship between depression and suicide

When examining the level of suicidal ideation in patients with depression, it is necessary to evaluate childhood traumas and coping strategies together. Childhood traumas are defined as a child experiencing an event that causes emotional pain or distress and often has long-term mental and physical effects. These experiences can be major natural events, terror, migration, war, domestic violence, neglect, or abuse [8]. Behaviors that negatively affect the child's development, cause some restrictions, and hurt them mentally, and are inappropriate are described as child neglect and abuse [9]. The concept of neglect is classified as emotional neglect and physical neglect; abuse is classified as physical abuse, emotional abuse, and sexual abuse. According to the report published by the World Health Organization in 2014, approximately 23% of adults were exposed to physical abuse during childhood, 16.3% to physical neglect, and 36.3% to emotional abuse. It has been stated that the rate of being subjected to abuse throughout life does not show significant differences between genders, but women experience sexual abuse at a higher rate. According to the data announced by TÜİK, 46% of the crimes committed are against children, and violence and sexual abuse against children are particularly prominent in these crimes [11].

Suicide resulting in death occurs very rarely outside of psychiatric disorders. Suicide itself is not a disease, but it can be seen together with many diseases. Conwell and Henderson determined that 90% of completed suicides have a psychiatric disorder [39]. About 50–70% of all suicide cases are caused by a mood disorder, and 80% of these cases are in patients diagnosed with major depression [40].

There are many factors that increase the risk of suicide in major depression. It has been suggested that some cognitive aspects of depression, such as hopelessness and pessimism, are more closely associated with suicide. In studies conducted in adult patients, hopelessness has been associated with suicidal behavior independently of depression [41].

There are limited studies in the literature on whether somatic symptoms found in the depression table increase the risk of suicide. A large study conducted in the elderly population in the United States found that low socioeconomic levels, deterioration in social functionality, increased anxiety, and the intensity of somatic symptoms significantly increase the risk of suicide [42]. In addition, in recent years, it has been emphasized that alexithymia and somatization tendencies are more common in the elderly and that depression suppresses other symptoms of depression seen in this age group [43]. However, patients with somatic complaints often first apply to non-psychiatric clinics, which can lead to these patients receiving incorrect and inadequate treatment, exacerbating their depression symptoms, and increasing their risk of suicide [44].

5. Conclusions

As previously stated, when the relationship between suicide and psychopathology is examined, it is seen that the concept most closely related is depression [45]. Half of the completed suicides are related to depression and other mood disorders (ICD-1, F3). In a study comparing clinical and non-clinical groups, it was reported that the risk of suicide in the clinical group was 20 times higher [46]. A recent review study reported that the lifetime prevalence of suicide attempts in individuals diagnosed with major depressive disorder was 31% [47] and the prevalence of suicidal ideation was 38% [48]. Another study reported that depression increases the risk of suicide in society by 2–30 times and that patients diagnosed with depression have the highest risk of suicide compared to patients with other psychiatric diagnoses [49]. In a study conducted in our country with 120 patients with depression, it was reported that there was a strong relationship between depressive symptoms and suicidal thoughts, that childhood traumas affected the severity of depression, and that dysfunctional coping attitudes negatively affected the disease picture [50]. A recent study examined the suicide probability of 406 adults and found moderately significant relationships between the individuals' depression level and the probability of suicide. It was also determined that, as the level of depression increased, suicidal ideation, hopelessness, and the probability of suicide also increased [51]. In a controlled study conducted with 118 adolescents diagnosed with depression with and without suicidal behavior, it was reported that adolescents with suicidal behavior had a higher probability of suicide compared to participants without suicidal behavior and without a diagnosis of depression [52]. Despite this, when the literature is examined, it can be found that there is no significant relationship between suicide attempt and the severity of depression in adolescents in our country [20].

In a study conducted in Turkey, the sociodemographic characteristics of 155 patients receiving inpatient treatment in a psychiatric clinic were examined in relation to the possibility of suicide.

The results of the study revealed that the suicide probability scores of patients diagnosed with depression were higher than those of patients not diagnosed with depression [53]. On the other hand, it was reported that the predictive role of depression and hopelessness on suicidal behavior was insufficient, and it was determined that the risk of suicide was much higher in patients with depression [54].

Suicidal thoughts, anxiety, hopelessness, and functionality levels of patients diagnosed with major depressive disorder who had and had not attempted suicide were examined.

When the results were examined, it was determined that the suicide attempt rate of treatment-resistant depression patients and patients receiving inpatient treatment reached up to 17%. In addition, it was reported that patients diagnosed with depression who attempted suicide had higher hopelessness and suicidal thoughts. However, it has been reported that patients who attempt suicide continue to have problems with unhappiness, social adaptation, suicidal thoughts, and occupational functioning even during remission periods [55].

Studies have shown that depression experienced during adolescence is associated with depression and suicidal ideation and risk experienced during adulthood and emerging adulthood [56]. Johnson and Johnson [57] examined the relationship between a diagnosis of depression during adolescence and psychological health problems during adulthood. In this review study, it was reported that individuals who were diagnosed with depression during adolescence had a high risk of being diagnosed with depression, suicide risk, and anxiety disorder during adulthood [57]. In another study examining the possible outcomes of depression experienced during adolescence during adulthood, the prevalence of depression was reported as 38.8% in adolescence and 37.7% in adulthood. However, the prevalence of suicidal ideation in adulthood among participants who experienced depression during adolescence was determined as 13.1%, while this rate was determined as 6% for suicide attempts. In another similar study, the prevalence of depression in adolescence was reported as 18.4% and the prevalence of depression in emerging adulthood as 21.3%. In addition, the prevalence of suicidal ideation in adulthood was found to be 12.2% in individuals diagnosed with depression in adolescence [58]. In a cohort study where the average age of participants was 16.6, the prevalence of depression in adolescence was reported as 17.4% and the prevalence of depression in emerging adulthood as 19.8%. The study found that depression in adolescence had an effect on suicide attempts in early adulthood and emerging adulthood [59].

Conflict of interest

The authors declare no conflict of interest.

Author details

Fatih Kara[1]* and Arzu Gülbahçe[2]

1 Atatürk University, Diyarbakır, Turkey

2 Atatürk University, Erzurum, Turkey

*Address all correspondence to: musap-21@hotmail.com

References

[1] What is the WHO Definition of Health? Available from: https://www.who.int/about/who-weare/frequently-asked-questions

[2] Koroglu E. American Psychiatric Association, Diagnostic and Statistical Manual of Mental Disorders. 5th ed. (DSM-5) Diagnostic Criteria Reference Manual, trans. Ankara: Hekimler Publishing Union; 2013

[3] Avenevoli S, Swendsen J, He JP, Burstein M, Merikangas KR. Major depression in the National Comorbidity Survey–Adolescent Supplement: Prevalence, correlates, andtreatment. Journal of the American Academy of Child and Adolescent Psychiatry. 2015;**54**(1):37-44

[4] Ulutas S, Ergin D. Evaluation of physicians' attitudes towards patients with mental disorders. The Journal of Turkish Family Physician. 2019;**10**(4):185-194

[5] WHO [Internet]. Available from: http://www.who.int/mental_health/media/en/426.pdf [Accessed: August 29, 2024]

[6] Çevik A, Volkan VD. Psychodynamic etiology of depression. Galenos Medical Journal. 2001;**5**:44-46

[7] Çevik A, Özcan H, Uysal E. Analysis of suicide attempts: Risk factors and follow-up. Clinical Psychiatry. 2012;**15**:218-225

[8] Tyler S, Allison K, Winsler A. Child neglect: Development alcons equences, intervention, and policy implications. Child and Youth Care Forum. 2006;**35**(1):1-20

[9] Taner Y, Gökler B. Child abuse and neglect: Psychiatric aspects. Hacettepe Medical Journal. 2004;**35**(2):82-86

[10] DenHerder T. Design and simulation of PV super system using simulink [thesis]. San Luis Obispo: California Polytechnic State University; 2006

[11] TUIK Justice Statistics. 2016. Available from: https://biruni.tuik.gov.tr/medas/?kn=98&locale=tr [Accessed: June 03, 2024]

[12] Agargün MY, Besiroğlu L, Kıran ÜK, Özer ÖA, Kara H. COPE (coping attitudes evaluation scale): A preliminary study on psychometric properties. Anatolian Journal of Psychiatry. 2005;**6**:221-226

[13] Roth S, Cohen LJ. Approach, avoidance, and coping with stress. The American Psychologist. 1986;**41**(7):813-819

[14] Folkman S, Moskowitz JT. Coping: Pitfalls and promise. Annual Review of Psychology. 2004;**55**:745-774

[15] Townsend MC, Özcan CT, editors. Fundamentals of Mental Health and Psychiatric Nursing: Evidence-Based Practice Care Concepts. Academician Bookstore; 2016

[16] Devrimci-Özgüven H, Eskin M. Psychometrics and Measurement Tools in the Assessment of Suicidal Behavior, in Understanding and Intervention in Suicide. Turkish Psychiatry Publications; 2019

[17] Barraclough BM, Shepherd D. A necessary neologism: The origin and uses of suicide. Suicide and Life-threatening Behavior. 1994;**24**(2):113-126

[18] De Leo D, Bertolote JM, Lester D. Self directed violence. In: Krug EG, Dahlberg LL, Mercy JA, et al., editors. World Report on Violence and Health. Geneva: World Health Organisation; 2002. pp. 185-212

[19] Odag C. Suicide (Self-Involvement) Definition-Theory-Treatment. Bornova-Izmir: Izmir Psychiatry Association. Ege University Printing House; 2008

[20] Cuhadaroğlu F, Sonuvar B. Adolescent suicides: A review of risk factors. Turkish Journal of Psychiatry. 1992;**3**:222-226

[21] Durkheim E. Le Suicide JA. Spaulding and G. Simpson (translated). London: Routledge and Kegan Paul Ltd.; 1952

[22] Jacobson E. Depression: The Oedipus conflict in the development of depressive mechanisms. The Psychoanalytic Quarterly;**12**:541-560

[23] Bauer MN, Leenaars AA, Berman AL, Jobes DA, Dixon JF, Bibb JL. Late adulthood suicide: A life-span analysis of suicide notes. Archives of Suicide Research. 1997;**3**(2):91-108

[24] Alptekin K, Duyan V. Suicide and Suicide Prevention. Istanbul: Yeni İnsan Publishing House; 2012

[25] Spirito A, Lewander C. Attempted and completed suicide in adolescence. Annual Review of Clinical Psychology. 2004;**2**:237-266

[26] Posner K, Oquendo MA, Gould M, Stanley B, Davies M. Columbia classification algorithm of suicide assessment (C-CASA): Classification of suicidal events in the FDA's pediatric suicidal risk analysis of antidepressants. The American Journal of Psychiatry. 2007;**164**(1):1035-1043. DOI: 10.1176/appi.ajp.164.7.1035

[27] Eskin M. A cross-cultural investigation of the communication of suicidal intent in Swedish and Turkish adolescents. Scandinavian Journal of Psychology. 2003;**44**(1):1-6

[28] Lester D. The role of shame in suicide. Suicide and Life-threatening Behavior. 1997;**27**(4):352-361

[29] Arslan-Çelik M. Comparison of patients hospitalized due to suicide attempt according to clinical diagnosis and suicidal behavior characteristics [unpublished medical specialization thesis]. Health Sciences University; 2018

[30] Wasserman D, Rihmer Z, Rujescu D, Sarchiapone M, Sokolowski M, Titelman D, et al. The European Psychiatric Association (EPA) guidance on 238 suicide treatment and prevention. European Psychiatry. 2012;**27**(2):129-141

[31] Parellada M, Saiz P, Moreno D, et al. Is attempted suicide different İn adolescent and adults? Psychiatry Research. 2007;**30**:1-7

[32] Phillips MR, Li X, Zhang Y. Suicide rates in China, 1995-99. Lancet. 2002;**359**:835-840

[33] Sharma B, Gupta M, Sharma AK, et al. Suicides in northern İndia: Comparison of trends and review of literature. Journal of Forensic and Legal Medicine. 2007;**14**:318-326

[34] Uluşahin A. General approach to depression. Turkish Medical Journal. 2003;**10**:79-88

[35] American Psychiatric Association. Diagnostic and Statistical Manual of Mental Disorders (DSM-IV). 2000. Press 4

[36] Kaplan HI, Saddock BJ. Synopsis of psychiatry. Presstime. 2003;**9**:24-35

[37] Simon GE, Von Korff M. Recognition, management, andoutcomes of depression in primary care. Archives of Family Medicine. 1995;**4**:99-105

[38] WHO. Suicide [Internet]. 2024. Available from: www.who.int/news-room/fact-sheets/detail/suicide [Accessed: August 29, 2024]

[39] Conwell Y, Henderson RE. Neuropsychiatry of Suicide. Neuropsychiatry. Baltimore: Williams and Wilkins; 1996. pp. 485-5213

[40] Akiskal HS. In: Sadock BJ, Sadock VA, editors. Mood Disorders: Introduction and Overview. Comprehensive Textbook of Psychiatry. 7th ed. Vol. 1. Philadelphia, Lipincott, Willams and Wilkins; 1999. pp. 1284-1298

[41] Beck AT, Steer RA, Beck JS, et al. Hopelessness, depression, suicidal ideation, and clinical diagnosis of depression. Suicide and Life-Threatening Behavior. 1993;**23**:139-145

[42] Cook JM, Pearson JL, Thompson R, et al. Suicidality in older African Americans. Findings from the EPOCH study. The American Journal of Geriatric Psychiatry. 2002;**10**:437-446

[43] Howard R. In: Howard R, editor. Syndromes of Depression in the Elderly. Depression in Elderly People. Martin Dunitz: United Kingdom; 1997. p. 33

[44] Simon GE, Von Korff M. Recognition, management, and outcomes of depression in primary care. Archives of Family Medicine. 1995;**4**:99-105

[45] Okan C, Bilson L, Zhong D, Weidemann G, Bailey PE. Validating the interpersonal theory of suicide among older adultspre- and peri-COVID-19 pandemic. Aging and Mental Health. 2023;**27**(8):1552-1558

[46] Lépine JP, Briley M. The increasing burden of depression. Neuropsychiatric Disease and Treatment. 2011;**7**(supp. 1):3-7

[47] Dong M, Zeng LN, Lu L, et al. Prevalence of suicide attempts in individuals with major depressive disorder: A meta-analysis of observational surveys. Psychological Medicine. 2019;**49**:1691-1704. DOI: 10.1017/S0033291718002301

[48] Cai H, Jin Y, Liu S, et al. Prevalence of suicidal ideation and planning in patients with major depressive disorder: A meta-analysis of observation studies. Journal of Affective Disorders. 2021;**293**:148-158. DOI: 10.1016/j.jad.2021.05.115

[49] Alpay Ü. The relationship between self-construals and suicide and problem-solving skills [master's thesis]. Adnan Menderes University, Institute of Social Sciences; 2015

[50] Üzel T, İnci F. Investigation of childhood traumas, coping attitudes, level of suicidal ideation and the relationship between them in patients with depression [master's thesis]. Nevşehir Hacı Bektaş Veli University; 2020

[51] Cakil G. The relationship between post-traumatic cognitions and suicide probability in a university sample [unpublished master's thesis]. 2018

[52] Akkaya-Kalayci T, Popow C, Waldhör T, et al. Impact of religious feast days on youth suicide attempts in Istanbul, Turkey. Neuropsychiatry. 2015;**29**:120-124. DOI: 10.1007/s40211-015-0147-9

[53] Sercan. The journey of self-suicide through time. In: Devrimci Özgüven H, Sercan M, editors. Understanding and Intervention in Suicide. Turkish Psychiatry Publications; 2019

[54] Demirkol ME, Namlı Z, Tamam L. Psychological pain. Current Approaches in Psychiatry. Journal of Affective Disorders. 2019;**11**(2):205-213

[55] Kaplan SJ, Pelcovitz D, Labruna V. Child and adolescent abuse and neglect research: A review of the past 10 years. Part I: Physical and emotional abuse and neglect. Journal of the American Academy of Child and Adolescent Psychiatry. 1999;**38**(10):1214-1222

[56] Jonsson U, Bohman H, von Knorring L, Olsson G, Paaren A, Von Knorring AL. Mental health outcome of long-term and episodic adolescent depression: 15-year follow-up of a community sample. Journal of Affective Disorders. 2011;**130**(3):395-404

[57] Johnson DW, Johnson RT. Implementing the teaching students to be peacemakers program. Theory into Practice. 2018;**43**(1):68-79

[58] Fergusson DM, Horwood LJ, Ridder EM, Beautrais AL. Subthreshold depression in adolescence and mental health outcomes in adulthood. Archives of General Psychiatry. 2005;**62**(1):66-72

[59] Briere FN, Rohde P, Seeley JR, Klein D, Lewinsohn PM. Comorbidity between major depression and alcohol use disorder from adolescence to adulthood. Comprehensive Psychiatry. 2014;**55**(3):526-533

Chapter 8

The Role of Self-Rumination from Psychological, Neurological, and Linguistic Viewpoints

Soheil Behdarvandirad and Maryamsadat Mirpour

Abstract

This chapter delves into the multifaceted relationship that self-rumination has with depression and suicidality through psychological, neurological, and linguistic lenses. It explores how self-focused thoughts and language contribute to depressive symptoms and suicidal behaviors. The psychological section examines the self-focus model, differentiates between rumination and reflection, and highlights their impacts on happiness and social functioning. The neurological section investigates brain areas like the default mode network, medial prefrontal cortex, and anterior cingulate cortex, focusing on the roles of these regions in self-referential processing and emotional regulation. The linguistic section discusses how language use, particularly self-focused language, reflects underlying psychological conditions and ruminative patterns. Finally, the chapter synthesizes the observations of the relevant studies, with the aim of providing a comprehensive understanding of how self-rumination exacerbates depression and suicidality.

Keywords: rumination, depression, suicidality, neurological, psychological, linguistic

1. Introduction

Self-rumination, a cognitive process where individuals repeatedly focus on themselves and their negative emotions, plays a meaningful role in the development and exacerbation of depression and suicidality. This chapter explores self-rumination from three distinct perspectives: psychological, neurological, and linguistic. Each section delves into how self-rumination influences and reflects depressive symptoms and suicidal behaviors. The psychological viewpoint examines theoretical models and empirical findings related to rumination and its impact on mental health. The neurological perspective investigates the brain mechanisms underlying self-rumination, highlighting key areas involved in self-referential processing and emotional regulation. Finally, the linguistic approach analyzes how language use, particularly self-focused language, mirrors and influences depressive and ruminative thoughts. Through an interdisciplinary perspective, this chapter attempts to provide a thorough understanding on the complex interplay between self-rumination, depression, and suicidality.

2. Psychological viewpoints

The first domain where the role of rumination in depression and suicidality was explored was psychology. This section begins by providing an overview of rumination and the self-focus model. It then distinguishes between rumination and reflection. Next, it examines the influence of rumination on depression, with a focus on happiness and social function. Following this, the role of rumination in suicidal behavior is explored. Finally, therapeutic approaches for managing rumination are briefly mentioned.

2.1 The self-focus model and self-rumination

Pyszczynski and Greenberg's self-focus model provides a compelling explanation of how depression is associated with self-rumination [1]. This model highlights the discrepancy between the desired and real worlds as the main reason for the self-rumination of the depressed. Besides the real world that we all live in, our minds are occupied with a different "desired world" that is fair, where things are how we want them to be. That world might be free of poverty, suffering, and unexpected distressing situations. According to the self-focus model, a depressive mind, which also suffers, cannot let go of the question, "Why isn't the world as we desire?" The world that a person with depression experiences is full of agonizing aspects, to the extent that the world itself seems to have an agonizing undertone. Depression causes one to be preoccupied with change and how things could be. But there must be a reason for the discrepancy between the world out there and the world inside the mind.

According to Pyszczynski and Greenberg [1], a depressed individual has a strong tendency to attribute the reason for this discrepancy to oneself. This attribution can manifest in various life occurrences. For instance, when failing a test, a depressed student might think, "I am not good enough," "There is something wrong with how I prepare for and take exams," or "Am I not stupid?" In contrast, a non-depressed classmate who also failed the exam is more likely to attribute the cause to other factors, thinking, "The questions were too difficult" or "The teacher didn't teach us the exam material well enough." Such self-rumination can be present everywhere in the experience of a depressed person, even in incidents where the person has almost no responsibility for the undesirable state. For example, at a party or gathering where the atmosphere seems cold and unenergetic, a depressed person might think, "Wouldn't this party and the people in it be happier if I could make good jokes?" or "Wouldn't this party be much better if it weren't for me?" More extreme versions of such self-blame can occur when seeing poverty and blaming oneself for not dedicating one's entire life to its eradication.

2.2 Types of self-focus: rumination versus reflection

According to Pyszczynski and Greenberg [1–3], depressed people's self-focus increases in cases of failure and decreases when they experience success, while the opposite pattern is true for non-depressed individuals. In one study by Pyszczynski and Greenberg [2], participants performed a task (successfully or not) and then had 10 minutes to work on two puzzles, one of which was located in front of a mirror, a self-focusing stimulus. Depressed participants significantly worked more on the puzzle in front of the mirror after failure compared to after success. Sakamoto [4, 5] and Pyszczynski and Greenberg [2] highlight the lengthier periods of self-focus after failure among depressed individuals.

Comparing 40 depressed patients with 40 non-depressed individuals, Watkins and Molds [6] outlined that the self-focus state has two distinct types with completely different impacts, especially on social problem solving. While the negative mood of depressed patients increases after ruminative self-focus (described as abstract self-focus), a concrete and cognizant mode of self-focus (concrete self-focus) has the opposite impact and enhances social problem solving. The functional properties of each self-focus mode are distinct. The lack of concreteness in abstract rumination is maladaptive; after reducing the ability to solve problems, personal mind-occupations remain unsolved, leading to more rumination. This observation aligns with reduced concreteness theory [7], which highlights that increasing concreteness in worrisome thoughts can significantly aid improvement and healing.

Treynor et al. [8] performed a factor analysis and categorized rumination into two separate factors: reflection and brooding. Reflection involves a purposeful turn inward to solve cognitive problems and address symptoms of depression. In contrast, brooding involves passively comparing one's current state with some desired and unachieved situation. Treynor et al. [8] reported that while reflection is correlated with concurrent depression, it is associated with less depression in the long run. Conversely, brooding is correlated with depression both concurrently and in the long run. More studies have supported this finding [9, 10]. Despite the positive role that reflection seems to play (as opposed to brooding), some have reported reflection as a predictive factor for suicidality [11, 12].

2.3 Self-rumination, happiness, and social functioning

Previous studies have indicated the association between depression and self-rumination. Rumination has been found to be negatively correlated with subjective happiness [13] and interpersonal skills [14], and positively associated with stress [15], the mind's tendency for distressed fantasies, failure, and anger [16]. Olatunji et al. [17] performed a meta-analysis examining 197 studies to investigate the relationship between rumination and both anxiety and depression. They found that different ruminative modes are meaningfully associated with depression and anxiety. Mood disorders were also correlated with higher degrees of rumination.

2.4 Self-rumination and suicidal behavior

According to Williams et al. [18] and Baumeister [19], suicidal behavior can be considered an attempt to escape from intolerable states and emotions. The discrepancy between one's perceived ideal and actual selves can intensify the tendency to end the lack of expectation fulfillment. The ideal self can be formed by others' and one's own expectations. Having a self that is far from this desired self can be suffocating for a depressed person, leading to insufficient feelings of self-worth under more pressure. When an individual's perception of their ideal self is "I should be happy," the fact that they are not adds to their unhappiness.

The influence of rumination on depression and suicidality has been repeatedly noted [11, 20–23]. A study by Smith et al. [23] showed that higher degrees of rumination could predict the likelihood and longevity of suicidal ideation over 2.5 years. Comparing the influence of brooding versus reflection as the two distinct types of self-focus in 230 healthy individuals, O'Connor and Noyce [20] reported the significant role that brooding plays in self-criticism and suicidal ideation. They also outlined that such self-criticism is linked to perfectionism, which makes one excessively critical of their behavior, drains the pleasure and value from successful performance, and causes serious worry about others' criticisms [24].

The association between self-rumination and depression/suicidality can fluctuate due to different contexts. For example, Cheref et al. [25] reported that rumination was negatively correlated with depression, an unexpected finding contradicted by a study by Bernard et al. [26], which focused on black youth. Further research can shed more light on this context.

Morrison et al. [27] conducted a systematic review identifying 11 studies that investigated the correlation between rumination and suicidality. Except for one study, the rest supported the existence of this correlation. In a study involving interviews and self-reports of 300 suicide attempters, Khosravani et al. [28] sought patterns and factors that decreased self-rumination and increased self-reflection. To measure these variables, they used the Rumination/Reflection Questionnaire [29]. A look at this tool's items better delineates the separation between self-rumination and self-reflection. Descriptive items like "Sometimes it is hard for me to shut off thoughts about myself" and "I spend a great deal of time thinking back over my embarrassing or disappointing moments" gauge self-rumination, while self-reflection items include "I love exploring my 'inner' self."

The meta-analytic review conducted by Rogers and Joiner [30] attempted to examine the relationship between self-focusedness and suicidal ideation. The results indicated a meaningful relationship between rumination and brooding (but not reflection) with suicidal attempts. This observation is consistent with previous ones reporting rumination as significantly correlated with suicidal attempts [12, 31].

As Mori and Tanno [32] highlight, the difference between self-reflection and self-rumination lies in the ability of self-reflection to enable a decentralized position, allowing better observation and judgment of the self. Examining 249 Japanese undergraduate students, their findings demonstrated that self-reflection was associated with more decentering features and decreased depressive symptoms, while it was the opposite for self-rumination. The correlation between brooding and suicidal attempts was highlighted by Sharaf et al. [33]. Surprisingly, they reported a relationship between suicidality and reflection as well. This contrasts with previous findings demonstrating the adaptive influence of self-reflection and the maladaptive influence of self-rumination regarding depression [14]. Further studies can shed more light on the role that self-reflection plays, especially concerning suicidal attempts and ideation.

2.5 Therapeutic approaches to managing self-rumination

Despite the relationship between self-focus and depression, constant distraction and staying entirely away from self-focused modes of thought do not seem to be appropriate strategies for dealing with recurring depressive states [34]. In addition to the unrealistic effort required for such an approach, total suppression of negative thoughts and emotions impedes the process of healing [35]. After all, wounds need to be inspected and should not be entirely hidden. Watkins and Teasdale [34] suggest that instead of resorting to distraction and completely getting rid of self-focused thoughts, a much better alternative is to refocus on the self in a structured way. This helps the depressed person re-examine their thoughts, feelings, and perceptions about the self more unbiasedly, without being distractedly sinking in the current of brooding. Consistently, Teasdale [36] highlights the difference between self-rumination and mindful self-awareness, where the first involves maladaptive thinking about the experience and the second involves present awareness of the moment's experience. This mindset also led to mindfulness-based cognitive therapy for depression (MBCT) [37, 38].

Mindfulness-based cognitive therapy for depression (MBCT) encourages people to observe the thread of their thinking in a cognizant way and notice the types of judgments and criticisms that are repeated in their thought processes. It promotes an attitude of unbiasedness, acceptance, and openness [39]. Being aware of the rumination process, which can be a mode of meta-awareness [40], prevents the distractedness that hinders one's path of thinking. Leashing this distraction in self-rumination and focusing on the self in a cognizant way is fruitful.

Crane et al. [39] investigated how the addition of MBCT to the usual treatment impacted self-discrepancies between "ideal" and "ought" selves in individuals who had experienced recovery from major depression (major depressive disorder (MDD)) and serious suicidal behavior or ideation. Higher degrees of discrepancy between the perceived actual and ideal selves have been shown to lead to higher degrees of dispirited affect and anxiety [41, 42]. Mindfulness therapy was used as treatment for preventing relapse. The control group comprised participants who met the same inclusion criteria as the experimental group but were on the waitlist for MBCT treatment. Although the discrepancy changes in the experimental group were not reported as significant after MBCT treatment, there was a significant difference between the self-discrepancies of the two groups. This meaningful difference resulted from the decrease in self-discrepancies in the experimental group and the increase in the control group. The results indicate that MBCT can be beneficially used as a self-regulatory and preventive strategy for individuals in recovery from suicidal depression.

3. Neurological viewpoints

Self-rumination and the role it plays in depressive symptoms and suicidality have been investigated in the realm of neuroscience. Understanding the neural mechanisms involved in depression and suicidal ideation/behaviors is of great importance. The literature indicates that self-ruminative neural activations are significantly associated with increased levels of depression and suicidality. Brain areas involved in self-focus, such as the default mode network, medial prefrontal cortex (mPFC), and anterior cingulate cortex (ACC), have been found to be more activated in cases of depression and suicidality. This section explores these areas and proceeds by examining functional connectivity and emotional processing.

3.1 The default mode network

The default mode network (DMN) is a brain network that involves areas which are active when the brain is at rest and not engaged in processing driven by the outside world [43, 44]. The DMN is composed of the medial prefrontal cortex, posterior cingulate cortex (PCC), precuneus, hippocampus, lateral temporal cortex, amygdala, and inferior parietal lobule (IPL) [45]. When the brain is at rest and not concentrated on the external world, more self-referential processing takes place, and activity in the DMN is enhanced [46].

Berman et al. [47] indicated that, compared to healthy individuals, depressed participants had atypical connectivity of the DMN during the resting state and not when they were engaged in the task of recalling emotional words. Consistently, enhanced resting-state connectivity of the precuneus (as a part of the DMN) and thalamus to the rest of the DMN has been observed among depressed subjects [48], and this association was also related to the length of the depressive episode. Maladaptive depressive rumination is known to increase activation in the DMN [49]. As a crucial node of the DMN, which is also involved in self-focus, the precuneus has been associated with the tendency to ruminate in the study conducted by Jacob et al. [50]. Comparing 20 patients with major depressive disorder (MDD) and 20 healthy controls, their findings supported the involvement of the DMN in the self-focus existing in the maladaptive rumination of patients with major depressive disorder.

Hamilton et al. [51] stated that the self-referential processing associated with major depressive disorder represents a significant increase in the connectivity that the DMN has with the subgenual prefrontal cortex. Zhou et al. [52] performed a meta-analysis that was aimed at identifying brain regions involved in ruminative processing. The results indicated a relationship between rumination and the involvement of the DMN, especially the dorsal medial prefrontal cortex (dmPFC) subsystem.

Ho et al. [45] compared the DMN of depressed versus non-depressed individuals. The depressed participants who had both suicidal ideation and non-suicidal self-injury had lower ventral DMN coherence compared to depressed individuals without suicidal ideation or non-suicidal self-injury, and also non-depressed participants. There was a relationship between lower degrees of coherence in all the DMN subnetworks and past-month suicidal ideation or non-suicidal self-injury. Consequently, both of these variables were correlated with difficulties in self-ruminative processing.

3.2 Medial prefrontal cortex (mPFC) and anterior cingulate cortex (ACC)

As key regions in the DMN, the mPFC and ACC play a crucial role when the brain is occupied with self-referential processing. Numerous studies have indicated the abnormal activity of these brain regions among depressed people, especially while performing self-referential tasks. Increased activity of the mPFC and ACC has been associated with negative self-referential processing as a contributing factor to rumination and negative self-focus [53, 54].

Nejad et al. [44, 50] demonstrated that, after comparing the activity of the mPFC and ACC between depressed individuals and healthy controls, these brain regions displayed significantly increased neural activity. Such enhanced activation is linked to the continuous negative evaluation of the self and the emotional distress that comes with rumination. Moreover, the pathophysiology of depression also highlights the importance of the mPFC and ACC. A study by Koolschijn et al. [55], which focused on depressed patients, showed structural abnormalities such as reduced gray matter volume in the mPFC and ACC.

3.3 Functional connectivity and emotional processing

Rumination can also be examined from the perspective of neural connectivity. Two main types of connectivity crucial for understanding rumination are those between the DMN and the task-positive network (TPN) and the limbic system. The TPN includes areas such as the dorsolateral prefrontal cortex (DLPFC) and is involved in external and goal-oriented tasks. Depression often leads to an imbalance between the DMN and TPN. According to Hamilton et al. [56], the DMN is more dominant in self-referential thought and the resting state among depressed individuals compared to healthy controls.

Previous studies focused on functional connectivity have indicated the abnormal interactions that the mPFC and ACC have with brain limbic regions and the amygdala in depression. The amygdala, a central part of emotional processing, has been found to be more active among depressed individuals during negative self-referential tasks [57]. According to Siegle et al. [58], such an enhanced amygdala response, coupled with the reduced regulatory role of the DLPFC, can lead to continuous negative emotions and affective dysregulation associated with rumination. The findings of Kessler et al. [59] and Ho et al. [45] also showed that the connectivity between the mPFC, ACC, and amygdala among depressed individuals is altered during neural processing involving self-focus. It can be concluded that the disruption of the emotion regulatory neural circuitry caused by depression can lead to increased negative self-focus and rumination. Serafini et al. [60] aimed to identify brain activation patterns conducive to suicidal behavior and considered self-focus and rumination as contributing factors.

4. Linguistic viewpoints

Language not only facilitates communication but also reflects our psychological states. The way individuals use language can significantly reveal their mental health, with specific patterns emerging in those experiencing depression. This section explores the relationship between depression and self-focused language, examining how linguistic choices can indicate underlying psychological conditions. By synthesizing existing research, we aim to understand how language serves as both a mirror and a mediator of mental health.

4.1 Depression and self-focused language

Innumerable factors, such as psychological ones, influence the way we learn and use language [61, 62]. Given the repeatedly observed correlation between depression and self-focusedness, it is expected that there would be an association between depression and self-focused language. The literature supports this association. The more depressed individuals are, the more likely they are to use self-focused language [63–66]. This self-focusedness appears in the form of increased use of first-person singular pronouns, mainly "I," "me," and "my." The rumination of a depressed person with its gloomy undertone tends to put the spotlight more on the self. "I" and the deficiencies it has are seen as most responsible for the discrepancy between the desired world and the current situation.

The study by Behdarvandirad and Karami [66] investigated different aspects of how language use is influenced by psychological constructs in the context of the Iranian population. Two hundred twenty participants were asked to write about their current state of life, how they feel about it, and what things have shaped their current life state. Participants were assigned to different experimental groups based on mood treatment and native versus foreign language in writing. Expectedly, depression was associated with more self-focused language in the use of the native language. However, this association vanished when participants used a foreign language, even though these participants were advanced in the foreign language they were writing. The absence of elevated self-focus as a depressive linguistic sign is consistent with previous studies that have highlighted the increased levels of rationality and decreased levels of emotionality when individuals use a language they are less proficient in compared to their mother tongue [67, 68].

The tool mostly used in the literature for measuring the self-focusedness of the elicited language is the Linguistic Inquiry and Word Count (LIWC2015) [69]. This program measures different aspects of the input text by dividing the number of words belonging to that aspect by the total word count. LIWC has a categorized dictionary, and each category belongs to a specific defined feature of language (self-focus, positive words, future language, etc.). The corresponding dictionary category for each linguistic feature involves the words belonging to it. For example, "I," "me," and "my" belong to the self-focus category. By identifying the number of words in this category, dividing this number by the total word count, and multiplying this number by 100, the percentage of the first-person singular pronouns in a text is calculated, serving as a criterion for self-focused language. LIWC supports and performs analysis in different languages.

One of the most cited studies examining the relationship between depression and self-focused language is Rude et al. [64]. In their study, college students were asked to write about their experience since starting college, and their depressive symptoms were also measured. A significant relationship was found between depression and the use of self-focused pronouns.

Two studies attempted to review and synthesize previous research on the increased self-focus due to depressive symptoms. The meta-analysis by Edwards and Holtzman [70] identified 21 studies that investigated the association between the use of first-person singular pronouns and depression. Similarly, Tackman et al. [65] synthesized data collected from different studies where 4754 participants had been examined. The observations of both studies supported the significant correlation between I-talk and depression. It should be noted that Tackman et al. [65] also examined neuroticism. According to their findings, neuroticism has a slightly stronger association with self-focused language, suggesting that this might be a wider correlation where depressive I-talk is a part.

4.2 Suicidality and ruminative language

Fernández-Cabana et al. [71] analyzed 23 suicide notes and reported an increased use of first-person singular pronouns, along with more denials and longer, more emotional, more tentative notes written in past and future tenses. Such unexpected findings could be due to the fact that the notes were the last thing individuals wanted others to read and might not be a good indicator of the thought process a suicidal individual goes through. Additionally, a similar examination of 25 suicide notes by Egnoto and Griffin [72] showed that the use of personal pronouns was prevalent in suicide notes.

In a study using machine learning and natural language processing to explore the role of self-focused pronouns in detecting suicidal ideation in the Chinese context, Huang et al. [73] found that all forms of first-person singular pronouns, including subjective, objective, dative, and possessive pronouns, were correlated with depression. Only the objective form ("me") had a significant relationship with suicidal ideation.

Homan et al. [74] conducted a systematic review to explore previous studies that examined linguistic features as predictors of suicidal thoughts and behaviors. Investigating 75 relevant studies, they observed that findings supported the association between the use of first-person singular pronouns and suicidality.

An interesting study compared poems written by poets who had committed suicide with those of non-suicidal poets. Stirman and Pennebaker [75] noticed preoccupation with self as a noticeable suicidal sign. Suicidal poets tended to detach themselves from others. Comparing the use of words related to communication (such as speak, listen, share, etc.), the poets who committed suicide showed lower levels of interest in social interactions. While the use of positive and negative emotion words did not significantly differ between the two groups, the poems of the suicidal poets demonstrated increased self-focusedness.

4.3 Negative mood and rumination among depressed vs. non-depressed

Another aspect examined by Behdarvandirad and Karami [66] in the context of native language use was the influence of mood. Before writing, native-writing participants were put into three groups based on the mood induced by pretested videos: negative, neutral, and positive. Each video was assigned to one group. Two interesting results were observed. Generally, negative mood was not associated with elevated self-focused language, or "I-talk." Instead, it was associated with "we-talk." This can be seen as an emotion regulatory strategy that individuals use in case of having a negative mood to distract themselves from self-rumination. This is consistent with Bernard et al. [63], where participants exposed to negative stimuli (in the form of pictures) used more "other-talk" in their writings after mood regulation.

However, there was one significant observation from Behdarvandirad and Karami [66]. While their study showed a relationship between negative mood and "we-talk," and there was no association between negative mood and self-focused language, when depressed participants received the negative mood stimuli, their self-focused language intensified. It seems that negative mood strengthens pronoun use tendencies. If a person is non-depressed, a negative mood makes them tend to focus on others or "we" (plurally), but when depressed individuals are exposed to a negative mood, their focus on the self is heightened and more noticeable in their language.

5. Conclusion

Self-rumination is a pervasive cognitive pattern that significantly contributes to the development and maintenance of depression and suicidality. By examining self-rumination through psychological, neurological, and linguistic perspectives, this chapter has highlighted the multifaceted nature of this phenomenon. Psychologically, self-rumination exacerbates negative self-focus and impairs social functioning and happiness. Neurologically, it involves specific brain areas and networks that are hyperactive in depressed individuals, disrupting emotional regulation and cognitive balance. Linguistically, self-rumination is reflected in the increased use of self-focused language, further reinforcing negative thought patterns. Understanding these intricate connections provides valuable insights for developing therapeutic interventions that are more effective. Addressing self-rumination through targeted psychological therapies, neurological interventions, and mindful language practices can potentially mitigate its detrimental effects and improve mental health outcomes.

Author details

Soheil Behdarvandirad[1*] and Maryamsadat Mirpour[2]

1 Texas State University, San Marcos, Texas, United States

2 Islamic Azad University Science and Research Branch, Iran

*Address all correspondence to: soheilbehdarvandirad@gmail.com

References

[1] Pyszczynski T, Greenberg J. Self-regulatory perseveration and the depressive self-focusing style: A self-awareness theory of reactive depression. Psychological Bulletin. 1987;**102**(1):122

[2] Pyszczynski T, Greenberg J. Depression and preference for self-focusing stimuli after success and failure. Journal of Personality and Social Psychology. 1985;**49**(4):1066

[3] Pyszczynski T, Greenberg J. Evidence for a depressive self-focusing style. Journal of Research in Personality. 1986;**20**(1):95-106

[4] Sakamoto S. The preoccupation scale: Its development and relationship with depression scales. Journal of Clinical Psychology. 1998;**54**(5):645-654

[5] Sakamoto S. Self-focus and depression: The three-phase model. Behavioural and Cognitive Psychotherapy. 2000;**28**(1):45-61

[6] Watkins E, Moulds M. Distinct modes of ruminative self-focus: Impact of abstract versus concrete rumination on problem solving in depression. Emotion. 2005;**5**(3):319

[7] Borkovec TD, Ray WJ, Stober J. Worry: A cognitive phenomenon intimately linked to affective, physiological, and interpersonal behavioral processes. Cognitive Therapy and Research. 1998;**22**(6):561-576

[8] Treynor W, Gonzalez R, Nolen-Hoeksema S. Rumination reconsidered: A psychometric analysis. Cognitive Therapy and Research. 2003;**27**:247-259

[9] Schoofs H, Hermans D, Raes F. Brooding and reflection as subtypes of rumination: Evidence from confirmatory factor analysis in nonclinical samples using the Dutch ruminative response scale. Journal of Psychopathology and Behavioral Assessment. 2010;**32**:609-617

[10] Burwell RA, Shirk SR. Subtypes of rumination in adolescence: Associations between brooding, reflection, depressive symptoms, and coping. Journal of Clinical Child and Adolescent Psychology. 2007;**36**(1):56-65

[11] Miranda R, Nolen-Hoeksema S. Brooding and reflection: Rumination predicts suicidal ideation at 1-year follow-up in a community sample. Behaviour Research and Therapy. 2007;**45**(12):3088-3095

[12] Surrence K, Miranda R, Marroquín BM, Chan S. Brooding and reflective rumination among suicide attempters: Cognitive vulnerability to suicidal ideation. Behaviour Research and Therapy. 2009;**47**(9):803-808

[13] Elliott I, Coker S. Independent self-construal, self-reflection, and self-rumination: A path model for predicting happiness. Australian Journal of Psychology. 2008;**60**(3):127-134

[14] Takano K, Tanno Y. Self-rumination, self-reflection, and depression: Self-rumination counteracts the adaptive effect of self-reflection. Behaviour Research and Therapy. 2009;**47**(3):260-264

[15] Samaie G, Farahani HA. Self-compassion as a moderator of the relationship between rumination, self-reflection and stress. Procedia-Social and Behavioral Sciences. 2011;**30**:978-982

[16] Shrimpton D, McGann D, Riby LM. Daydream believer: Rumination,

self-reflection and the temporal focus of mind wandering content. Europe's Journal of Psychology. 2017;**13**(4):794

[17] Olatunji BO, Naragon-Gainey K, Wolitzky-Taylor KB. Specificity of rumination in anxiety and depression: A multimodal meta-analysis. Clinical Psychology: Science and Practice. 2013;**20**(3):225

[18] Williams JM, Barnhofer T, Crane C, Beck AT. Problem solving deteriorates following mood challenge in formerly depressed patients with a history of suicidal ideation. Journal of Abnormal Psychology. 2005;**114**(3):421

[19] Baumeister RF. Suicide as escape from self. Psychological Review. 1990;**97**(1):90

[20] O'Connor RC, Noyce R. Personality and cognitive processes: Self-criticism and different types of rumination as predictors of suicidal ideation. Behaviour Research and Therapy. 2008;**46**(3):392-401

[21] Nolen-Hoeksema S, McBride A, Larson J. Rumination and depression: A two-wave study. Cognitive Therapy and Research. 1997;**21**:297-308

[22] O'Connor RC, Noyce R, Williams JMG. The relationship between brooding and reflection with suicidal ideation. Behaviour Research and Therapy. 2007;**46**:392-401

[23] Smith JM, Alloy LB, Abramson LY. Cognitive vulnerability to depression, rumination, hopelessness, and suicidal ideation: Multiple pathways to self-injurious thinking. Suicide and Life-threatening Behavior. 2008;**38**(4):445-455

[24] Dunkley DM, Blankstein KR, Masheb RM, Grilo CM. Personal standards and evaluative concerns dimensions of "clinical" perfectionism: A reply to Shafran et al.(2002, 2003) and Hewitt et al.(2003). Behaviour Research and Therapy. 2006;**44**(1):63-84

[25] Cheref S, Lane R, Polanco-Roman L, Gadol E, Miranda R. Suicidal ideation among racial/ethnic minorities: Moderating effects of rumination and depressive symptoms. Cultural Diversity and Ethnic Minority Psychology. 2015;**21**(1):31

[26] Bernard DL, Halliday CA, Are F, Banks DE, Danielson CK. Rumination as a mediator of the association between racial discrimination and depression among black youth. Journal of Racial and Ethnic Health Disparities. 2022;**9**(5):1937-1945

[27] Morrison R, O'Connor RC. A systematic review of the relationship between rumination and suicidality. Suicide and Life-threatening Behavior. 2008;**38**(5):523-538

[28] Khosravani V, Baseri A, Kamali Z, Mohammadzadeh A, Amirinezhad A. Direct and indirect effects of behavioral inhibition/activation systems on depression and current suicidal ideation through rumination and self-reflection. Archives of Suicide Research. 2020;**24**(4):568-588

[29] Trapnell PD, Campbell JD. Private self-consciousness and the five-factor model of personality: Distinguishing rumination from reflection. Journal of Personality and Social Psychology. 1999;**76**(2):284

[30] Rogers ML, Joiner TE. Rumination, suicidal ideation, and suicide attempts: A meta-analytic review. Review of General Psychology. 2017;**21**(2):132-142

[31] Grassia M, Gibb BE. Rumination and lifetime history of suicide attempts.

International Journal of Cognitive Therapy. 2009;**2**(4):400-406

[32] Mori M, Tanno Y. Mediating role of decentering in the associations between self-reflection, self-rumination, and depressive symptoms. Psychology. 2015;**6**(5):613-621

[33] Sharaf AY, Lachine OA, Thompson EA. Rumination, social problem solving and suicide intent among Egyptians with a recent suicide attempt. Archives of Psychiatric Nursing. 2018;**32**(1):86-92

[34] Watkins E, Teasdale JD. Adaptive and maladaptive self-focus in depression. Journal of Affective Disorders. 2004;**82**(1):1-8

[35] Wenzlaff RM, Bates DE. Unmasking a cognitive vulnerability to depression: How lapses in mental control reveal depressive thinking. Journal of Personality and Social Psychology. 1998;**75**(6):1559

[36] Teasdale JD. Emotional processing, three modes of mind and the prevention of relapse in depression. Behaviour Research and Therapy. 1999;**37**:S53-S77

[37] Mason O, Hargreaves I. A qualitative study of mindfulness-based cognitive therapy for depression. British Journal of Medical Psychology. 2001;**74**(2):197-212

[38] Segal Z, Williams M, Teasdale J. Mindfulness-Based Cognitive Therapy for Depression. Guilford Press; 2012

[39] Crane C, Barnhofer T, Duggan DS, Hepburn S, Fennell MV, Williams JM. Mindfulness-based cognitive therapy and self-discrepancy in recovered depressed patients with a history of depression and suicidality. Cognitive Therapy and Research. 2008;**32**:775-787

[40] Chin J, Schooler JW. Meta-awareness. Encyclopedia of Consciousness. 2010;**2**:33-41

[41] Carver CS, Lawrence JW, Scheier MF. Self-discrepancies and affect: Incorporating the role of feared selves. Personality and Social Psychology Bulletin. 1999;**25**(7):783-792

[42] Scott L, O'Hara MW. Self-discrepancies in clinically anxious and depressed university students. Journal of Abnormal Psychology. 1993;**102**(2):282

[43] Fox MD, Snyder AZ, Vincent JL, Corbetta M, Van Essen DC, Raichle ME. The human brain is intrinsically organized into dynamic, anticorrelated functional networks. Proceedings of the National Academy of Sciences. 2005;**102**(27):9673-9678

[44] Nejad AB, Fossati P, Lemogne C. Self-referential processing, rumination, and cortical midline structures in major depression. Frontiers in Human Neuroscience. 2013;**7**:666

[45] Ho TC, Walker JC, Teresi GI, Kulla A, Kirshenbaum JS, Gifuni AJ, et al. Default mode and salience network alterations in suicidal and non-suicidal self-injurious thoughts and behaviors in adolescents with depression. Translational Psychiatry. 2021;**11**(1):38

[46] Gusnard DA, Akbudak E, Shulman GL, Raichle ME. Medial prefrontal cortex and self-referential mental activity: Relation to a default mode of brain function. Proceedings of the National Academy of Sciences. 2001;**98**(7):4259-4264

[47] Berman MG, Peltier S, Nee DE, Kross E, Deldin PJ, Jonides J. Depression, rumination and the default network. Social Cognitive and Affective Neuroscience. 2011;**6**(5):548-555

[48] Greicius MD, Flores BH, Menon V, Glover GH, Solvason HB, Kenna H, et al. Resting-state functional connectivity

in major depression: Abnormally increased contributions from subgenual cingulate cortex and thalamus. Biological Psychiatry. 2007;**62**(5):429-437

[49] Sheline YI, Barch DM, Price JL, Rundle MM, Vaishnavi SN, Snyder AZ, et al. The default mode network and self-referential processes in depression. Proceedings of the National Academy of Sciences of the United States of America. 2009;**106**(6):1942-1947

[50] Jacob Y, Morris LS, Huang KH, Schneider M, Rutter S, Verma G, et al. Neural correlates of rumination in major depressive disorder: A brain network analysis. NeuroImage: Clinical. 2020;**25**:102142

[51] Hamilton JP, Farmer M, Fogelman P, Gotlib IH. Depressive rumination, the default-mode network, and the dark matter of clinical neuroscience. Biological Psychiatry. 2015;**78**(4):224-230

[52] Zhou HX, Chen X, Shen YQ, Li L, Chen NX, Zhu ZC, et al. Rumination and the default mode network: Meta-analysis of brain imaging studies and implications for depression. NeuroImage. 2020;**206**:116287

[53] Lemogne C, le Bastard G, Mayberg H, Volle E, Bergouignan L, Lehéricy S, et al. In search of the depressive self: Extended medial prefrontal network during self-referential processing in major depression. Social Cognitive and Affective Neuroscience. 2009;**4**(3):305-312

[54] Yoshimura S, Okamoto Y, Onoda K, Matsunaga M, Ueda K, Suzuki SI. Rostral anterior cingulate cortex activity mediates the relationship between the depressive symptoms and the medial prefrontal cortex activity. Journal of Affective Disorders. 2010;**122**(1-2):76-85

[55] Koolschijn PC, van Haren NE, Lensvelt-Mulders GJ, Hulshoff Pol HE, Kahn RS. Brain volume abnormalities in major depressive disorder: A meta-analysis of magnetic resonance imaging studies. Human Brain Mapping. 2009;**30**(11):3719-3735

[56] Hamilton JP, Etkin A, Furman DJ, Lemus MG, Johnson RF, Gotlib IH. Functional neuroimaging of major depressive disorder: A meta-analysis and new integration of baseline activation and neural response data. American Journal of Psychiatry. 2012;**169**(7):693-703

[57] Cooney RE, Joormann J, Eugène F, Dennis EL, Gotlib IH. Neural correlates of rumination in depression. Cognitive, Affective, & Behavioral Neuroscience. 2010;**10**(4):470-478

[58] Siegle GJ, Thompson W, Carter CS, Steinhauer SR, Thase ME. Increased amygdala and decreased dorsolateral prefrontal BOLD responses in unipolar depression: Related and independent features. Biological Psychiatry. 2007;**61**(2):198-209

[59] Kessler RC, Berglund P, Demler O, Jin R, Walters EE. Lifetime prevalence and age-of-onset distributions of DSM-IV disorders in the National Comorbidity Survey Replication. Archives of General Psychiatry. 2005;**62**(6):593-602

[60] Serafini G, Pardini M, Pompili M, Girardi P, Amore M. Understanding suicidal behavior: The contribution of recent resting-state fMRI techniques. Frontiers in Psychiatry. 2016;**7**:69

[61] Behdarvandirad S. A systematic review of second language acquisition from the perspective of complex dynamic system theory. Theory and Practice of Second Language Acquisition. 2024;**10**(1):1-39

[62] Tackman AM, Baranski EN, Danvers AF, Sbarra DA, Raison CL, Moseley SA, et al. 'Personality in its natural habitat' revisited: A pooled, multi–sample examination of the relationships between the big five personality traits and daily behaviour and language use. European Journal of Personality. 2020;**34**(5):753-776

[63] Bernard JD, Baddeley JL, Rodriguez BF, Burke PA. Depression, language, and affect: An examination of the influence of baseline depression and affect induction on language. Journal of Language and Social Psychology. 2016;**35**(3):317-326

[64] Rude S, Gortner EM, Pennebaker J. Language use of depressed and depression-vulnerable college students. Cognition & Emotion. 2004;**18**(8):1121-1133

[65] Tackman AM, Sbarra DA, Carey AL, Donnellan MB, Horn AB, Holtzman NS, et al. Depression, negative emotionality, and self-referential language: A multi-lab, multi-measure, and multi-language-task research synthesis. Journal of Personality and Social Psychology. 2019;**116**(5):817

[66] Behdarvandirad S, Karami H. Depression, neuroticism, extraversion and pronoun use in first and foreign languages following mood induction. Language Sciences. 2022;**94**:101503

[67] Pavlenko A. Emotions and Multilingualism. Cambridge University Press; 2005

[68] Caldwell-Harris CL. Emotionality differences between a native and foreign language: Theoretical implications. Frontiers in Psychology. 2014;**5**:1055

[69] Pennebaker JW, Boyd RL, Jordan K, Blackburn K. The Development and Psychometric Properties of LIWC2015. Austin, TX: University of Texas; 2015

[70] Edwards T, Holtzman NS. A meta-analysis of correlations between depression and first person singular pronoun use. Journal of Research in Personality. 2017;**68**:63-68

[71] Fernández-Cabana M, Jiménez-Féliz J, Alves-Pérez MT, Mateos R, Gómez-Reino Rodríguez I, García-Caballero A. Linguistic analysis of suicide notes in Spain. The European Journal of Psychiatry. 2015;**29**(2):145-155

[72] Egnoto MJ, Griffin DJ. Analyzing language in suicide notes and legacy tokens. Crisis. 2016;**37**(2):140-147

[73] Huang R, Yi S, Chen J, Chan KY, Chan JWY, Chan NY, et al. Exploring the role of first-person singular pronouns in detecting suicidal ideation: A machine learning analysis of clinical transcripts. Behavioral Sciences. 2024;**14**(3):225

[74] Homan S, Gabi M, Klee N, Bachmann S, Moser AM, Michel S, et al. Linguistic features of suicidal thoughts and behaviors: A systematic review. Clinical Psychology Review. 2022;**95**:102161

[75] Stirman SW, Pennebaker JW. Word use in the poetry of suicidal and nonsuicidal poets. Psychosomatic Medicine. 2001;**63**(4):517-522